Favorite Operas

BY GERMAN AND RUSSIAN
COMPOSERS

FAVORITE OPERAS
BY GERMAN AND RUSSIAN COMPOSERS

by Paul England

Dover Publications, Inc., New York

137762

This Dover edition, first published in 1973, is an unabridged reprint of appropriate sections from *Fifty Favorite Operas,* by Paul England, second enlarged (1929) edition, London (George G. Harrap & Co., Ltd.) .

International Standard Book Number: 0-486-22933-5
Library of Congress Catalog Card Number: 72-96409

Manufactured in the United States of America
Dover Publications, Inc.
180 Varick Street
New York, N. Y. 10014

CONTENTS

OPERAS DESCRIBED

Orfeo ed Euridice (1762) . .	*Gluck* . . .	1
Die Entführung aus dem Serail (1782)	*Mozart* . . .	9
Le Nozze di Figaro (1786) . .	*Mozart* . . .	15
Don Giovanni (1787) . . .	*Mozart* . . .	29
Die Zauberflöte (1791) . . .	*Mozart* . . .	44
Fidelio (1814)	*Beethoven* . .	58
Der Freischütz (1821) . . .	*Weber* . . .	65
Martha (1847)	*Flotow* . . .	80
Der fliegende Holländer (1843)	*Wagner* . . .	91
Tannhäuser (1845)	*Wagner* . . .	105
Lohengrin (1850)	*Wagner* . . .	126
Tristan und Isolde (1865) . .	*Wagner* . . .	136
Die Meistersinger (1868) . .	*Wagner* . . .	147
Der Ring des Nibelungen . .	*Wagner* . . .	165
Das Rheingold (1869) . . .	*Wagner* . . .	169
Die Walküre (1870) . . .	*Wagner* . . .	174
Siegfried (1876)	*Wagner* . . .	182
Götterdämmerung (1876) .	*Wagner* . . .	191
Parsifal (1882)	*Wagner* . . .	206
Hänsel und Gretel (1893) . .	*Humperdinck* . .	221
Boris Godounov (1874) . . .	*Moussorgsky* . .	229
Le Coq d'Or (1910)	*Rimsky-Korsakoff* .	241
Der Rosenkavalier (1911) . .	*R. Strauss* . .	249
A Short Historical Summary	269

Favorite Operas

BY GERMAN AND RUSSIAN COMPOSERS

ORFEO ED EURIDICE

Music by GLUCK. *Words by* CALZABIGI.
Vienna, 1762 ; *London,* 1770 ; *New York,* 1863.

IT is one of the happiest of chances that what is
generally regarded as the oldest opera in the repertory
should bear the name of Orpheus, the legendary
singer, minstrel, magician—the symbol through all ages
of the power of music. As Dryden has told us :

> Orpheus could lead the savage race,
> And trees uprooted left their place,
>   Sequacious of the lyre ;

but his fame derives its greatest lustre from those songs
which

> Drew iron tears down Pluto's cheek,
> And made Hell grant what love did seek,

and the classic story of Orpheus and Eurydice has been
the inspiration of musicians for close on four centuries.

With the very earliest experiments we are not here concerned, but the first real Italian opera, or drama for
music, was the *Euridice* of Peri and Caccini, produced at
Florence in 1600. In those early days the subject was
treated again and again, and generally under the title of
Orfeo.

At the end of the 17th century, when opera had already
departed sadly from its first ideals, a version was put
forward in which the motive was oddly altered by turning
Orpheus into a '*galant' uomo,*' so that Euridice dies, not
from the traditional snake-bite, but from jealousy !

Several settings of the legend were produced in Gluck's
lifetime, notably one by Bertoni, an air from which was

sometimes introduced into Gluck's opera. Haydn wrote an *Orfeo* specially for London in 1794—the last of the serious versions. Sixty years later Offenbach's *Orphée aux Enfers*, an *opéra bouffe* produced at Paris in 1858, was for some time the delight of the Second Empire. To-day Gluck's *Orfeo* still holds its place in the repertory, where the pure gold of its quality makes too many of its companion operas seem like tarnished Brummagem by comparison.

As the success of Gluck's opera depends almost entirely on the personality of a single artist its revivals must always be comparatively infrequent. The most famous Orfeo of the last century was the famous contralto Pauline Viardot-Garcia, for whom Berlioz rearranged the part; she played the rôle in the Paris revival of 1859 for one hundred and fifty nights in succession, and repeated her triumph at Covent Garden the following year. Within living memory the two most notable revivals in London have been one for Giulia Ravogli in 1890, and another for Marie Brema in 1898.

The short and simple fable is unfolded in four principal Scenes, the division into Acts varying with the several revivals.

Scene I. The curtain rises on a vale in Thessaly, where Eurydice, but lately dead, lies buried. Nymphs and shepherds, her former companions, pay the solemn rite of mourning at her tomb ; there is a sad procession, and the strewing of flowers, while they call on the departed, if she still can hear them, to give some sign of her presence. Above the subdued and sombre strains of the chorus rises the poignant cry of Orpheus, the bereaved lover—" *Euridice ! Euridice !* " He bids them leave him to his grief. Alone with the dead, he invokes her dear shade in a passionate recitative, and calls the trees, the streams, all nature, to testify to his undying love. In a short, plaintive melody thrice repeated he finds what comfort he may in talking with Echo, who at least makes music of the beloved's name. At last his growing passion moves him to resolve on the greatest of all adventures; he himself will go down to Hades, down to the underworld, to claim his bride and bring her back to earth—such love as his, he feels, must move even the Stygian realms to pity.

Nor does love fail him—Amor, the God of Love, appears; the gods have heard his cries and approve his courage. "Go, then, with thy lyre," says Amor, "to the gates of Hades; thy songs, thy mighty love, shall surely prevail even with those awful Powers." But one condition the gods impose. "In leading home thy lost Eurydice, thou mayst indeed speak with her—*but thou shalt not look upon her*—if thou dost, her life and thine are forfeit. Go, and joyfully obey the will of heaven!"

But even in his first outburst of joy and thankfulness Orpheus foresees the failure that threatens him; how is it possible to hold his love once more in his arms, yet not to look at her? How shall he bear it? What will she think? Yet the gods must be obeyed—and love will surely triumph over all.

[The recitative in which Orpheus expresses these feelings should rightly end the Scene; but the singer's requirements induced Gluck to add a long and unusually elaborate song for the Paris production of 1774, since when it has been the frequent custom to substitute an air from another of Gluck's operas, or by another composer, *e.g.*, Bertoni; but it is better to omit the number altogether.]

Scene II. The entrance to Hades, the kingdom of the dead—darkness and Stygian fumes and dreadful gleams from subterranean fires. The Furies, snake-tressed monsters, who guard those gates, are already aware of some strange influence, and stir uneasily; as Orpheus approaches they spring fiercely forward to challenge him in harsh and gloomy chorus, with the clash of brazen cymbals. "What impious mortal dares invade the realms of Erebus? Here none may enter but by the gods' permission!" As the singer preludes on his lyre they break into a frenzied dance, while the horrid bark of three-headed Cerberus mingles with their cries of defiance. Still Orpheus holds his ground, trusting to the charm of song and lyre to move even the powers of Hell to pity. At first, to all his pleadings, their only answer is a thunderous "No!" reiterated thirteen times at intervals with tremendous effect. Nothing daunted, the hero urges the claims of his own transcendent sorrows: "I fear not the tortures of Hell!" he sings. "Yourselves would count them little, could ye but know the pangs of a bereaved lover!"

When even the power of song has failed, the mighty name of love prevails. The spell begins to work; strange feelings of compassion stir in those monstrous forms; their angry voices sink gradually into an almost wistful softness; slowly the awful gates roll back, and Orpheus passes through unharmed into the underworld.

[It is hardly possible to give any idea in words of the music to this short but perfect Scene; the tense, picturesque action, the contrast of contending passions, are depicted with an economy and restraint without a parallel, and the result is the most vivid embodiment possible of the poetic conception; but this can only be realized by seeing and hearing it performed as the composer intended.]

Scene III. Short and simple as this opera is, it profits more than almost any other by the effect of striking contrasts. After the gloom and terror of the last Scene we pass to the golden calm of the Elysian Fields. The short introductory minuet strikes at once a note of serene beauty which reigns unbroken. The following chorus, with soprano solo—sometimes sung by a " Blessed Spirit," sometimes assigned to Eurydice—is full of a tender grace which the flute obbligato helps to invest with a " something afar from the sphere of our sorrow."

But the climax of beauty is achieved in the next number : *Che puro ciel ! Che chiaro sol !* Here we have such a musical picture as has never been surpassed ; by purely orchestral means Gluck has rapt us into the very heart of Elysium ; here are the light, the airs, the streams, of Paradise—they are no earthly trees on which those birds are singing. In this number Gluck is at the height of his inspiration, and the illusion of musical description can go no farther.

[The composer's masterly employment of the woodwind is here the most notable feature of the instrumentation ; as with the flute in the previous number, so here he gets his most poignant effect with a solo oboe.]

Even Orpheus, on entering this abode of bliss, yields to its tranquil spell ; his first melodious phrases are well attuned to the peace and beauty that flood the scene. But soon the old yearning stirs within him ; parted from love, beauty itself is void of recompense—he can have no peace until his quest is accomplished. A chorus of invisible spirits breathes consolation, and tells him that his reward is close at hand. After another of those delicious ballets which in Gluck never seem intrusive Eurydice appears, in glowing beauty, attended by her sister-spirits.

" Fear not to leave us," so they sing, " and to return to earth ! Thy husband claims thee—and where love is, there is Elysium ! "

So Orpheus and his Eurydice are once more united.

Scene IV. We are still in the underworld, but in another region; the difficult earthward journey has begun. Orpheus, who knows too well the danger of delay, is impatient to regain the upper air; in his haste he has even released his hold on the beloved's hand, and presses onward, exhorting her to follow.

But the trial is too severe for poor Eurydice. "How can he bear to leave my side so soon! His words are few and cold, and not one glance of love! What can it mean! Am I so changed? Am I no longer fair? Go then!" she cries, "return to earth without me! What happiness awaits me there, now thou hast ceased to love me?" Torn by anguish and suspicion, Eurydice will move no farther.

Orpheus, distracted, still urges her to follow—but he does not turn, his glance is still averted from her. "Look on me once, beloved!" she pleads. He dares not—and he despairs of making her understand his reason. In impassioned song and dialogue the unequal contest goes on —but her tears, her reproaches, her entreaties, are too strong for even a hero's resolutions—he turns, he clasps her in his arms, he looks into her eyes with all the hunger of love—and even as he does so, she droops and fails in his embrace; she is withdrawn from his mortal vision, and is once more his lost Eurydice.

Then follows that famous solo which, it would seem, age cannot wither nor custom stale. *Che farò senza Euridice* is the dear possession of many thousands who have never seen the opera, and know nothing of Gluck but this one air. From the dramatic point of view the accompanied recitative which precedes it is a still finer inspiration, an intenser expression of tragic passion. This second cruel parting from his love is more than Orpheus can bear;

in desperation he is about to stab himself, when his guardian God of Love again appears and averts the fatal stroke. The hero's trial is over, his faithful love has moved the gods again to pity. Eurydice is restored to him, and the earthward journey is resumed to the strains of a triumphant march. After a succession of dances the scene is changed. We are on earth once more, in the temple of Love, whose praises are sung in a short mellifluous trio. The dances are then resumed, and finally culminate in a long, elaborate, and very spirited *chaconne*.

Exquisitely graceful as Gluck's ballet-music always is, there is certainly too much of it in the Paris version of *Orfeo*, the one usually performed. Gluck himself made a stand against the dramatic impropriety of transferring the courtly dances of the 18th century to the Elysian Fields and the vales of Thessaly ; but the traditions of the ballet overruled all other considerations, and the Vestris family, that long line of famous dancers, was just then in the ascendant : " Monsieur Gluck," said Papa Vestris at a rehearsal of *Orfeo*, " I want a *chaconne* here, if you please ! " " *Chaconne ! Chaconne !* " cried Gluck, " this is a Greek drama ! Do you suppose the Greeks knew anything about *chaconnes* ? " " Did they not ? " replied Vestris, with lifted eyebrows ; " then they are much to be pitied ! " But the dancer got his *chaconne* as we have seen.

Nor was this the only concession that Gluck had to make against his better judgment ; for the Paris production (1774) he was obliged to assign the rôle of Orfeo, written for a male contralto, to a tenor, a change unfavourable to the musical effect, besides necessitating incidentally the introduction of inappropriate alterations and additions. In the original exponent of the part, Guadagni, the composer was exceptionally fortunate. This admirable singer had been in London in 1745, and was specially chosen by Handel to sing the alto parts in *Samson* and the *Messiah*. He seems to have been specially devoted to the dramatic side of his art, and in the course of his frequent visits to England he became the friend and pupil of Garrick. Indeed, his reverence for dramatic propriety has earned him a reputation unique, one supposes, in the annals of the stage—it is said that he never gave an encore, and even refused to return to the scene in acknowledgment of the loudest applause.   By persisting in this course " he so greatly offended individuals and the opera audience in general that at length he never appeared without being hissed."   Nevertheless, he continued a great favourite in London, where he played Orfeo in 1770.   It is worthy of note that this remarkable man reaped further laurels in a very different field ; he was known as " the best billiard-player in Europe."   Such a combination of talents has probably been equalled only in the French composer Philidor (1726–95), whose musical reputation was almost eclipsed by his fame as a chess-player.

DIE ENTFÜHRUNG AUS DEM SERAIL

Music by MOZART. *Words by* BRETZNER.
Vienna, 1782 ; *London,* 1827.

THIS little opera, more generally known as *Il Seraglio*, can be made one of the most delightful of entertainments; the fresh and homely humour of it intrigues us from the start, the sentiment fortunately fails to move us, except to enjoyment of the music. As to the words, it is said that Mozart himself had a large share in them. It may be ; in any case they serve their turn well enough for the musical setting, and for the conduct of the simplest of plots.

Picturesqueness of scene is secured by giving the little play a Turkish setting—the palace of the Pasha Selim, on the shores of the Bosphorus. Here Costanze, a noble lady who has been carried off by pirates, is held captive in the harem, together with her maid Blonde, and Pedrillo, the droll, faithful servant of Costanze's *fiancé* Belmonte. Costanze, pining for her absent lover, is embarrassed by the attentions of the Pasha, while little Blonde is plagued by those of old Osmin, the surly gardener—who is, moreover, the Pasha's right-hand man and the great comic figure of the piece. Pedrillo manages to introduce Belmonte into the palace, and together they plan an escape which nearly succeeds, when Osmin intercepts the elopers and drags them bound before the Pasha Selim. In the course of conversation it comes out that Belmonte's father once did the Pasha some tremendous wrong, which would seem to call for even severer punishment than the immediate circumstances demand. Selim, however, is every inch a gentleman, and sees his chance here for a show of splendid magnanimity. He, who, in spite of his ardent passion for the fair Costanze, has never tried to force her to his will, now resigns her to Belmonte, the son of his bitterest enemy, grants them a free pardon, and provides all with a safe passage to their native land.

Act I. In the grounds of the Pasha Selim's palace, part of which gleams white through the trees, while the waves of the Bosphorus sparkle blue in the background. Enter Belmonte, devoured by all a lover's impatience. Though he has managed to find his way to the place of Costanze's captivity, he is at his wits' end how to communicate with his beloved. He has just time for a plaintive little air, *Hier soll ich dich denn sehen*, when approaching footsteps send him into hiding.

It is Osmin who enters—a magnificent figure of fun, with his surly humour and huge bass voice, " that can sing both high and low." (The part was written for a certain Ludwig Fischer, who had a compass of two octaves and a half.) The old man, with a basket on his arm, mounts a ladder that stands against a fig-tree, and sings grotesquely as he gathers the fruit. He seems to have the harem rather on his mind ; women *will* be women—even his little Blonde gives him a lot of trouble— and he has a life's experience behind him, which he sums up in the song, *Wer ein Liebchen hat gefunden* :

> When a maiden takes your fancy,
>   And you want her for your own,
> Be a hero in your wooing,
> Always kissing, always cooing,
>   Never leave the girl alone ! [1]

Belmonte, who has just found his way into the palace

---

[1] These extracts from the English version are printed by kind permission of Messrs Boosey and Co., Ltd.

grounds, interrupts him : " Hey, friend ! is this the Pasha Selim's house ? " Osmin eyes him sourly, but deigns no answer ; he goes on with his song :

> But when once she's safely landed,
> Lock the door and turn the key !
> For you'll find the charming creature
> Has a restless, roving nature,
> Far too fond of liberty !

The two men soon go at it hammer-and-tongs in a lively duet, in which Belmonte is driven off the stage. The arrival of Pedrillo and his cool request for figs rouse Osmin to still greater fury. His longish solo, *Solche her-gelauf'ne Laffen* is a masterpiece in the *buffo* style ; he gets almost inarticulate toward the end, as he enumerates the things he would like to do to Pedrillo, if only he got the chance :

> Hang you first ! Draw and quarter !
> Souse you next in boiling water !
> On a spit then I'd pin you !
> Last of all I'd take and skin you !

A spirited chorus of janissaries, together with the ladies of the harem, welcomes the arrival of Pasha Selim in his state barge, from which he gallantly hands the lovely captive-heroine on to the stage.

" Still drooping, fair Costanze ? " he questions. " Still in tears ? "

Alas, yes ! it is the poor girl's fate to move weeping through the opera, as a foil to so much gaiety ! However, her first air, *Ach, ich liebte,* affords at least some consola-tion (to a prima donna) by being extremely florid and extremely high, a remark which is still more applicable to the great solo allotted to the heroine (*Martern aller Arten*) in Act II. The part was, in fact, written for an exceptionally high soprano, Aloysia Weber, Mozart's first love, subsequently his sister-in-law, and

sister to the Mme Hofer who 'created' the rôle of the
Queen of Night in *The Magic Flute*. However, Costanze's song (of devotion to her lost love) touches the
heart of Selim, who vows never to put constraint upon
one so tender and so true.

Pedrillo, meanwhile, has persuaded the Pasha to take
Belmonte into his service as architect, and the scene
closes with a merry knockabout trio, *Marsch, marsch,
marsch!* in which Osmin tries to stop Belmonte and
Pedrillo from going into the palace, but is himself over-
powered and rolled in the dust, while the pair make a
triumphant entry.

Act II. We begin with a lively quarrel between Osmin
and Blonde, daintiest of soubrettes, who, " as a freeborn
English woman," flatly declines to take her orders from
any heathen Turk—least of all an elderly one! Blonde's
music throughout absolutely sparkles with gaiety and high
spirits, and in their duet, *Ich gehe, doch rath' ich es dir*,
the way in which she flaunts the old fellow, mocks his
manner, and leaves him gasping with amazement at her
audacity, is quite delicious. Osmin being thoroughly
routed, Pedrillo enters to tell Blonde of the brightening
of their prospects—of Belmonte's admission to the palace,
and their plans for escaping that very night. Blonde breaks
out into an exuberant little song, *Welche Wonne, welche
Lust!* which obviously calls for an accompanying dance,
and is perhaps the most captivating solo in the opera.

Costanze, meanwhile, is well provided for in the great
air, *Martern aller Arten*, one of the most exacting pieces
of *coloratura* in the soprano repertory; this outburst
is occasioned by the Pasha informing Costanze that his
patience will not last for ever, and that she really must
reconsider her position. But the fun is resumed in a
rollicking duet, *Vivat Bacchus!* in which Pedrillo plies

Osmin with unaccustomed drink and so puts him *hors de combat.* Belmonte, Costanze, Blonde, and Pedrillo now join in the quartet of rejoicing which ends the Act. Any possible monotony of mood is cunningly broken by the introduction, in the middle of this number, of one of those inevitable little tussles between the sexes. Belmonte and Pedrillo are both struck by a horrid suspicion that their respective mistresses may not have been *quite* so firm against the temptations of the harem as they vow they have been. This is too much for the patience of the fair ones ; Costanze, of course, is soon in tears ; Blonde promptly boxes Pedrillo's ears—

> (Me, forsooth, to be suspected
> With an ugly waddling Turk !),

and the men are quickly brought to their senses.

Act III. The escape is planned for midnight. As the hour draws near, Belmonte invokes the God of Love to aid him, in a suave Mozartian air, with much Italian ornamentation, *Ich baue ganz auf deine Stärke.* But all in vain ! Osmin and the guard are on the watch, cut off the fugitives, and bind them fast to await the coming of the Pasha, while the old ruffian bursts out into an almost fiendish song of triumph, *Ha ! wie will ich triumphiren !* a song which with its compass of two octaves and its strenuous hammering on the high notes must remain the admiration and despair of all but exceptional basses. In a long and pathetic duet Costanze and Belmonte resign themselves to their fate, but the entrance of Selim with his halo of magnanimity and a free pardon for everybody brings the play to an end with a chorus of gratitude, the departure of the happy lovers for their fatherland, and the popular collapse of that old wind-bag, Osmin.

" The Escape from the Seraglio," to give the title its

true English meaning, may well be considered as the beginning of the German School of Opera ; it breaks away from Italian traditions in many particulars, chiefly in the attempt to secure a closer union of words and music, and the introduction of a large amount of spoken dialogue, a novelty in an operatic work of any importance. Its form is actually that of the *Singspiel*, a category which includes *The Magic Flute*, Weber's *Freischütz*, and even Beethoven's *Fidelio*. Although there are certain conventional Italian airs in *Seraglio*, these must be counted as its weakness ; its strength lies in the sweet simplicity of some of its tunes, the sprightly gaiety of others, and the rich humour to be found in the concerted pieces and throughout the whole part of Osmin. This little opera is of a thoroughly intimate *genre*, and can be given properly only in a small theatre. Until recently it has not had a fair chance in England because of a tasteless ' arrangement ' —say, rather, distortion—produced nearly a hundred years ago at Covent Garden, with " original additions " by one Kramer. It was successfully revived, however, in England about fifteen years ago in its original purity, and with a new English libretto, and is now a well-established favourite, while Osmin's first song, " When a maiden takes your fancy," has become one of the most popular *buffo* songs in the concert-room.

LE NOZZE DI FIGARO

Music by MOZART. *Words by* DA PONTE, *from* BEAUMARCHAIS.
Vienna, 1786; *London*, 1812; *New York*, 1823.

THIS is an opera which, owing to the delicious gaiety of many of the scenes, the charm of certain of the characters, and, above all, the ever-present enchantment of Mozart's music, it is possible to enjoy to a great extent without any real understanding of the plot. It would be a mistake, however, to go no farther, for the music is so illustrative of the drama that our enjoyment is doubled when we are able to appreciate how subtly Mozart has moulded it to every changing mood and to every twist and turn of the rapid action. Some knowledge at least is necessary of Beaumarchais' two great comedies, *Le Mariage de Figaro*, from which this opera is taken, and its predecessor in point of time, *Le Barbier de Séville*, so familiar to all opera-goers in connexion with Rossini's *Barbiere*. It is essential, for instance, to bear in mind that the Count and Countess of Mozart's creation are the Almaviva and Rosina of the earlier play (and of Rossini's opera), that poor Rosina has been long neglected by her roving husband, and that Figaro is no longer a mere 'barber,' but a valet, and the actual rival of his master in love.

A writer at the beginning of this century described the 'book' of *Figaro* as "a moral blister"; a fantastical comedy of intrigue would seem perhaps a truer description. In Beaumarchais' play, *Le Mariage de Figaro*, upon which da Ponte based his libretto—and which was said to have had its share in hastening the French Revolution

—there are, of course, darker undertones and threads of serious interest, but he must have a morbid mind indeed who can discover anything in the words and action of the opera but the most delightful flummery, touched here and there with tender sentiment.

The scene is laid appropriately in a castle in Spain, and the persons of the drama may be said to act accordingly. The chief characters are not the Count and Countess, but his valet Figaro and her maid Susanna. The two are about to get married, and Figaro has good reason to be anxious about the Count's unwelcome attentions to Susanna, his plans to prevent their marriage, and his purpose to revive certain seigneurial privileges, of a kind which would certainly come as a shock to our modern ways of thinking. The maid and the valet, who are very much in love, combine with the neglected Countess to defeat the Count's designs, and incidentally by a public exposure to shame him into a better way of life. The plan is entirely successful; we enjoy the rake's discomfiture, even if we cannot put much faith in his permanent reformation.

The under-plot is concerned with the intrigues of a rather farcical duenna, Marcellina, who, at the outset, is bent on marrying Figaro herself, a plan in which she is backed up by the Count and old Bartolo, for whom she keeps house; but no one who has any acquaintance with the stage devices of that period will be in the least surprised to learn how " the unexpected discovery that Figaro is her son leads to a generally happy *dénouement* ! "

So much for the ' moral blister ' ! In the midst of this unsubstantial but very complicated plot, at every corner we find lurking that pearl of all operatic Pages, the delightful Cherubino, the roguish, sentimental youngster, standing, but with no reluctant feet, on the threshold of manhood. Whatever can be alleged against the Chérubin of Beaumarchais, Mozart's Cherubino must not be so aspersed; he is a figure of purest fantasy, and a sheer delight.

Act I. After an overture which promises nothing but gaiety the curtain rises on a piquant situation. Figaro is measuring the walls of a large apartment, while Susanna, before the looking-glass, is making herself more than usually attractive by trying on the bridal wreath and veil. " Fifteen ! Eighteen ! " sings Figaro, with his footrule; " Yes, 'tis really sweet and dainty," sings Susanna to herself in the glass. It is their wedding eve; the Count has kindly given them this fine room for their own. " Just between the Count's room and the Countess's—so handy ! " says the simple Figaro. " Handy ! yes—for the Count ! " replies Susanna ; " *you* can use it if you like— *I* won't have it ! " She then tells him certain facts which make him fairly caper with rage and break into the jolly air *Se vuol ballare* :

> Let me but catch you here,
> My pretty master,
> Straight to disaster
> I'll lead you a dance ! [1]

And so Figaro dances off.

Enter that cattish duenna Marcellina with Bartolo, who is very willing to help her in catching Figaro. Susanna re-enters, and, in a sprightly duet, each lady, while ' making politeness ' at the door, tells the other what she thinks of her (*Via resti servita*):

> MAR. I bow to my lady
> So dainty and fine !
> SUS. Nay, nay, ma'am, believe me,
> The honour is mine !
> MAR. Now pray go before me !

Sus. No, no ! 'tis for you !
Mar. I'm not so uncivil——
Sus. I know what is due !
Mar. The bride of the moment !
Sus. A lady—though plain !
Mar. The Count's little fancy !
Sus. The doxy of Spain !
Mar. Your innocence——
Sus.   Dignity !
Mar. Your influence——
Sus.   Your age !
Mar. (By heaven, I could throttle her !
        I'm bursting with rage !)

With every sentence the ladies bow and curtsy with ever greater politeness, until Susanna's last shot—" Your age ! "—drives Marcellina from the field.

Now comes Cherubino, almost in tears ; the Count has caught him flirting with the gardener's daughter, Barberina—(Fanchette in Beaumarchais' comedy)—and has dismissed him from the castle. Never again will he see his dear Susanna—no, nor the Countess either ! He is equally in love with both, it seems—nay, with all the women in the world, as his delicious solo so well sets forth (*Non so più cosa son, cosa faccio*) :

Yes, it's true ! I don't know what I'm doing !
Such a fever within me is brewing !
Every maiden I meet makes me flutter,
Any fair one can set me on fire !

It is necessary to record that in this scene Cherubino contrives to snatch from Susanna a ribbon belonging to the Countess, and gives her in exchange a little song he has composed, and which he hopes Susanna will sing to her mistress ; for this is the *Voi che sapete* which the Page sings himself in the Second Act.

Suddenly the Count's voice is heard outside, and the plot immediately thickens in a way which demands our closest attention. Cherubino, in a fright, hides behind

the big armchair. The Count, who has come to beg
Susanna for a rendezvous, has not got far with his gallantry
when the voice of Basilio, the music-master, makes him
jump. The Count, of course, must not be found in
Susanna's room (least of all by Basilio, who has a serpent's
tongue)—he will hide behind the armchair ; just in the
nick of time Cherubino slips round to the seat of the chair
and is covered up by Susanna.

Enter Basilio, to tease Susanna, who hates him, with
the most scandalous insinuations about Cherubino and
herself—" and as for the Page and her ladyship the
Countess—well, everybody is saying——" "*What* is
everybody saying ? " thunders the Count, springing up
from behind the chair. The trio *Cosa sento !* paints the
general confusion, in the course of which Cherubino is
naturally dragged from his lurking-place. The Count
acts promptly ; there is a commission vacant in his regi-
ment, Cherubino shall have it, and he must be off at
once. Susanna and the Countess are both a little sorry,
but Figaro thinks it fine fun, and nobly has Mozart
provided for his mood : there is surely not an opera house
the world over that has not been 'brought down' by
Non più andrai, the most admirable example of robust
humour to be found in the whole range of vocal music.

> So, Sir Page, your vagaries are over !
> Far too long you've been living in clover,
> Till at last they've begun to discover
>   That you're turning the house out of doors ! [1]

How gaily he mocks the airs and graces of the lad, pulls
his curls, tweaks off his feathered cap ! Ah, life's a very
different thing in the army !

> You'll forget your parlour dances
> When the sweltering line advances.

---

[1] These four incomparable lines are by the late W. H. Bellamy ; it
would be sacrilege to substitute any other version.

Over mountains ! through the river !
First you sweat and then you shiver !
Up you get and on you blunder,
Trumpets blare and cannons thunder,
While the shots come whizzing round you
Till you wish yourself away !
Cherubino's all for glory !
He's the boy to win the day !

Act II. In contrast to the lightness and gaiety of the First Act a deeper note is sounded on the second rise of the curtain. The Countess, alone in her apartments, a pathetic figure of neglected love, voices her sorrow in the cavatina, *Porgi amor qualche ristoro.* This is a crystal stream of Mozartian melody, " pouring unto us from the heaven's brink."

Plaintive as are the words, the music soars above all earthly melancholy ; whether the song is dramatically appropriate may be questioned—we are more than content to accept it as a perfect piece of abstract beauty.

But soon all is once more in movement. Susanna comes to talk with her mistress, and the entrance of Figaro promises further plots and intrigues.

It is well to notice the way in which the stage is set for this Scene : the room has a closet, a curtained recess, two doors, and a window ; all of which prepare us for a certain liveliness of action.

Figaro has a plan for diverting the Count from opposing the coming nuptials. " Our only hope of defeating his lordship," he says, " is to turn the tables upon him—keep his thoughts away from other people's wives by making him apprehensive about his own ! " With this object he has sent him an anonymous letter warning him that the Countess has an assignation with a gallant in the park that very evening. That will give him something to think about ! Meanwhile, Susanna must promise to grant the

Count his wished-for rendezvous at the same time and place. " But surely," says the Countess, " you will not let Susanna do that ! " " Not exactly ! " he answers; " Cherubino shall go, disguised, in her place ! "

So Sir Page is not yet off to the wars !   He enters now, and after all this dialogue of intrigue his little song is welcome, *Voi che sapete*—who does not know it ?

> One feeling moves me,
> All else above—
> Tell me, fair ladies,
> Can this be love ?

Susanna proceeds gaily to dress the youngster in the garments he is to wear as her substitute that evening. The chatter and laughter are at their height when an angry knock is heard at the door, which Susanna had locked in view of the ' trying on.' It is the Count—heavens ! and Cherubino, only half dressed, in the Countess's chamber !   He flies into the bedroom and bolts the door behind him ; Susanna hides behind the curtains of the recess. The Countess lets in her furious lord, full of suspicion, with Figaro's letter in his hand. A chair is overturned in the bedroom. " Only Susanna ! " says her ladyship. The Count demands entry, to see for himself ; the Countess bars the way ; the door is locked, she says, and shall not be opened. The Count goes in search of a hammer to break it down, and takes the Countess with him. Cherubino opens the door, kisses his Susanna good-bye, and jumps through the window into the garden, while Susanna takes his place in the bedroom. Re-enter the Count and her ladyship ; and then begins one of those long and elaborate finales—*Esci omai, garzon malnato*—which Mozart had a special genius for devising.

So far as the music is concerned, movement succeeds movement in sprightly variety, and with admirable clearness ; not so the plot, however, in which no less than eight persons are involved. The complications are so numerous and so tangled that it is impossible to recount them in detail. The chief effect is made by the entrance of Marcellina, Bartolo, and Basilio, who present to the Count an alleged contract of marriage between Figaro and Marcellina, and demand that justice be done to the aggrieved duenna. The Count, of course, is privy to this conspiracy, and promises to have the matter tried before the court. Mention must be made of the episodic entry of the gardener, old Antonio, with a damaged pot of choice carnations. Someone—Cherubino, of course—had jumped on to them from the Countess's bedroom window that very morning! But even this awkward incident is explained away by the ready wit of Figaro and Susanna, who swear that the jumper was none other than Figaro himself.

Act III. *Scene* 1 opens with a short dialogue very essential to the plot, in which the Countess tells Susanna that she has determined to go herself to the rendezvous with the Count, who, taking her for Susanna, will thus be detected in paying lawful attentions to his own wife! Then follows one of the loveliest and best-known numbers of the opera, the duet *Crudel, perchè finora*, in which Susanna agrees to meet the Count that evening in the park. The music exactly illustrates both the amorous ardour of the Count and the delicious coquetry of Susanna, and blends them together into a flawless whole. [It is very well worth while to compare the duet with the equally well-known *Là ci darem* in *Don Giovanni*, and to note the subtle and perfectly appropriate differences in the method of treatment.]

The following showy air for the Count, *Vedrò mentr'io sospiro*, expressive of jealousy and rage against Figaro, is perhaps the least interesting number in the whole opera ;

dramatically it has hardly any justification, and might well be omitted, as it is most obviously 'written in' to gratify the demands of the singer. At the same time, it makes a most effective piece for the concert-room, where it has always been a great favourite.

Now enters Marcellina with her supporters, Basilio and old Bartolo, together with Don Curzio, the stuttering lawyer who is to decide on the claims against Figaro. "The defendant must either pay the plaintiff the sum demanded or marry her this very day," says Don Curzio. The second alternative, however, is soon ruled out by the discovery that Figaro—who has "a strawberry mark on his left arm!"—is the long-lost son of Marcellina and Bartolo! A short but pregnant sestet follows in which many things happen. Figaro is welcomed by his new-found parents; Susanna enters just in time to see him embracing Marcellina, and, under a misapprehension, boxes his ears; but an explanation follows and the usual 'happy *dénouement*' is greatly assisted by the bag of gold with which Susanna discharges Figaro's obligation to Marcellina; how she came by it was her own secret—and the Count's!

Scene II. The scene now changes to the Countess's apartment and we have in quick succession two of the loveliest lyrical numbers of the opera—the great air *Dove sono i bei momenti*, similar in sentiment (but very different in musical form) to the *Porgi amor* of the previous Act— and what is perhaps musically the most enchanting of all Mozart's duets, *Sull'aria*, in which Susanna writes, at the Countess's dictation, a letter to the Count fixing the exact spot for their rendezvous.

[This letter, it is important to remark in view of subsequent developments, they secure not with a seal, but a *pin*.]

Now to the strains of a robust march the wedding procession enters, and Figaro and Susanna with much ceremony receive the blessing of their master and mistress. A stately *fandango* is then danced, and a short chorus sung in praise of the Count, who invites them all to the grand festivities of the evening.

Kindly note the *pin* again! Susanna has managed to pass her letter to the Count, who pricks his finger with the pin; Figaro observes this, but without suspecting Susanna.

Act IV.   *Scene* 1.   A room in the Castle.

A careful study of the short scene with which this Act opens is absolutely essential for the understanding of the tangled *imbroglio* which is to follow. It begins with a dainty miniature of an air for Barberina, the gardener's daughter: *L'ho perduto.* The girl is looking for a pin—the one with which Susanna had ' sealed ' her note to the Count, and which she had entrusted to Barberina to take back to her as an acknowledgment of its receipt. Figaro enters and learns all the circumstances from the unsuspecting child; he hastily concludes that Susanna is faithless to him after all, and intends to yield that evening to the Count's solicitations; stung to a fury of jealousy, he denounces the entire race of women in the song *Aprite un po' quegl'occhi* :

> These are your so-called goddesses
>   That claim your whole devotion,
> Whose very skirts and bodices
>   You worship from afar !
>   *I'll* tell you what they are !
>
> They're vampires that cling to you
>   With poisonous breath,
> They're sirens that sing to you
>   And lure you to death !
>   .   .   .
> They vex us and grieve us,
>   They always deceive us,
> And then at the last
>   In the lurch they will leave us !

A perfect tornado of abuse is this song, and a wonderful piece of musical ingenuity.

Scene ii. In the park, under the pine-trees, where the final entanglement is to be knit and unravelled.

Susanna has heard from Marcellina of Figaro's unwarranted suspicions ; she is very angry, and determined to make him smart for it: " One gentleman coming to make love to me, and another to spy upon me ! Well, I'm ready for both of them ! "

She takes her seat in one of the arbours in the dim and perfumed garden ; she knows that Figaro will be lurking near ; she is masked and dominoed. Indeed, the whole atmosphere on the stage, as in the orchestra, is one of masks and dominoes and moonlight, were it not that even moonlight would be too indiscreet for the conduct of the intrigue that is to follow.

It is late evening and the moon has not yet risen. It is the very hour of love, and Susanna sings such a lovesong as was never heard before and has never since been equalled, *Deh vieni, non tardar*. It would be ungrateful to suggest that the mood of the music is far too exalted for the situation—no situation could be worthy of it, for it is no earthly music.

> In heaven there shines no star, the moon is hidden—
> Now all the world to love's high feast is bidden.
> Then come, no more delay, my heart's dear treasure !
> Here, where the darkness broods, we'll take our pleasure.

Alas that such a piece of " linkèd sweetness long drawn out " should do worse than " waste its sweetness on the desert air " ! It exactly fulfils Susanna's intention by confirming the suspicions of the listening Figaro, who regards it as the genuine expression of Susanna's passion for the Count—and determines on an instant revenge.

With the arrival of the Count, the Countess, and

Cherubino, we plunge at once into such a game of cross-purposes as is rarely to be found even in the *imbroglio* of an 18th-century comedy of intrigue. Not only have we the confusion of masks and dominoes, but even the voices must lend themselves to the deception while the Countess plays Susanna to the Count and Susanna passes herself off on Figaro as the Countess.

When Figaro finds out the truth, and the lovers are reconciled, Susanna still keeps up her disguise in order that together they may enact a little love-scene for the benefit of the Count, who discovers his wife, as he supposes, actually encouraging the attentions of his own valet. This is too much : the Count calls loudly for his people to arrest Figaro, the stage is crowded with the complete *personnel* of the piece (not omitting even the gardener Antonio and the stuttering Don Curzio), and the *dénouement* is swiftly reached. The supposed Countess is revealed as Susanna, the supposed Susanna as the Countess ; Figaro is innocent ; the Count is guilty enough in intention, but through the ready wit of the two women is landed in a purely farcical situation, being detected in making proposals of gallantry to his own wife ! So fast and furious are the complications of this last and most elaborate scene that it is almost a relief to reach the final tag :

> To this day of dire confusion,
> Queer adventure, fond illusion,
> Let us make a gay conclusion
>   With a merry wedding ball !

All now are happily provided for : old Bartolo does his duty by Marcellina, Cherubino concentrates on Barberina, the Countess, the long-suffering Rosina, gives Count Almaviva another chance, and, best of all, Figaro, the one-time Barber of Seville, is free at last to marry his faithful Susanna.

A word as to the libretto of *Figaro*. It is laid out effectively for musical setting, its lyrics are generally graceful and often most ingenious ; nevertheless, it is a failure owing to the fact that da Ponte, the author, tried to do too much. Successfully to compress the contents of Beaumarchais' long and witty comedy within the cramping limits of a four-act opera is manifestly impossible—it is certainly astonishing to find how little, even of the less important quality, has been omitted, yet the result is still but a baffling confusion. The opera, we must remember, was produced when the play was only two years old, and was in everybody's mouth, so that nearly all who listened to da Ponte's version were already familiar with the original, and such familiarity is essential if we wish to understand the action of the opera. Even were the dialogue clearly heard and understood, that would not be enough, as so much of the development is carried on obscurely in the concerted pieces and finales. The earlier English versions, indeed, were so unsatisfactory that people tacitly agreed to leave them alone and enjoy the glorious music for its own sake ; they were content to admire the outstanding characters, Figaro, Susanna, Cherubino, to wonder what on earth the other mysterious figures, Bartolo, Basilio, Barberina, etc., were doing on the stage, and, by the time the dense *imbroglio* of the fourth Act began, to give the whole thing up as a bad job. As if these unhelpful English versions were not hindrance enough to the understanding of the plot, it became too often the custom to make senseless ' cuts,' which entirely destroyed such thin threads of continuity as existed. At last in 1915 a version was prepared by Sir Thomas Beecham for his original Opera Company, in which, by the judicious readjustment of certain scenes, and the introduction of much additional dialogue from

Beaumarchais' comedy, the whole becomes an intelligible and delightful frolic. Played in this way it immediately caught the public taste, with the result that what was once a collection of 'favourite airs' for old-fashioned lovers of music has now become one of the most popular entertainments for general enjoyment.

DON GIOVANNI

Music by MOZART.   *Words by* DA PONTE.
Prague, 1787 ; *London*, 1817 ; *New York*, 1826.

OF all operas *Don Giovanni* would seem to have the best chance of what mortals call immortality ; there is certainly no other about which musical as well as popular opinion is so unanimous. Hailed as a masterpiece on its first production, its reputation has steadily increased in the course of nearly one hundred and forty years ; Beethoven (frowning on the subject of the libretto) kept a portion of the score beside him for study and admiration, Rossini knelt in reverence before the autograph original in Viardot-Garcia's possession ; Wagner's enthusiasm for it increased with his own development, and Gounod, on the occasion of its centenary, wrote the most splendid panegyric that any composer has ever penned of another's work. It is still an inexhaustible treasure-house of ideas for musical students of to-day, and it is probable that, as the late H. E. Krehbiel prophesied, when the next great Master shall arise, he will be found to be a descendant not of the Titan Wagner, but of the ' divine Mozart ' who wrote *Don Giovanni*.

Da Ponte, the librettist of *Figaro*, has served Mozart only fairly well in this second collaboration. The subject was not new ; the story of the Libertine and the Statue that came to supper had been familiar for at least two centuries. Both Molière and Corneille had been attracted by it—the English laureate Shadwell had used it in *The Libertine Destroyed* (1676)—Gluck had written a ballet round it. Da Ponte's 'book,' *Il dissoluto punito: ossia il Don Giovanni*, is taken directly from a Spanish version called *El Combidado de Piedra* ("The Stone Guest"). The scene is laid in Seville, and the producer who wishes to get the right atmosphere would do well to seek his inspirations in the grim, occasionally *macabre*, humour of the Spanish painter Goya.

With one exception, every person in the opera is a distinct piece of careful characterization. We have the reckless, all-conquering libertine, Don Giovanni, whose only virtues are his persistent gaiety and his indomitable courage ; Donna Anna, a haughty and tragic figure, inconsolable for the loss of her father the Commendatore (who is killed in the first Scene, and reappears as the spectral statue in the last) ; Donna Elvira, the too credulous victim of the Don's fascinations ; Zerlina, the rustic coquette, with her boorish lover Masetto ; lastly, Leporello, the Don's droll dog of a valet, always a coward, always grumbling, but still attached to his master. The only 'wooden' figure is Don Ottavio, the *fiancé* of Donna Anna, to whom Mozart has assigned by way of compensation two of the loveliest tenor songs ever written.

It is difficult to place Mozart's masterpiece in any particular category—the original label of *dramma giocoso* or *opera buffa* is obviously inadequate ; in fact *Don Giovanni* as an opera stands alone, though the libretto in its naïve blending of supernatural horror with scenes of gaiety and even low comedy reminds us somewhat of Horace Walpole's *Castle of Otranto* and must have seemed just such a daring innovation. The serious element is confined almost entirely to the beginning and to the end of the opera. In the opening Scene the dissolute 'hero' kills in a duel the father of a noble Spanish lady whom he has insulted; retribution is deferred until the final Scene, when the spectre of the slain man appears in the banquet hall to shatter the revelry, and drag the unrepentant libertine away to that place of torment where the worm dieth not and the fire is not quenched.

The greater part of the opera is given up to further amorous adventures of the incorrigible Don Giovanni, and the ineffectual attempts on the part of his victims to bring him to justice; the rather loosely knit scenes are treated almost entirely in a spirit of comedy, and their dramatic value is not very great, but the entire opera is made glorious by the radiant atmosphere of beauty with which Mozart's music has invested it.

Act I. *Scene* 1. We are introduced to our libertine hero in an unlucky moment; the all-conquering Don Giovanni has made a sad mistake for once. The scene is a court in the palace of the Commandant of Seville; it is past midnight, and Leporello, drowsing in a corner, is tired of waiting for his master, busied with amorous adventure inside. The *buffo* music of Leporello's opening air, *Notte e giorno faticar*, soon passes to dramatic excitement as two figures hurry from the palace—Don Giovanni, concealing his face with ample cloak and downdrawn hat, and a lady clinging to him, in frantic endeavour to tear his disguise away; it is Donna Anna, the Commandant's daughter, whom the insatiable Don had hoped to add to his list of conquests. The lady is furious, and her indignant cries soon bring her father to her assistance; he forces Don Giovanni to a duel, in which the elder man is slain; Donna Anna, who has not succeeded in discovering the identity of her insulter, has gone in search of further aid.

[Attention should be given to the music of this short scene, in which the swift action and the varying emotions are most vividly expressed with a marvellous economy of means.]

The lady now returns with Don Ottavio, her affianced lover, to lament her father's death in heartrending phrases ; in the agitated duet *Fuggi, crudele!* the two swear to devote themselves to the detection and punishment of the murderer.

Scene II. Outside the walls of Seville. Leporello, as is his habit, is engaged in lecturing his master on his evil ways, when the sound of footsteps sends them both into hiding. Enter a lady in distress—it is Elvira, an old flame of the Don's, not long deserted ; in the vigorous trio *Ah, chi mi dice mai* she pours out her indignation against her betrayer, while Leporello and his master make their characteristic comments. Don Giovanni, not recognizing the voice, steps forward, eager to console the lady ("Console! that's good!" says Leporello. "How many hundreds has he 'consoled' already!"); to his confusion she discovers his identity, but before she has exhausted her reproaches he manages to slip away, leaving his servant to do such 'consoling' as he may. Leporello's method is certainly an odd one. "Madame," says he, "you are not the first whom my master has used in such fashion—nor will you be the last! Permit me to give you some account of the fair ones, not a few, whom he has already honoured with his attentions!" Then follows the famous *Madamina!* perhaps the most amazing example of unctuous humour to be found in Mozart. Drawing a formidable parchment from his pocket, Leporello proceeds to rattle off a sort of catalogue, illustrated by his own gestures and grimaces, of his master's amorous exploits. The number of his conquests is certainly prodigious. In Italy alone they amount to 640; Germany, France, Turkey, all contribute, the last a mere trifle of 90; Spain,

of course, comes out on top with a glorious total of
1003! Duchesses and real princesses, country damsels,
city ma'amselles—fair or swarthy, tall or tiny—he has
'consoled' them all with an impartial benevolence;
true, he prefers the plump in winter, reserving the
slender for the summer heat, and—but there is no need
to go farther into Leporello's lively description! The
song is, in fact, a piece of extravagant clowning which
the alchemy of Mozart's genius has transformed for us
into delicious gaiety, a thing of pure delight. It must be
confessed that it is hardly calculated to console the poor
forsaken lady. However, in order that our sympathies
may be still further enlisted on her side, it has become
the custom to let her bring down the curtain on the fine
air (No. 25), transferred from Act II, *Mi tradì quell'alma
ingrata*, in which the fair Elvira expresses her willingness
to pardon the dear rogue and give him yet another trial.

Scene iii. A scene of rustic gaiety in a village not far
from Don Giovanni's palace. It is the wedding day of
Zerlina and Masetto; the peasants are all assembled for
the festivities, and the radiant bride is exhorting the
maidens to follow her example and make the best use of
their time (*Giovinette che fate all'amore*). The Don, who
enters with Leporello, casts an approving eye on the
dancing beauty, and grasps at once the possibilities of the
situation. With a courtier's affability he approaches and
invites them all to consider his palace and gardens as their
own for that day; Leporello is told off to conduct them
thither, while, in spite of Masetto's protest, Zerlina is
persuaded to stay behind with her new admirer. Indeed,
the wide-awake coquette offers little resistance to the
Don's advances, and, by the time the bewitching duet
Là ci darem la mano is finished, is quite willing to accompany him to the neighbouring summer-house—but for

the arrival of the indignant Elvira, who, taking in the situation at a glance, warns the peasant girl of Don Giovanni's real intentions and leads her off to a place of safety.

Enter Donna Anna in deep mourning, leaning on Ottavio's arm; they are still looking for the man who slew her father, and are about to enlist the Don's aid when Elvira returns and tries to make them realize the true state of affairs. In the quartet which follows, *Non ti fidar, o misera,* Elvira's excited protestations are admirably contrasted with Don Giovanni's subtle insinuations that the poor lady is mad, and the hesitation of the other two in coming to a decision. As the baffled woman makes a despairing exit, the Don follows, in pretended anxiety for her safety; in bidding the others a courteous *au revoir,* something in his voice awakens Donna Anna to the truth at last—there goes the wretch who insulted her, the slayer of her father! She declaims her fierce longing for vengeance in the superb aria *Or sai chi l'onore,* probably the severest test for a dramatic soprano to be found in any of Mozart's operas. Admirable is the contrast afforded by Ottavio's song of sympathy, *Dalla sua pace,* one of those restful oases of serene beauty to which all true Mozartians look forward with especial delight. Ottavio having retired, Leporello appears, followed by his master; the former has cleverly disposed of Elvira— the coast is clear, the guests already assembled. Don Giovanni gives orders for the most lavish entertainment and bids Leporello take care that the wine gets well into the dancers' heads. Leporello, indeed, is expected to act as master of the ceremonies, the Don having certain private affairs on hand that will keep him fully occupied. In *Fin ch'han dal vino,* a perfect tornado of a song, the very incarnation of devil-may-care gaiety, the incorrigible rake gleefully anticipates the coming revels, in the course of which he hopes to add another score to the already prodigious roll of his conquests.

Scene iv. The garden-front of Don Giovanni's country house; through the rose-covered colonnades, the open doors and windows, we see a vista of brilliantly lighted halls and galleries; in the grounds is a summer pavilion, and groups of trees, favourably disposed for amorous hide-and-seek; the scene is plainly set for one of those elaborate *finales* of complicated action in which Mozart fairly revelled. But first he gives us one of those heavenly simplicities of his which make a universal appeal: if any melody may be said to be " not for an age but for all time," surely it is Zerlina's song of *Batti, batti, o bel Masetto.* The bridegroom is naturally aggrieved at the young woman's behaviour in the previous Scene. " Encouraging his lordship in that way!" he grumbles. "Hussy! I've a very good mind to give you the beating you deserve!" But Zerlina knows better: at once her arms are round the sulky neck, and all her cajoleries brought into play: " Beat me, then, dearest, if it please you! See, here I stand, as meek as any lamb! Strike me, pull my hair out, do your worst! And then when all is over, I will kneel at your feet and kiss the dear hands of the only man I love!" But it is Masetto, of course, who is beaten: at the first sign of his relenting she seizes those ' dear hands ' and sings and dances him once more into subjection.

Don Giovanni now appears, followed by a crowd of peasants gaily decked for the masquerade; as they pass into the ballroom the Don again attempts to detain Zerlina, but Masetto interposes, and all three go in together. The musicians are already striking up—we hear snatches of a minuet with which we shall soon become familiar—when three masked figures in sombre dominoes make an impressive entry. Leporello, spying them from a balcony, invites them to the dance ; they accept, but, before entering, advance to the footlights and, removing their masks, reveal themselves as Donna Anna, Donna Elvira, and Don Ottavio ; they are searching for the slayer of the Commendatore, and unite in a fervent prayer that heaven will protect the innocent and punish the guilty.

[This trio, *Protegga il giusto cielo*, is a splendid instance of Mozart's power of expressing essential grandeur in a little space ; though only twenty bars in length, the music leaves an ineffaceable impression of solemn beauty of which one never tires.]

Scene v. We are at last inside the palace, where the revels are in full swing. If Don Giovanni has made lavish provision for his guests of food and wine, Mozart has been even more prodigal in the matter of dance-music. No less than three small orchestras are placed in the various apartments ; one is playing a gavotte, another a ' German,' the third a minuet—surely the most famous minuet in the world—all three blending in satisfying harmony, clear and unconfused.

Confusion enough, however, is soon astir among the actors. Don Giovanni, who has Zerlina for partner in the gavotte, manages to steer her toward a private apartment, into which he drags her and locks the door behind them. Loud cries for assistance are shortly heard, and the dancing stops, as Ottavio and his two companions hurry to the spot; the door is forced, and Zerlina rushes out, disordered and terrified — the truth is plain to all. Leporello slips into the room to warn his master, who promptly drags him back into the company and denounces him as the villain who has insulted Zerlina ! The Don's guilt, however, is too evident ; Donna Anna and her party are resolute in their attack, and the general anger grows hot against the shameless libertine. A violent storm in the orchestra, thunder and lightning ' off,' proclaim the consenting wrath of heaven, and it almost seems as if the villain's career were ended; but cool courage, our ' hero's ' greatest quality, comes once more to his aid, and the curtain falls on Don Giovanni, sword in hand, clearing his way through the ranks of his enraged assailants.

Act II. The closest attention is needed for the understanding of the Scenes that are now to follow; if the complex situations are of no great assistance to the drama, they at least give rise to an almost continuous succession of musical masterpieces such as Mozart himself has never surpassed.

Scene 1. We begin with a delightful little patter duet, *Eh, via buffone !* in which Leporello, really scared by his recent experiences, seeks once again to break away from his dare-devil master, but is soon brought to heel by the clink of a purse of gold. Don Giovanni, undaunted, nay, in the highest spirits, is bent on fresh gallantries. The two are standing at nightfall in the spacious square where Donna Elvira has her mansion. Has Leporello noticed the lady's bewitching little chambermaid ? Well, his master's heart is already on fire for her, and he means to begin the siege at once ; as a preliminary it will be advisable for him to change cloak and hat with Leporello—little chambermaids have grown so shy, lately, of dashing gentlemen !

No sooner is the change effected—and little does poor Leporello dream of all the woes this disguise will bring upon him !—than a high casement is flung open, and Elvira leans out to sigh her sorrows to the evening breeze ; her heart, it seems, is still heavy for her faithless lover. The opportunity is too good to be lost ; pushing Leporello into the moonlight and crouching down behind him, he protests to the lady, in melting accents, his sincere penitence, his renewed devotion.

[In the trio *Ah, taci, ingiusto core !* Elvira's music is of an exquisite beauty which is apt to suffer in performance from the *buffo* extravagances of the other two. It should be noted that the shameless Don, in his appeal to the lady, ' tries on ' some of the phrases from the serenade that he is shortly to sing to her maid.]

Elvira's foolish heart succumbs once more to that seductive voice ; without more ado she descends and flies to her former lover, as she supposes, though it is Leporello, of course, who receives the poor lady in his willing arms. " Dear love," she says, " behold me all on fire for you ! " " And I," says Leporello, " am already burnt to ashes ! "

His master, impatient to have the coast clear, scares them away with uncouth cries, and, taking his mandoline, sings the serenade *Deh vieni alla finestra*, with which he hopes to melt the heart of the pretty chambermaid.

[Although the English versions and analyses of the opera assume that the serenade is intended for Zerlina, whom Elvira, they say, has taken into her household, there is no warrant for this idea in the original, and it is more reasonable to assume that Don Giovanni is tracking down a new victim.]

Hardly is the song over when Masetto enters with a band of peasants armed with muskets and searching for the villain Don. That gentleman, secure in the disguise of Leporello, is quite ready to assist in so worthy a cause ; giving elaborate directions as to how they may best find the object of their search, he gets rid of them all except Masetto, whom he detains for a little private conversation. Under pretence of anxiety for his safety he inquires as to the sufficiency of the weapons he carries; Masetto hands them over for inspection, and thus disarmed is suddenly seized by the indignant Don, beaten black and blue, and flung into the ditch. This broadly farcical scene is rounded off in true Mozartian fashion; attracted by poor Masetto's groans, Zerlina hastens to the spot, and sings a song so sweet as to make Masetto, or any lover, think lightly of his pain. Certain it is that *Vedrai, carino* has brought a healing balm to many thousands of hearers, and will continue to do so while music still has power to soothe.

Scene II. In the twilight *imbroglio* of this Scene it is Leporello who is the central figure; all the characters, with the exception of Don Giovanni, find their way by night, for operatic reasons, to a spacious courtyard of Donna Anna's—formerly the Commandant's palace—most unfortunately for Leporello, but with the happiest musical results; the sestet *Sola, sola in buio loco*, is one of the outstanding glories of Mozartian opera.

The first to appear are Leporello and Elvira, seeking refuge from their late alarms; he, of course, is still playing the part of his master, and is soon to reap the bitter consequences of such an impersonation. He soon manages to lose Elvira in the darkness, and is just about to make his escape when the door he is trying opens, and Donna Anna enters, leaning on Don Ottavio's arm. His second attempt is even more disastrous, as he runs right into Masetto, Zerlina, and all the peasants in hot pursuit of the wicked Don, whom they now imagine they have caught at last. The torches they carry throw a damning light upon the fine hat and mantle; the others join in the attack, and Leporello, in some danger of his life, finds it best to cast off his disguise, fall at their feet, and claim their pity as another victim of Don Giovanni's treachery. But many accounts have to be settled, and Leporello soon

finds that he must answer for his master's misdeeds as well
as his own. Zerlina begins it : " So you," she screams,
" are the ruffian who beat my Masetto black and blue ! "
" And you," cries Elvira, " are the base villain who so
shamefully tricked me ! " (" I wonder," thinks Leporello, " which is the better actor—my master or I ? ")
Don Ottavio, too, is on the point of arresting him for being
on the premises for an unlawful purpose when Masetto,
armed with a stout cudgel, and smarting with the memory
of his sores, interposes and claims the privilege of dealing
with the culprit out of hand. Leporello, however, contrives to gain time with some clever patter, and finally
gives them all the slip. Don Ottavio is now given another
chance to emerge from his insignificance, and brings down
the curtain on *Il mio tesoro*, that supreme test of the
lyric tenor, a song which enjoys the same unquestioned
supremacy in the realm of classical opera as does the
Prize Song from *The Mastersingers* in the modern world
of music-drama.

[A short scene that follows between Zerlina and Leporello comes rather as an anti-climax, and is generally
omitted ; the grand aria for Elvira (*Mi tradì quell'alma
ingrata*) which follows here as No. 25 is usually transferred, as has been noted, to an earlier place in the opera.]

Scene III. Pale moonlight floods the space in front of
Seville Cathedral ; in the middle of the square gleams an
equestrian statue of marble, fresh from the sculptor's
hand, to the memory of Don Pedro, the murdered Commandant—it dominates the scene and prepares us for the
fantastic terrors that are to come. It is not long past
midnight ; Don Giovanni, still dressed as Leporello,
enters, fresh from some discreditable adventure which he
describes with gusto to his servant. They are carrying
on their ribald dialogue in the usual *recitativo secco* when

suddenly, to the accompaniment of sombre chords from the orchestra, an awful voice is heard : " Laugh on until the dawn ! Then—no more laughter ! " Leporello's heart sinks within him—his master, angry but unafraid, noisily challenges the unseen speaker. Again comes the awful monotone : " Be silent, thou madman ! Leave the dead to their slumbers ! " There can be no longer any doubt ; it is the statue that is speaking. Leporello is now half dead with fright ; his master, on the other hand, breaks out into boisterous mirth : " Tell the old dotard," he says to Leporello, " that I invite him to sup with me this very night ! " When the trembling wretch has stammered out this message, the statue seems to bend its marble head. Don Giovanni is still unimpressed ; swaggering up to the Commandant he looks him full in the face : " Speak, old man, if you are able ! Say, will you sup with me to-night ? " Once more that awful voice is heard—and with the one word " Yes ! " Don Giovanni's doom is sealed.

[The action is delayed at this point by the interpolation of a long solo for Donna Anna, *Non mi dir, amato bene,* one of Mozart's elaborate concert arias in the Italian manner ; it has little to do with the drama, but it is a most welcome refreshment to prepare us for the grotesque horrors of the closing scene.]

Finale. Although Don Giovanni had gone straight home with Leporello, intending to prepare for the entertainment of his strange expected guest, he would seem to have thought little more of the matter ; for in the sumptuous hall on which the curtain rises we find him (to quote the stage directions) " seated at the table, surrounded by several young and beautiful women, who jointly partake of the banquet with him."

The scene is of the gayest ; the musicians in the gallery

play a selection from operas popular at the time, by composers whose very names are now almost forgotten. Leporello, guzzling furtively in the intervals of service, knows all the tunes, and nods approval more especially when the band strikes up *Non più andrai* from *Figaro*, the favourite opera of the day.

Even now, when the sands are nearly run, one last chance of repentance is offered to the hardened libertine ; Elvira, of all persons the least expected—Elvira who has never ceased to love the worthless Don, and is gifted now it would seem with some prophetic instinct of his coming fate—bursts into the room and flings herself at his feet. She pleads not for herself, but for him, passionately imploring him to forsake his evil ways before it is too late. But all in vain ; the wretched man is deaf to such appeals —mockery and insult are all he gives for answer. Indignant, broken-hearted, she leaves the room—but only to turn back with shrieks of horror and to make her escape through another door. The guests and musicians all follow her in wild disorder—horror is in the air ! Don Giovanni, angry but undismayed, sends Leporello to inquire into the cause of the panic. There comes a cry more terrible than Elvira's, as the wretched valet staggers back into the room and babbles of what he has seen and heard : " The Marble Man, señor—as white as death ! If you could only see him—and hear him, as he comes down the corridor, *thump ! thump ! thump !* " Even as he speaks a loud knocking is heard—Don Giovanni pushes Leporello aside and opens the door. There stands the invited guest, the Man of Stone, who has come to supper ; on horseback no longer, heavily, step by step, he advances into the room—*thump ! lump ! thump ! lump !*

Even now Don Giovanni retains a perfect composure ; he receives his guest with courtesy, and gives orders for his entertainment. But this visitor is from another world —he would have his host remember that all earthly things are over and done with. " I am here," he says, " to invite thee to *my* dwelling—to bid thee sup with *me* ! Say— wilt thou come ? " Don Giovanni's courage has never failed him yet; " I fear thee not," he says, " nor hell, nor heaven ! And I will come to supper ! " " Then," says the Marble Man, " give me thy hand in pledge ! " The haughty Don stretches out a hand of flesh, and a hand of stone closes upon it in the grip of death. The libertine has lost his hold of earth, the wildest terror seizes him, but his pride is still unbroken. " Repent ! Repent ! " thunders the awful voice of the Stone Guest. " Never ! " shrieks the captive, as he writhes and struggles vainly to get free.

But there is a term to Heaven's forbearance ; the last offer of mercy has been rejected, the messenger can stay no longer. The stony fingers are relaxed, the Man of Stone has vanished ; hell opens, and through the belch- ing flames Don Giovanni is seen struggling to the last, desperately struggling with the fiends who drag the un- repentant libertine down to his doom of torment without end.

DIE ZAUBERFLÖTE

Music by MOZART.   *Words by* SCHIKANEDER.
Vienna, 1791 ; *London,* 1816 ; *New York,* 1833.

A BAD libretto has generally proved fatal even to a great composer; too often it has dragged his music down to an early grave. *Die Zauberflöte* is the glittering exception ; not only is it well in its second century, but to-day, in England at least, it seems to have acquired a new vitality, and has become a popular ' draw ': no one but Mozart has ever achieved so great a triumph with such a heavy handicap.   Dr Johnson said of Richardson's *Pamela* that anyone who tried to read it for the sake of the story would be likely to cut his throat, and surely the man who goes to see *The Magic Flute* for the sake of the dramatic interest might be forgiven any rash act before the performance was ended.   Fortunately the music saves us from any such risks ; it raises us to a state of ecstasy where dramatic propriety and the logical sequence of events are of no account whatever ; we are quite content to lay common sense aside so long as we can breathe in the rarer atmosphere of absolute beauty. However, for out present purpose, the plot must be faced ; let us handle it boldly, " nothing extenuate, nor set down aught in malice."

The action takes place either in temples—Egypto-Masonic—or in the groves that surround them.   Sarastro, as High Priest of Isis, is of course entitled to his temple ; the Queen of Night (Astrafiammante) also has one, and three ladies to do her bidding, whose names in the Italian version are Aretusa, Iperatusa, and Egle.   There is a blackamoor called Monostatos, the bird-catcher Papageno, dressed all in feathers, and a withered old woman who, later on, for the bird-catcher's benefit, is turned into the young and lovely Papagena. In addition to these remarkable personages we have Tamino, a prince, Pamina, daughter of the Queen of Night, three Genii, two Men in Armour, two Priests, and an Orator.

The plot, which employs so formidable an array of fantastic characters, may be told in a few lines. Sarastro, the embodiment of lofty wisdom, has removed Pamina from the evil guidance of her mother, the Queen of Night, and keeps her guarded in his temple, where she is trained in the ways of virtue. The Queen persuades Tamino to attempt her abduction, promising him Pamina in marriage as his reward. Tamino, however, on meeting with Sarastro, comes at once under his influence, and chooses to remain in the Temple of Isis, where he and Pamina successfully pass through the ordeals essential for initiation into the Mysteries, and are at last united. This very simple action is complicated by a number of queer episodes which apparently have little to do with the plot, though some of them provide a ' comic relief ' which is very welcome.

Act I. Outside the temple of the Queen of Night. Enter Tamino, pursued by a serpent—so runs the first stage direction! The unhappy youth falls fainting to the ground, while three Ladies, attendants on the Queen, come from the temple, armed with spears, and destroy the ' monster.' At once enamoured of Tamino's manly beauty they join in the sprightliest of trios, in which each expresses her determination to remain and tend the unconscious prince ; but as they seem unable to agree on this matter, all three re-enter the temple together.

Tamino recovers from his swoon, and has only just

time to ask himself where he is when a merry tooting is heard, and Papageno, the bird-man, appears—the quaintest figure, in his gay dress of feathers, and playing on his pan-pipes as he sings *Der Vogelfänger bin ich ja!* a jolly air which sets all heads wagging to the rhythm.

In the spoken dialogue which follows, Papageno boasts that it was he who slew the serpent—a lie which brings its swift punishment, as the ladies are quickly on the spot once more with gifts from the Queen; to Tamino she sends a portrait of her daughter, Pamina, while for Papageno there is a golden padlock with which they effectually shut his mouth, adding insult to injury by their advice " not to drink too much! "

Tamino at once falls in love with Pamina's beauty, which he praises in the sweetest of arias, *Dies Bildniss ist bezaubernd schön*, when mysterious strains proclaim the coming of the dreaded Queen of Night. This character is perhaps the most baffling in the whole range of opera—impossible to act, almost impossible to sing. The part was written—dropped in, we might say—for Josepha Weber (Madame Hofer), Mozart's sister-in-law and cousin to the composer of *Der Freischütz*, a *coloratura* soprano with an incredibly high voice; it consists of two airs, which require a working-compass of over two octaves and a volume of voice quite incompatible with their extravagant range. The Queen's aria, *O zittre nicht*, has a lovely *andante* deploring the loss of her daughter, followed by an elaborate *bravura* section in which she urges Tamino to bring Pamina back to her.

She vanishes, and the Ladies appear once more, remove Papageno's padlock, and tell him to attend Tamino on his quest; they also furnish him with a little set of chiming bells, and Tamino with a golden flute, both instruments of power, to help them in time of trouble—

and for their further comfort promise them the assistance
of three Genii to guide them on their way.

[The quintet *H'm ! h'm ! h'm !* has not a dull moment
in it ; it is a succession of artless little melodies, sweet
and gay, first cousins to the folk-song, which exercise an
inexplicable fascination ; even with moderately good performers this number can never fail of its effect.]

Scene II. We are now introduced to the queerest
character of the drama, Monostatos, a blackamoor, who
resides in Sarastro's palace and is referred to as ' Chief of
the Slaves.' Perhaps we should regard him as the comic
villain of the piece, in contrast to Papageno, who is the
pure and simple clown. We find Monostatos in a room
of the temple, forcing his attentions on Pamina ; as she
repulses him, she is bound in chains by two black slaves
and swoons with fright. At this moment Papageno appears
in his gaudy plumage ; he has never seen a black man
before, and never in his life has Monostatos seen a man
who looks so like a monstrous parrot. Each believes the
other to be the Devil, and the little scene of comic terror
that ensues compensates for the apparent irrelevancy of
the incident. But something better is to follow. Papageno turns to Pamina, who has awakened from her swoon,
and persuades her to join him in a search for Tamino. The
duet which follows, *Bei Männern welche Liebe fühlen*,
dear to our ancestors as " The Manly Heart," belongs to
that realm of serene unearthly sweetness to which Mozart
alone of all composers can admit us.

The *finale* of this Act is a not very coherent medley of
incidents which take place in the grove before the Temple
of Isis. The three Genii lead in Tamino, and leave him
to seek admittance at one of the three doors confronting
him. His first two attempts are repulsed by voices from
within, but as he approaches the central door a Priest

comes forth ; he informs him that Pamina is safe, and that, with patience and obedience, he may hope to see her that very day. Tamino, remembering his magic flute, begins to play on it, in the hope of bringing his beloved to his side—with what surprising results may be gathered from the stage directions : " Various birds of every hue and plumage appear amongst the branches of the trees, and carol in concert to his music ; various wild beasts, apes, etc., also appear, and draw round Tamino, soothed and charmed by the magic spell of his flute." Toward the conclusion of his lovely air *Wie stark ist nicht dein Zauberton !* he hears Papageno's pan-pipes not far away and hurries off to seek him. The bird-man immediately enters with Pamina, and is quickly followed by Mono- statos with his black slaves, still bent on carrying off the lady. Fortunately Papageno bethinks him of his ring-o'- bells, which he sets chiming with remarkable results. At the very first sound Monostatos and his sooty fellows drop their chains and their villainy at the same time, and stand rooted to the ground, while a smile of ecstatic delight spreads over their features ; then the music takes them in their feet, and with arms upraised and uncouth gestures they dance in time to the bird-man's rhythmic jingle ; like another Pied Piper he draws them after him across the stage, and, having got rid of them in the wings, he and Pamina in a duet of entrancing simplicity bring to an end a delicious little scene that is all too short.

A march and chorus behind the scenes herald the approach of Sarastro. From the depths of the grove comes a long procession of Priests and Priestesses with wreaths and baskets, cats and crocodiles, and all the symbolic pomp attendant on the rites of Isis ; these form in double line and sing a solemn chorus to welcome the even more impressive procession that follows, in the midst of which Sarastro is seen, standing in a slave-drawn chariot, "magnificently attired; a wreath of laurel is on his brow, and in his right hand he holds a long, golden wand with the emblem of the Sun at its top." Pamina instantly throws herself at his feet to implore pardon for having left the temple in order to escape from Monostatos' persecution. Sarastro at once reassures her; he knows the secret of her heart, and approves her choice of Tamino. At this juncture Monostatos, leading Tamino in chains, enters; he expects praise from Sarastro for his zealous capture, but, to his surprise, hears himself condemned to be soundly bastinadoed. Meanwhile Tamino and Pamina have recognized each other at sight, and are happy in their first embrace. Sarastro now proposes to depart, and bids Pamina mount beside him in the chariot, while Tamino and, oddly enough, Papageno also, are given into the hands of the Priests to be veiled and vested for the rite of initiation.

Act II. A forecourt in the Temple of Isis. A dim vista of columns, sphinxes, pyramids—mysterious rumblings underground, and thunder in the distance—all these are meant to attune our minds to solemn mood. Far more effectual are the two musical numbers with which the Act opens, a march and a solo for bass (*O Isis und Osiris*), which can best be described by the cheapened word 'sublime.'

Looking down the long lines of white-robed Priests, each with lighted torch and silver trumpet, we see the High Priest, Sarastro, mysterious lord of wisdom and of love; he tells them of Tamino, the new postulant for initiation into the rites of the temple—he is virtuous, discreet, benevolent, in all ways worthy of admission— here all raise their silver trumpets and, by three long, sonorous blasts, signify their approval.

Further, the gods have ordained that Pamina too shall enter on her probation, so that the two may be in the end united. The wonderful song *O Isis und Osiris* is a prayer to those deities that the young pair may be strengthened for the coming ordeals or, should they perish, may pass to the realms of everlasting light.

Sarastro having retired, Tamino and Papageno are brought in, to be instructed by the Priests : silence is the first duty enjoined on them ; the second, to be on their guard against the wiles of women. Left to themselves, they are put to an instant test ; the Queen of Night's three Ladies rise out of the ground, to Papageno's great dismay, and prophesy dire misfortune to both should they remain in the temple. Tamino is proof against all temptations and disobedience, and manages to keep the bird-man's terrors within bounds ; the Ladies vanish at the sound of threatening voices from the temple, from which the Priests appear, who veil Tamino and his clown-companion, and lead them off for further instruction.

Changes of scene now follow with such kaleidoscopic frequency that an exact chronicle would be tedious, especially as much depends on the judgment, or the resources, of the particular producer ; it is sufficient to say that the action takes place either in the temple of Isis or in the grove surrounding it.

On a flowery bank, flooded with moonlight, Pamina is discovered asleep by Monostatos, who, after a rather unconvincing solo, *Alles fühlt der Liebe Freuden*, proceeds to take advantage of the situation ; he is about to steal a kiss from the unconscious girl when, to the accompaniment of thunder and lightning, the Queen of Night rises through the earth, and the blackamoor slinks into hiding. On learning from her daughter that Tamino is determined to become an Initiate in the temple, the enraged Queen lays a solemn charge on Pamina to slay Sarastro, and recover from him the golden Symbol of the Sun which had once been in her possession, and on which all his power depends ; for this purpose she thrusts a dagger into the amazed Pamina's hands, sets off such a series of vocal crackers as never before were heard, and vanishes as she had come.

[The *bravura* air *Der Hölle Rache* is certainly the most exacting in the repertory ; not only is the voice kept throughout at an abnormally high pitch, but the character of the piece calls for such a forcible delivery as is rarely at the command of a *soprano sfogato* ; so seldom, indeed, is a satisfactory performance achieved that one is inclined to ask whether it would not be better to cut it out altogether, as unworthy to keep company with some of the loveliest and most vocal music that even Mozart ever wrote.]

Monostatos now comes out of hiding and, snatching the dagger from Pamina's hand, threatens to stab her if she will not yield to his wishes, but is put to flight by the timely arrival of Sarastro. Pamina, assuming that he is aware of the Queen's evil design, pleads for her mother. Sarastro assures her that his way is to return only good for evil, and soothes her with his majestic song *In diesen heil'gen Hallen.*

Another change of scene allows of some more fooling on the part of Papageno, this time with the old woman who is destined later to become his youthful bride. The three Genii next arrive, with a banquet ready spread, Tamino's flute, and Papageno's bells—a sign that their real ordeal is about to begin.

[These Genii are described in some editions as Boys ; if any doubt could exist as to the essential spirituality of their nature, it would at once be dispelled by the little

trio : *Seid uns zum zweitenmal willkommen.* Like many
other happy little tunes throughout this opera, it gives
one the impression of having been made up, just for fun,
in " the nurseries of heaven."]

Pamina now makes a joyous entry, only to find herself
repulsed, as she imagines, by Tamino, whose recent vow
forbids him to acknowledge her greeting by word or look.
The broken-hearted girl, unaware of the reason for his
attitude, pours out her sorrow in an air, *Ach, ich fühl' es,*
which floats above the heights of beauty, and at the
same time is full of a pathos which has no parallel in
Mozartian opera. It was Sontag, an incomparable exponent of the part, who used to say : " A Pamina who
in this air cannot move the public to tears has no idea
of Mozart."

We now get a rather bewildering succession of short
scenes. In a crypt of the temple, lit by the fires of many
altars, Sarastro and all the Priests are assembled in solemn
conclave ; Tamino is led in, " clothed in a long garment
of pure white, girt about at the waist with a plain gold
fillet, a chaplet of roses on his brow "—ready for the rite
of initiation which is about to be performed. Pamina is
also introduced, to take farewell of her beloved, though
Sarastro cheers her with hints that they will meet again ;
leading them both by the hand, and followed by the
long succession of Priests, he passes into the innermost
recesses of the temple, and the brazen gates close behind
them.

After these impressive proceedings it is rather a shock
to find the irrepressible Papageno intruding, quite un-
abashed, among such strange surroundings. It is well to
note, however, that this queer parrot-fellow is not without
some claim to our consideration ; if Sarastro represents
the higher wisdom, Papageno may well stand for the rare

quality of common sense. In a previous dialogue, when a Priest asks him whether he too does not yearn to follow Tamino in the pursuit of truth and wisdom, he replies that he has no desire to meddle with what does not concern him ; his real business is with meat, drink, and sleep—yes, and a buxom little wife would ensure his best attention. So on the present occasion when the Priest sternly reminds him that he has forfeited his chances of attaining to the higher life, Papageno stands firm—he does not in the least regret his decision ; what he really sighs for is a glass of good wine. This is immediately provided, and inspires him with a most rollicking, amorous ditty, *Ein Mädchen oder Weibchen*, in which he shakes his magic bells with delightful effect. The old woman again appears, but changes at once into the young maiden of his desires, who is, however, snatched away from him at his first approach, for no intelligible reason.

In another garden scene the Genii again appear, just in time to prevent Pamina from using her mother's dagger on herself in her despair at Tamino's fancied desertion ; they are able to assure her that he is still faithful to her, and lead her away happy in the prospect of a joyful reunion.

We now come to the great business of the ordeal by fire and water through which the lovers must pass in order to achieve their union and obtain admission to the kingdom of light and love.

The original stage directions are so terrific and so little followed in modern times that it will be best to quote them in a curtailed version. " The stage represents a wild and gloomy region at the foot of a black and rocky mountain . . . vast caverns are perceived stretching far into the interior . . . dim flashes of sulphurous light flash forth from these caverns . . . a ruddy glare may be seen within, which gradually increases. On the left, an opening in the precipice is closed by a pair of massive and lofty iron gates, over which an inscription is carved on the face of the rock, the characters thereof seeming to emit a phosphorescent light ; a similar gate on the right." From the latter gate Tamino is led forth by " the two Guardians of the Threshold, men of gigantic stature, clad in full black armour ; from their helmets a flame of ruddy fire is blazing " ; the tips of their spears also " send forth a ruddy glow." These imposing personages draw Tamino's attention to " the characters of living fire over the opposite gates." The words of the inscription are :

> Who dares the varied storms of yon dark realm to weather,
> Made pure by fire, by water, earth, and ether,
> Shall soar triumphant, conqueror o'er sin and death,
> To heav'n, as angel-priest of our true faith.
> If at her shrine the suppliant humbly kneel,
> To him shall Isis then her mysteries reveal.

[This duet, for tenor and bass, *Der welcher wandert diese Strasse*, gives occasion for some of the noblest music in the opera. Mozart has employed, for the vocal theme, a fine old German choral, solemn, suave, and broad, and has woven for it an orchestral accompaniment of such cunning beauty, in striking contrast to the previous temple music, that we ask ourselves if this is not rather the great Bach himself.]

Pamina now enters, determined to follow her beloved through fire, through water, through the very gates of death. After a duet of rapturous reunion, followed by a magnificent contrapuntal quartet in which the Guardians join, the great gates on the left are thrown open and— but here we must have recourse again to the formal stage directions : " Tamino takes his flute, Pamina clings to his arm. . . . Eddies of flame rush from the caverns, which are rent asunder as with an explosion, burning lava pouring down on all sides, etc., etc. In the midst of this elemental strife Tamino, playing manfully on the flute, and Pamina, clinging to him, are seen to pass." Successful and undaunted, the pair are the next minute " perceived buffeting with the billows of a foaming and impetuous torrent, still clinging to each other, Tamino steadily playing his flute: after being nearly torn asunder by the force of the waves, they are finally cast on the rocky shore."

The scene immediately changes to the inmost sanctuary of the temple, where Sarastro is ready at the altar to bless the brave and faithful lovers.

The short chorus of triumph which follows should certainly be the end of the opera; but Papageno and Papagena have not yet had their scene together, and there is also the Queen of Night to be disposed of. Mozart would seem to have had a special affection for his quaint parrot-man; even at this late hour he chooses to provide him and his partner with page after page of delicious foolery, musically as fresh and charming as anything that has gone before.

First, Papageno enters in despair; he has lost his Papagena—what has he to live for now? So he resolves on a most prudent attempt at suicide. Standing on a largish stone at the foot of a tree, he throws a rope over the branch above, adjusts it loosely round his neck, and is about to kick the stone away—with not so much as the risk of a sprained ankle—when the good Genii come to his relief, and advise him rather to have recourse to his magic bells. At the first peal his pretty Poll is at his side, and in a lively duet the two resolve to go into partnership, with unlimited power to add to their number.

Now for the baleful Queen of Night! In a cavern immediately beneath the inmost shrine of the temple she is discovered, with her three Ladies and the black Monostatos, putting the finishing touches to some fiendish plot which shall involve Sarastro, the temple, and all within it in final and irrevocable ruin.   But the Powers of Darkness have had their day, and Sarastro must now assert his power.   The conspirators " are interrupted by a loud succession of peals of thunder from within the rocks, and the rushing sound as of mighty waters ; the rocks rapidly surround and close in upon them as they strive to fly "—and the opera ends, as it was bound to do, in the Temple of Isis with Sarastro's blessing of the triumphant lovers, and a final chorus in praise of Wisdom, Truth, and Virtue.

The reader who has had the patience to plough through the above mass of confused happenings may be surprised to hear that anyone should be found to take it seriously ; yet many have done so ; in fact it would require quite a long shelf to hold all that has been written about the ' inner meaning ' of *Die Zauberflöte*. Without going deeply into the matter, it seems worth while to examine the origin of this strange affair. Emanuel Schikaneder, a friend of Mozart who ran a small theatre in Vienna, approached the composer with a libretto of a comic opera which he had taken from a fantastic Eastern tale, *Lulu, or the Magic Flute*. A low-comedy actor, he had elaborated the part of Papageno for himself, and as Mozart's sister-in-law, Mme Hofer, was engaged at his theatre, the part of the Queen of Night was specially designed for her peculiar talent.   However, before the opera was ready, a musical version of the same story was produced at a rival theatre with great success, and there was nothing for it but to change the character of Schikaneder's libretto.

The question of Freemasonry was very much in evidence at that time, owing to the repressive measures taken against it by the Emperor Leopold and his Empress Maria Theresa, and it seemed to Schikaneder that this material might be worked up into a popular attraction for the theatre ; he and Mozart both being Freemasons, it was easy enough to devise the temple scenes and the final business of the ordeal, which contrast so strangely with the flimsy texture of the original fairy-tale. There seems to have been little attempt to blend the two elements, and the result is a scarcely intelligible succession of loosely related incidents. Those who insist on the cryptic significance of the piece inform us that Sarastro stands for Freemasonry, as the guardian of all truth and wisdom, Monostatos for the Clerical Party, Papageno for the lusty Viennese *bourgeoisie*, and the baleful Queen of Night for the great Maria Theresa. This is interesting, but does not reconcile us to the tedious folly of the action, which is a jumble of contradictions, confusions, and sheer buffoonery, all the more irritating when contrasted with the dignified solemnity of the temple scenes ; as Mr Krehbiel puts it, the best way to regard *The Magic Flute* is as " a sort of Christmas pantomime which Mozart has glorified by his music."

FIDELIO

Music by BEETHOVEN. *Words by* BOUILLY, *and others.*
Vienna, 1st *version* 1805, 2nd *version* 1814 ; *London,* 1832 ;
New York, 1839.

ALTHOUGH Beethoven's only opera is rather a tradition than an experience with opera-goers of to-day, it has a brilliant record of success behind it. Before the coming of Wagner not only was it regarded by serious musicians as the fine flower of German lyric drama—and even the Perfect Wagnerite allowed that *Fidelio* had certain claims to consideration—but the enthusiasm with which it was received by the public was quite extraordinary. During the period of its greatest popularity, in the first half of the last century, it was not unusual to repeat the Prisoners' Chorus, and the whole of the *finale* to the second Act. On one occasion, we read, " the splendid overture was also performed twice ; indeed, owing to the multitude of encores, the audience might almost as well have waited to the end, and insisted on a repetition of the whole opera." Further, in the dungeon scene, " loud and excessive applause drowned the music, and testified the delight of the house."

There is no fear of any such demonstrations, so strange a mingling of good and bad taste, at the present day ; musicians will always welcome the infrequent revivals of an interesting classic, but its hold on the public is not likely to be renewed. The truth is that *Fidelio*, in spite of its profound musicianship and its many noble qualities, has aged considerably. To make the inevitable comparison, the simplicities of Weber's *Der Freischütz* convey a much fresher, more vital impression of beauty to-day than all the heroic pretensions and wonderful symphonic achievements of *Fidelio*. If Weber, as he has recorded, strove for " nothing save truthfulness of expression, passion, and delineation of character," Beethoven's aim was assuredly not less noble ; nevertheless, in writing for the voice he not seldom fails to reach it. For instance, in the famous quartet *Mir ist so wunderbar*, where four separate emotions call for expression, the composer employs the form of the ' canon,' which obliges each person to repeat the same melody, note for note, a method which scarcely lends itself to " delineation of character." So throughout the opera ; while the grandeur of the conception is often apparent, and the orchestra rises to heights of dramatic significance hitherto unparalleled, the vocal writing frequently fails in right expression, owing to the cramping rigidity of the conventional forms employed. It is the work of a giant unable wholly to shake off the chains that bind him. However high we may rate Beethoven's symphonic genius, we must recognize that, in writing for the voice, he had not Mozart's gift of making beauty smile upon us even through narrowing prison bars.

Fidelio, oder die eheliche Liebe is the accepted title of this opera, in spite of Beethoven's preference for the alternative *Leonore*, which is the real name of the heroine. Produced at Vienna in 1805, during the French occupation of that city, it was a failure, and, though revived in the following year, was withdrawn after a few performances. Not till 1814 did it start on a successful career, when it was put on at the Kärnthnerthor theatre, with a greatly improved libretto. The part of Leonore was sung by Mme Milder-Hauptmann, for whom it had been written nine years previously. This lady, whose good gifts seem

to have been all on the heroic scale—" You have a voice
as big as a house, my child ! " was old Haydn's remark—
complained, nevertheless, of the too strenuous nature of
her music, and actually succeeded in getting Beethoven
to alter certain passages which she declared to be ruinous
to the voice.   If, with Wagner's heroines in mind, we are
inclined to smile at such a protest, it cannot be denied
that the part of Leonore makes exceptional demands on
both actress and singer ; the difficulty of finding an artist
worthy of the work goes far to account for the infrequency
of its revivals.

Schröder-Devrient, who followed Milder-Hauptmann
in the part (and lived to satisfy Wagner by her impersona-
tions of his earlier heroines) was probably its greatest
exponent.   Malibran sang it (in English) in the thirties,
her sister Viardot-Garcia somewhat later ; Johanna
Wagner, Sophie Cruvelli (German in spite of her name),
Lilli Lehmann, Marianne Brandt, are all remembered as
distinguished representatives of a part which yields to
none in dramatic dignity.   One of the most memorable
performances was at Her Majesty's in 1851, the year of
the Great Exhibition, when Cruvelli played the heroine
and Sims Reeves the part of Florestan, while a number
of prominent artists, including such names as Lablache
and Gardoni, did homage to the great composer by
appearing in the Prisoners' Chorus at the end of Act I.
More than this, however, was needed to atone for the
outrage committed by interspersing Beethoven's music
with recitatives composed for the occasion by Balfe, the
begetter of *The Bohemian Girl.*

Technically, *Fidelio* does not come under the category
of Grand Opera ; like *The Magic Flute, Il Seraglio,* and
Der Freischütz, it ranks as a *Singspiel,* or *Opéra Comique,*
i.e., an operatic work in which music and spoken dialogue

are intermingled. The 'book' as we now have it is the work of many hands; based on a French original by Bouilly, a well-known librettist of the time, it was adapted in the first instance by Sonnleithner (Kotzebue's theatrical successor in Vienna), reduced later by von Breuning from three Acts to two, and finally revised by Treitschke in 1814 with excellent results. The story, as its sub-title shows, is one of wifely devotion. The heroine Leonore is the wife of Don Florestan, a noble Spaniard, who has been seized by a political opponent, Don Pizarro, and thrown into the foul dungeon of a castle near Seville, where he has languished for two years before the action of the piece begins. Although he is reported to have died, Leonore, suspicious of the truth, has disguised herself as a youth, Fidelio by name, and entered the service of old Rocco the jailer, whose confidence she has contrived to gain. From him she has heard much of a mysterious prisoner who is confined in the deepest dungeon of all, and treated with ever-increasing severity—only lately has his ration of bread and water been cut down to starvation point, and the very straw on which he lay been taken from him; it is plain that nothing less than his death is aimed at. Leonore, convinced of the prisoner's identity, schemes how she may yet save her husband's life. She induces Rocco, who is growing feeble, to let her help him in his arduous duties in connexion with the many cells he has to visit daily. There is no time to lose. Pizarro, as she hears, has that very morning received a letter from Don Fernando, the Minister of the Interior, announcing his speedy arrival—he has heard reports of undue severity and other irregularities in the management of the prison, and is coming himself to inquire into the matter. Pizarro, panic-stricken, resolves to make an end of Florestan and to remove all traces of his existence ; he orders Rocco to dispatch him at once ; but this the old man refuses to do, so the Governor is driven to act as his own executioner. Leonore, who has overheard their conversation, determines to prevent the murder even at the cost of her own life. [Here comes the great scena *Abscheulicher !* so well known on the concert-platform.] The first Act ends effectively in the celebrated Chorus of Prisoners, who are allowed for a brief space to breathe the fresh air of the garden, only to be driven back again by Pizarro's orders to their dismal cells below.

The second Act shows us the dungeon in which the wretched Florestan is confined—a place of unimaginable horror, in the remotest depths of the foundations. Although Rocco declines to be the prisoner's murderer, he consents to dig his grave, and in this task Fidelio is to help him. As the two enter the dungeon, which is lit only by a solitary feeble lamp, they can hardly recognize the prisoner, seated on a block of stone, loaded with fetters, and chained to an iron ring fastened in the masonry of a massive column.

Near at hand are the ruins of a long-disused cistern, now choked with rubbish, in which Pizarro has decided to conceal the body of the murdered man ; it is Leonore's task to assist Rocco in preparing it for that purpose. In the short pauses of her heavy toil she is able to satisfy herself that the wretched being she sees before her, wasted with misery and only half alive, is really Florestan, her own beloved husband.

Pizarro enters, eager to despatch his old enemy without delay, as he fears every moment to hear the signal announcing the approach of Don Fernando, who comes to judgment. Advancing on his victim, he is just about to strike when Leonore, the supposed Fidelio, rushes

in between them; with the cry " First kill his wife ! "
she takes her stand in front of her dear husband, to live
or die with him.

In spite of his astonishment and confusion the villain
thrusts her roughly aside and is about to deal the fatal
blow when Leonore again interposes with a loaded pistol
pointed at Pizarro's forehead, and at the same moment
is heard from the battlements of the castle the solemn
trumpet-call which announces the coming of the Minister.

[This, of course, is the great moment of the opera, and
grandly has the composer treated it; the trumpet-call
is the fitting climax to one of the most dramatic scenes
in the whole range of musical drama.]

Don Fernando, after a hasty investigation of the true
state of affairs, soon brings matters to a happy issue;
the villainous Pizarro is led away to receive his just
punishment, and Florestan, in whom Fernando recognizes
an old friend, is at once set free, the actual loosing of his
chains being allotted to the heroic wife who alone is
worthy of so high an office. The prisoners are released
and brought once more into the light, and the opera
closes with a chorus of rejoicing, and of praise for Leonore
—well named ' Fidelio '—the glorious example of wifely
devotion.

Besides the characters already mentioned, two others
are introduced with the object of lightening the gloom
which broods rather heavily over the entire performance
—Marcellina, the jailer's daughter, in love with the
imaginary youth Fidelio, and Jacquino, the turnkey, in
love with Marcellina. But *Fidelio* is actually a one-part
opera; its successful revival must always depend upon
the rare occurrence of an ideal Leonore, an artist with
the ' Give me the dagger ' method of a Sarah Siddons,
and " a voice as big as a house."

Beethoven wrote no less than four different overtures for this work, the first three being known as " Leonore," 1, 2, and 3 ; " Leonore No. 3 " has always been a great favourite in the concert-room, where the " Overture to *Fidelio*," which always precedes the opera, is also frequently heard.

DER FREISCHÜTZ

Music by WEBER. *Words by* F. KIND.
Berlin, 1821 ; *London,* 1824 ; *New York,* 1825.

FEW masterpieces interest us from so many points
of view as *Der Freischütz* ; it is the first purely
German, the first purely romantic opera ; it anticipates the Wagnerian reforms in a truly remarkable
manner ; its delicious music, with something of the
heavenly candour of Mozart about it, appeals alike to
musicians and the laity. Finally we are attracted irresistibly by the figure of Weber the composer ; the contrast
between the wildness of his earlier days and the serene
happiness of his married life, his heroic struggle with
disease, his pathetic death in the very flush of his English
triumph, his burial in a London grave—these things
cannot fail to arouse our sympathies.

Weber's letters from London during the last weeks of
his life are good reading. He had come to London to
conduct his *Oberon,* specially composed for this country,
and was the guest of Sir George Smart in Portland Place ;
although it is to be feared that our raw climate tried
the poor consumptive severely, he found the social atmosphere invariably genial. " The people are really too kind
to me," he writes to his wife (5th March, 1826). "No king
had ever more done for him out of love ; I may almost
say they carry me in their arms." Of his reception by
the public he speaks in sheer astonishment : " Smart led
me to my place, and what followed baffles description.
. . . The calling, shouting, and waving of handker-
chiefs throughout the whole house seemed to have no

end ; nobody can call to mind a parallel enthusiasm."
Again : " Are these your ' cold English ' of whom I have
been told so often ? Their enthusiasm is incredible."
This from one who, as the composer of *Der Freischütz*,
had been for five years the musical idol of Europe is no
slight testimony to the warmth of a London audience a
hundred years ago.

Carl Maria von Weber was buried in the Catholic
Church of St Mary Moorfields (21st June, 1826), but those
who wish to lay a wreath upon his tomb must direct
their steps elsewhere. In 1844 the composer's body was
removed to the family vault at Dresden, where the
musical arrangements for its solemn reception and re-
interment were fittingly entrusted to the reverent care
of Richard Wagner.

Der Freischütz is a romantic opera in the true sense of
that term ; the supernatural incidents in the action, as tire-
some as such things usually are, though redeemed in this
case by the glamour of the music, merely contribute to
the general effect—it is the lighting-up of common things
that makes Weber's opera the enchanting masterpiece we
know. The dark mysterious forest for a background, the

> Plaint of the horn, where it moaneth
> Deep in the heart of the woods,

the lusty huntsmen, the simple, joyous woodlanders with
song and dance and drinking under the tavern lime-tree
—these sights and sounds of common day Weber, with
the help of a not unskilful librettist, has flooded with the
light of true romance, that " light that never was on land
or sea." Both music and book are full of that atmosphere
of natural magic, that deeply rooted forest-feeling be-
gotten of song and legend and lovely fancy, that made Old
Germany, every whit as much as Italy, " the land of

Romance." As Teutonic as *Die Meistersinger von Nürnberg*, *Der Freischütz* makes even a more universal appeal, and by its very simplicity may outlast the more elaborate structure of Wagner's creation. The title itself presents a difficulty ; it is impossible to translate the word *Freischütz*, and hard even to explain it ; "The Free-shooter," *Le franc archer*, *Il franco arciero*, fail to give the real meaning, and *Robin des Bois*, the title of the first Paris version (1824), merely shelves the problem. The most one can say is that a *Freischütz* is one who shoots with magic bullets that never fail to hit the mark, and, at the same time, are sure to bring disaster on him who uses them.

The well-known overture invites inevitable comparisons with that of *Tannhäuser* ; far shorter and simpler, it is hardly less successful than the later work in foreshadowing the action of the drama. In the opening section the delicious melody for the horns sets us in the fragrant heart of the sunlit forest, a shrine of peace and beauty ; but even there an evil power intrudes, the clouds gather, and with a change to the minor we pass into an atmosphere of wild tumult. We are conscious of the awful figure of Zamiel, the Demon Hunter, walking in darkness and exercising his unseen influence over the young ranger ; we hear Max's despairing cries, and all the clash and horror of the Incantation Scene is rising around us, when the sunshine is restored with the entrance of the *allegro* from Agathe's great *scena* in Act I—the *motif* of exultant love—and after some tussle between this and the darker themes the overture ends, like that of *Tannhäuser*, with the victory of Love, the triumph of Good over Evil.

The plot is simple enough. The scene is laid in Bohemia, but this localization is of slight importance—it is enough that we are in the heart of a woodland country ; the late Mr Krehbiel hits the mark when he says of this opera : " Instead of shining with the light of Florentine Courts, it glows with the rays of the setting sun filtered through the foliage of the Black Forest." Agathe, the daughter of Cuno, Head Ranger to Prince Ottokar, is betrothed to the young forester Max, Cuno's favourite pupil ; Caspar, his senior, and a rejected suitor of Agathe, is bent on revenge. Caspar is the villain of the piece— he is in league with the Powers of Darkness ; he has sold himself to Zamiel, the Demon Hunter, whom to en- counter is death, as he rides with his hellhounds at mid- night through the forest. Under the spell of Zamiel, Max, who has long been the finest shot for miles around, finds himself deprived of all his powers ; for weeks he has brought home neither fur nor feather from his forest walks, and not a single prize from the *Schützenfeste* (shooting-competitions), of which he was formerly the champion. As the time approaches for the most impor- tant event of all, the contest in the presence of the Prince himself, of which the reward is the succession to the Head Rangership, together with the hand of Agathe, Max becomes desperate, and Caspar is not slow to seize his opportunity. After convincing Max of the efficiency of a Magic Bullet (*Freikugel*) which he has in his possession, he persuades him to meet him at midnight in the Wolfs Schlucht (Wolf's Glen)—for only there, in the moon's eclipse, and by the aid of Zamiel, can such infallible bullets be procured. At the hour appointed, with every possible accompaniment of a rather grotesque *diablerie*, the deed is done ; seven bullets are cast, six of which are guaranteed to hit the mark designed by their possessor, but the seventh (a fact of which Max is kept in ignorance) obeys the guiding hand of Zamiel alone—where he will, there it finds its billet. Meanwhile Agathe, though quietly preparing for her approaching wedding, is not without her misgivings and forebodings ; these have been confirmed by the Hermit of the Forest, a sage greatly revered for his holy life, who has always had a fatherly regard for the girl. On a recent visit he had warned her of some unseen danger that threatened, and given her a knot of consecrated roses, powerful to protect her in the hour of peril.

On the day of the great shooting-match, when the decisive trial is to be brought off, Caspar is present in the certain hope of witnessing his rival's destruction ; he is persuaded that Zamiel is prepared to accept the soul of Max in exchange for his own, and his time for discharging his debt is almost up.

He climbs into a high tree to watch the event. Agathe has not yet arrived when the Prince orders the trials to begin and requests Max to aim at a white dove just flying past. Max fires—at the same moment Agathe enters and apparently receives the shot, as she falls senseless to the ground. It is soon realized, however, that it is Caspar who has been mortally wounded ; Zamiel appears, to claim his soul, and the wretched man dies with curses on his lips.

Meanwhile the venerable Hermit—whose roses have done their part in shielding the innocent girl—comes forward from his cave to restore the unconscious Agathe and to champion the cause of Max, with whom the Prince is inclined to deal sternly on account of his traffic with the Devil. All join in the Hermit's plea for mercy, and it is finally agreed that the young forester's recovered integrity shall be put to the test of a year's probation, at the end of which he is to be rewarded with the post of Head Ranger and the hand of the faithful Agathe.

Act I. The open space in front of a village tavern, on

the edge of a forest; groups of huntsmen and country folk are watching a shooting-match, which is just coming to an end. As the curtain rises, Kilian, a strapping young peasant, has just succeeded in bringing down the stuffed bird attached to the star which forms the centre of the target, and is rewarded by a noisy chorus of congratulation. A procession is formed, of men and maidens arm-in-arm, to conduct Kilian in triumph round the village; only Max, once the champion, who has failed completely on this occasion, sits at a table, his head on his arm, in solitary dejection. As the procession comes his way, Kilian stops to jeer at him, and to demand the homage due to the victor. His song, *Schau' der Herr mich an als König*, backed by the cackling laughter of the chorus, gives a capital impression of rough country banter— mischievous rather than ill-natured, for Kilian is a genial boor at heart. But it is too much for Max—he, a self-respecting forester, to be jeered at by a common peasant lad, and, alas, with reason! He hurls himself furiously upon his tormentor, and the peasants close in on them in an endeavour to rescue their man, when Cuno, the Head Ranger, arrives on the scene, with Caspar and others in attendance. Grieved to hear of Max's repeated failures, he bids him take heart and summon all his powers, for the morrow is the day of the decisive Trial Shot, on which depends the succession to the post of Ranger, and the hand of Agathe, to both of which Cuno hopes to see his favourite establish his title.

The long and tedious dialogue which follows, chiefly concerned with the legend connected with the Trial Shot serves at any rate to develop the character of the trea- cherous Caspar, who frequently mutters the name of Zamiel, his familiar demon, and otherwise betrays his villainous nature.

In the trio and chorus, *O diese Sonne*, in which Max
gives way to his despondent mood, all express their
sympathy, and try to cheer him, with the exception of
Caspar, whose harsh voice takes on a very different colour.
Very characteristic of the composer is the melodious choral
passage, *O lass Hoffnung*, in the accompaniment of which
he employs horns and bassoons with delicious effect, after
which the huntsmen's voices make a lusty entrance, and
work up a joyous *finale*, in which they hail the bride and
bridegroom of the morrow.

On Cuno's departure the village band strikes up the
simplest of waltzes, in which all take part except Max.
The light is fading now ; and the dancers disappear,
some to the tavern, some to the forest ways, leaving Max
to his despondency. His great *scena* that follows is an
alternation of light and shadow ; after the first gloomy
outburst, *Nein, länger trag' ich nicht die Qualen*, he passes
to the lovely melody *Durch die Wälder, durch die Auen*,
in which he recalls his former happy days, the careless life
of the forester, and the bliss of returning at nightfall to
the welcome of Agathe's smile.

[Flutes and clarinets here combine to give that outdoor
feeling, that atmosphere of sunshine in woodland glades,
which we find again in *Euryanthe* and in many of the
songs, and which seems to have been Weber's peculiar
secret.]

The sky now grows dark and threatening and in the
orchestra the drums give gloomy warning. In the background, invisible to Max, appears the gigantic figure of
Zamiel, the demon of the forest, "clothed" (according to
the stage directions) " in dark green, with a mantle of fiery
red ; a large hat adorned with a plume overshadows his
terrible countenance." Under the influence of his presence Max relapses into his former despondency, but

Zamiel's stay is short, and the young lover indulges in a delicious reverie of Agathe watching from her window for his coming. Zamiel again returns to plague Max still more sorely, and at the concluding movement Max expresses his abandonment to utter despair. "Are we the sport of idle Fate? Is there no God in heaven?" is his bitter cry.

In this dangerous mood he is found by Caspar; he, by contrast, is all roaring jollity, calls for drink in which Max must join him, and sings a capital tavern song in praise of Wine, Women, and Cards: *Hier im ird'schen Jammerthal.* The words are hardly to his hearer's mood:

> Wine, be thou my ABC!
> Woman, my divinity!
> Cards and dice, my Bible!

Max, however, cannot refuse to drink with him, and Caspar manages from time to time to drop something into his comrade's glass, calling at the same time upon Zamiel in a hollow whisper.

The drugged wine is taking effect upon Max, who rises to go home, but Caspar finds a way to keep him. How can he venture to face his sweetheart in such a sorry state, with a long tale of ill-luck, and no hope for the morrow. Still, all this may be remedied—there are ways and means —he, Caspar, knows a thing or two!

Max is incredulous of any sudden retrieving of his fortune, until the other gives him proof that his is no idle talk. "Here!" says Caspar, "take my rifle, and aim at yonder eagle!" It is nearly dark, the bird is far out of range, a mere speck in the clouds; yet, in the apathy of desperation, Max fires, and a huge golden eagle falls dead at his feet. Max knows it was an impossible shot; incredulous no longer, he allows himself to be persuaded to share in the secret powers which Caspar undoubtedly possesses. He will meet him at midnight in the Wolf's Glen for the casting of the Magic Bullets ; but it must be that very night, for the moon is then in eclipse, and only under such conditions, Caspar explains, can the infernal traffic be carried on.

Max, with the eagle's plume stuck proudly in his hat, goes off to bid Agathe good-night, while Caspar ends the scene with a song of fiendish triumph over his rival's approaching destruction : *Der Hölle Netz' hat dich umgarnt.*

Act II. A spacious and rather ' romantic ' chamber in what had formerly been a princely hunting-lodge ; there are faded tapestries, antlers, and other sporting trophies, an altar in a curtained recess, heavy furniture black with age. But though the setting may savour of a mouldering past, the two occupants of the room afford a delightful contrast to it ; these are Agathe, old Cuno's daughter, Max's affianced bride, and Aennchen, her young cousin, a piece of demure roguery—" just husband-high." Agathe's bridal dress is lying on a table, and Aennchen's spinning-wheel stands idle. Each of the girls is somewhat oddly occupied ; Agathe is tying a bandage round her forehead, which has been bleeding, and her cousin is rehanging a large picture which has fallen from the wall and evidently been the cause of Agathe's injury. It is a portrait of one of Cuno's ancestors, and Agathe is inclined to look upon its fall as an evil omen, but young Aennchen will listen to no such talk—she is all for laughing dull care away. The contrasted characters of the pair are admirably displayed in the pretty duet *Schelm ! halt fest !* Agathe, even on her bridal eve, cannot shake off a presentiment of coming disaster, her broad, sombre phrases standing out strongly against Aennchen's rippling gaiety, which sparkles as brightly in the passage *Grillen sind mir böse*

Gäste. Still livelier is her solo *Kommt ein schlanker Bursch gezogen,* in which she declares herself quite ready to say " Yes ! " when her turn comes. This short scene has a peculiar and unique charm ; it is a *genre* painting, a domestic interior, that would scarcely have seemed old-fashioned in the Germany of thirty years ago.

After Aennchen's exit, Agathe begins her famous scena, *Leise, leise,* which, for so many amateurs, is the great attraction of the opera.

It is past her time for retiring, but her anxiety for Max will not let her rest ; she must go to the window to watch until he comes. As she draws aside the curtain, the room is flooded by the light of the full moon which has just risen over forest and mountains, all clearly seen, though in the farther distance the sullen gathering clouds portend a thunderstorm. Awestruck at the majesty of the sight, she kneels beside the altar and prays for heaven's protection. This simple melody of sixteen bars (*Leise, leise*) must surely be known to thousands who have never heard of *Der Freischütz,* through its introduction into the religious services of various denominations, where, however out of place, it seems to satisfy the demands of popular piety. From Agathe's lips the air is appropriate and beautiful, though it must yield in musical value to the following section, *Alles pflegt schon längst der Ruh.* She has flung back the lattice and leans out, all eyes and ears for the faintest sign of her lover's approach ; there is no sound but the rustle of the beech-woods, the sighing pines, the tinkling of the falling rill, and all these are brought close to us, through the medium of the orchestra, in a way that is wholly magical.

At last ! a horn's low note—a hurrying step—'tis Max ! and in his hat, as she fondly thinks, the sign of victory that augurs all good for the morrow. Heaven opens wide before Agathe's eyes, and she pours out her joy and thankfulness in the fiery *allegro vivace* which forms the chief theme of the overture, *All' meine Pulse schlagen*. It might be well, musically, if the scene ended here ; but a final trio is demanded, and develops naturally enough out of the situation. Agathe's perfect happiness is soon clouded over by Max's agitated manner, and his announcement that he must shortly leave her, to bring home a stag which he has left lying in the Wolf's Glen. The mention of this ill-reputed spot renews Agathe's worst forebodings, and the final number is divided between her entreaties to Max to remain at home, his insistent plea of necessity, and Aennchen's lively endeavours to put everything in as favourable a light as possible.

Scene ii. The Wolf's Glen : the Incantation.

It is difficult to give a just impression of this Scene in mere words ; the amazing music baffles description, while the trivialities of the libretto hardly invite it.

The hour is midnight, the place the depths of a tremendous gorge, with waterfalls, and twisted pines and blasted oaks, fantastically lit by the stray beams from the full moon just above. We have skulls and crossbones, owls and ravens, ghostly apparitions of the living and the dead —all the tawdry paraphernalia of the cheap supernaturalism so popular in Germany at the time.

We begin with a dismal hooting of spectral owls—the stage directions go so far as to demand one specially large owl with fiery eyes, which open and shut at rhythmic intervals—while invisible demons chant the following words in monotone :

> Moon's milk fell upon the weed—
>   (*Uhui ! uhui !*)
>
> Now the spider's web doth bleed—
>   (*Uhui ! uhui !*)

> Ere another eve succeed—
> (*Uhui ! uhui !*)
>
> Dies the bride, a stricken reed—
> (*Uhui ! uhui !*).

Caspar, with the conventional magic rites, calls upon Zamiel to appear ; he tells how Max has fallen into the snare, and bargains with the Demon to accept the young man's soul in exchange for his own—for Caspar had long since sold himself to Zamiel, and his time for fulfilling the pact is nearly come. Zamiel apparently agrees to the proposal and vanishes.

Max is now seen on the crazy wooden bridge that spans the height of the ravine, hesitating whether to descend. The ghost of his mother, the phantasm of Agathe, appear and try to turn him from this dreadful project, but Caspar, with the aid of Zamiel, lures him down to the depths, and the casting of the Magic Bullets begins. To the accompaniment of rending boughs, screaming night-fowl, corpse-fires, and will-o'-the-wisps, the unhallowed work proceeds, with ever-increasing tumult and uproar of the elements—two thunderstorms are demanded by the librettist !—until, with the sixth bullet, the earth seems to rock, the gates of Hell to open, and the Wild Huntsman with spectral hounds and horses is seen galloping through the sky ; at the casting of the fatal seventh, Zamiel again appears, towers threateningly over Max, and vanishes. Both men are thrown violently to the ground, where Caspar lies senseless, but Max, who has contrived to make the sign of the Cross at Zamiel's approach, is seen to raise himself upright as the curtain falls.

With only this stale and unprofitable material to work in, Weber's imagination has produced a symphonic masterpiece of weird fantasy, which suggests far more than a merely physical horror. How much Wagner owed to this earlier master of romance is becoming more and more fully recognized as time goes on, and nowhere are the germs of the great reformer's ideas more clearly traceable than in this Incantation Scene in the Wolf's Glen.

Act III. After an orchestral *intermezzo*—on the theme of the famous Huntsmen's Chorus, which for more than half a century was the obsession of every man, woman, and child who could hum, strum, or whistle—the action is resumed in Agathe's chamber in the Forester's Lodge. She is in a simple dress of white trimmed with the green ribbons which befit a huntsman's bride ; on the little altar the Hermit's white roses have a conspicuous place.

Her rather hymn-like melody, *Und ob die Wolke sie verhülle*, breathes a spirit of hope and trustful resignation, but she is still unable to shake off her forebodings, which have been confirmed by her dreams of last night. The lively Aennchen, to whom she confides her fears, laughs them all away, and, in a delightful mock 'romanza,' *Einst träumte meiner sel'gen Base*, relates her own experience of a frightful apparition with fiery eyes and clanking chains, which turned out to be nothing worse than—" Nero the watch-dog ! "

The bridesmaids now enter to finish the adorning of the bride ; the little tune they sing, *Wir winden dir den Jungfernkranz*, was known for a long time as " The Bridal Chorus " *par excellence*, until the statelier march in *Lohengrin* came to supplant it. Poor Agathe !—evil omens still pursue her. The ancestral portrait of old Cuno has again fallen from the wall during last night's storm, and, worst of all, when the box which should contain the bridal-wreath is opened, it is found to contain a funeral wreath instead. However, the Hermit's roses are obviously destined for this special purpose, and, after a wreath has been hastily twined, the bridesmaids repeat their song, though in subdued tones, and the orchestra closes in the minor key as the little procession leaves the house.

Scene 11.   The concluding Scene of the Trial Shot is one of rather crowded incidents and of no special musical interest except for the Huntsmen's Chorus, which is now fully developed in the opening number.   The stage represents a green expanse, with a mountainous background, where the whole countryside is assembled to witness the exciting contest.   Prince Ottokar's pavilion occupies one side of the scene ; on the other are long tables set for the foresters and huntsmen, and feasting and drinking are the general order of the day.   The Prince rises from his daïs to hasten the conclusion of the business in hand ; Max has already acquitted himself well and won his approval—but one shot now remains to establish him in the position of Head Ranger.   The Prince bids him aim at a white dove that is flying from tree to tree ; Max fires with the last Magic Bullet in his possession, the Fatal Seventh.   At that instant Agathe arrives on the scene, and apparently receives the shot, falling senseless to the ground.   It is soon seen, however, that it is not Agathe, but the villain Caspar who has got his death wound—for it was Zamiel who directed the shot, and over the sinless maiden he had no power.   Caspar's body comes tumbling from the high tree to which he had climbed in the hope of witnessing Agathe's death by her lover's hand ; Zamiel, invisible to all but his victim, comes to claim Caspar's soul, while his body is dragged off to be thrown into the Wolf's Glen.

Agathe has now revived, in time to hear her lover's contrite confession of his entanglement in the snares of Zamiel and his possession of the Magic Bullet.   The

Prince, horrified by what he considers such unpardonable wickedness, banishes Max for ever from his realms, nor will he listen to the entreaties of Agathe, Aennchen, and the old Cuno. But the venerable Hermit now comes forth from his cave and dominates the situation; it is against the will of Heaven, he says, that one solitary lapse on the part of a youth so brave and honest should be so severely punished; Max must have another chance. Ottokar agrees; the culprit shall be put on a year's probation, at the end of which time he may look to attain his heart's desire. Agathe and Max are jubilant at the prospect of their now assured happiness, and the opera ends with a chorus based on the motive of Exultant Love —the *allegro* of the overture—wedded to words which celebrate the unfailing power of virtue and enjoin submission in all things to the will of God.

MARTHA

Music by FLOTOW. *Words by* VERNOY *and* ST GEORGES.
Vienna, 1847 ; *New York,* 1852 ; *London,* 1858.

*M*ARTHA, after enjoying an enormous popularity
for over half a century, has fallen into un-
deserved neglect in England, the last performance at Covent Garden dating as far back as 1896 ; in
New York, however, it still keeps its place in the repertory,
and there seems to be no reason why a London revival
should not succeed, if given in a smaller theatre and in the
intimate manner which it demands. The music, though
it makes no great pretensions, is consistently graceful and
melodious, and notably free from the commonplace pad-
ding which bores us in many a more ambitious work of the
period. Moreover, it has the advantage of a thoroughly
amusing libretto which goes its easy way unimpeded by
complications or obscurities of any kind. Approached
from the proper point of view, *Martha* is a delightful
entertainment, and only an incorrigible ' highbrow ' will
shrug a contemptuous shoulder at it.

The story, like the music, is of the slightest texture and
clear as daylight ; it needs no preliminary analysis. The
time is early in the 18th century, and the scene is Richmond, near London.

Act I. The Lady Harriet Durham is maid-of-honour to
Queen Anne ; she is young, she is lovely, she is a reigning
toast—yet she has come already to the conclusion that
life is a hollow sham and has nothing more to offer. True,
the world of London is at her feet, but crowded cities

have lost their charm for her ; amid all the splendours
of the Court she

> Sighs for a park, but, when a park she sees,
> At once she cries : " Oh odious, odious trees ! "

We make her acquaintance first in a pleasant apartment
in the royal palace of Richmond, where the Court is in
residence. Poets have sung the praise of Richmond Park,
but the Lady Harriet finds the trees here more than
ordinarily odious ; her spirits are at their lowest ebb, yet
she knows not what she lacks. Nancy, her confidential
waiting-maid, shrewdly guesses that it may be love.
Love ? Oh dear no ! Of lovers she has enough and to
spare, and they are all more odious, if possible, than the
trees.

Sir Tristan de Mickleford, who now enters, is one of
them ; too elderly, perhaps, to be taken seriously, he is,
nevertheless, her most devoted swain, and his mistress's
sad condition causes him great distress. He is there to
serve her—will her ladyship go with him to the donkey-
races ? or to see some cockfighting ? Her ladyship will
do nothing of the sort ; at the same time, the absurd airs
and graces of the foppish old beau cause her to break into
a hearty fit of laughter, which Sir Tristan takes as a
favourable sign. Certainly the Lady Harriet seems more
inclined to shake off her fit of the vapours, and laughter,
fortunately, is in the air ; it floats in through the open
window, mingled with a melodious chorus of fresh young
voices. These are the country wenches from miles around
on their way to the Mop Fair at Richmond. A Mop
Fair, Nancy explains, is a sort of festal gathering at which
servants of every kind assemble, once a year, and take
their stand in the market-place, to be hired by those
farmers and their wives who are in need of such com-

modities. The girls, it is plain, look upon it all as a great joke—their gaiety is so infectious that the Lady Harriet forgets all about her own blighted existence. How bright the world is looking! What lovely weather! What fun it would be to dress up in peasant guise and go with these merry wenches to Richmond Fair to take their chance of getting a comfortable place and good wages for the next twelve months! Nay, but they must act without delay: "Nancy, fetch me the peasant costumes we wore at the Queen's rout last week. Good—quite becoming! Now let me think—we must change our names, of course; I will be Martha! Nancy, I shall call you Julia [or Betsy in some versions]—and you, Sir Tristan, will be just plain John!" The stiff old courtier protests loudly against so wild a scheme, but to no purpose—the girls are now fully possessed with the idea. A little conscious, but charming in their peasant garb, they proceed to practise a rustic dance, into which they drag the gouty old beau, and the curtain falls on poor Sir Tristan exhausted and breathless from his exertions, and the two girls in fits of laughter at the uncouth gambols of their victim.

With *Scene* II we are in the thick of Richmond Fair. The opening chorus of farmers and their wives is soon reinforced by the voices of the servants in the lively melody we have already heard; but before the actual business of the hiring begins we make the acquaintance of two young farmers, obviously of the better class. Plunket, a baritone, is of the robust order, Lionel, as befits a tenor, is of finer mould, with a certain air of distinction that hardly belongs to his station. Their duet, which contains one of the best-known airs, *Solo, profugo, reletto,* lets us partly into the secret. Lionel, we learn, is Plunket's foster-brother; as an infant he had been confined to the care of Plunket's mother by a mysterious stranger, of whom nothing had since been heard ; he had, however, left behind him a ring, with instructions that his son, if ever he find himself in danger or difficulty, should forward it to the Queen, on whose favour he might confidently rely. Up to now Lionel has had no occasion to test the virtue of the ring, nor has he any desire for royal patronage ; the Court does not attract him ; he and Plunket are the best of friends, and well content to spend their days in the peace of the country. Alas, the destroyers of that peace are already close at hand !

Now the pompous old sheriff comes puffing on to the scene. " Silence ! in the name of the Queen ! " while he reads out the conditions of the statute by virtue of which the Fair is held. For a few minutes the Mollies and the Dollies keep as quiet as mice and listen to the proclamation ; all must clearly understand that when once a maid has pledged herself to service by taking the first instalment of her wages, the earnest-money, in her hand, there can be no drawing back—she is bound to her master or mistress until the year is out. Are they all agreed ? Very well—then let the girls step forward and show their paces ! The sheriff seems to know them all by name ; he calls on

Kitty Bell and Liddy Well,
And Nelly Box and Sally Cox

to state what each can do ; after hearing a recital of her qualifications he fixes the amount of wages to which she is entitled, and some lucky farmer hastens to secure the treasure. Business is brisk, the girls go off like hot cakes, and the chorus ends with a general hubbub of eager bargaining, and the passing of money from hand to hand.

But here come the disturbers of our rural happiness. The rustic dance of the previous Scene is played as Martha and Julia, demurest of rustic beauties, come jigging on, with the wretched Sir Tristan still in tow. Fine mistress and smart maid are hardly convincing in their peasant guise, while their elegant escort is thoroughly out of place as plain John. His uneasiness is greatly increased by the Lady Harriet's evident delight in their adventure, and her determination to make the most of it ; in his opinion nothing but trouble can come of it, and he is impatient to get them away. But the poor gentleman may as well keep quiet, for now comes young Cupid to take a hand in the game, and to move the puppets as he will. Lionel and Plunket are quick to note the new arrivals, and only too ready to make acquaintance with two such dainty rogues ; here indeed is a new variety of serving-maid, and one exactly to their taste. Nor are the girls altogether displeased by the admiring glances of two such comely and presentable young fellows, though they are hardly prepared for the suddenness with which events are moving. After a short preliminary skirmish, and almost before they realize what is happening, they have taken the earnest-money and find themselves engaged for a whole year as servants to the two young farmers—ten pounds a year for each, beer found, and pudding on Sundays! They refuse, of course, to take the matter seriously and are anxious now to get away as soon as possible. But it is too late—the gold pieces are in their hands ; the young men will not take the money back, and the sheriff's authority is appealed to. His verdict is final :

> Once the coin is in your keeping
> You must serve the twelvemonth out !

These words, chanted in a solemn monotone, are repeated by the chorus, and finally by Lady Harriet-Martha and Miss Nancy-Julia, with ludicrous effect.

Sir Tristan, of course, is in a terrible taking, but quite unable to render aid ; since his arrival he has been a helpless victim in the hands of the merry country wenches, who find him an excellent butt for their mischievous pranks ; they now close round him and hold him prisoner while Lady Harriet and her companion are bundled into a wagon with the two young men and driven off to scrape the pots and pans in a farmhouse kitchen.

This Scene is quite admirable as an example of much action packed into a small space without suffering confusion in the process ; the sequence of incidents is perfectly clear and intelligible, while the music, of the lightest possible texture, is graceful and melodious, free from banality, and entirely suitable to the subject. Would that many a more pretentious opera were so genuinely entertaining !

Act II. Pretty as a picture, the present Act contains little of dramatic importance, and will not detain us long.

Having got their fair baggages safely home, the two young men are not long in discovering that they have two rather queer customers to deal with. On being shown their own room, these newly hired ' servants ' are for shutting the door at once and retiring for the night ! What ! there is work to be done first ! But they know very little about domestic duties—and, besides, they are much too tired. Plunket is inclined to resent such independent behaviour, but Lionel is too tender-hearted not to yield at the sight of beauty in distress. To let them down lightly he proposes that they shall start with a little spinning. Here again they profess their ignorance, so the young men undertake to instruct them—after all, to sit beside a pretty girl and guide her hand on wheel and spindle is no unpleasant way of passing the time. So the ' Spinning Quartet,' *Presto, presto, andiam !* runs on harmoniously, even hilariously after a time, for the girls cannot long restrain their laughter at the young men's clumsy attempts at what they themselves, of course, understand perfectly well, and their tittering sounds pleasantly against Plunket's *Br'm! br'm! br'm!* as he bends solemnly to his task.

At last the lively Julia grows restive, kicks the wheel over, and makes for the door with Plunket in hot pursuit. We are now ready for a duet of sentiment between the other two.

The susceptible Lionel has had time to fall head-over-ears in love with his charming pupil, who can hardly be said to have kept him at a distance. Her instinct tells her that here is a young man who would not be out of place in polite circles, and toward whom she may allow herself to unbend without loss of dignity. When she frankly confesses that she would much sooner play than work, and that she dearly loves a hearty laugh, Lionel finds himself in perfect agreement ; work is certainly not to be expected from such a pretty creature—but will she not delight him with just one little song ? After some coquetry with a flower she is wearing, of which, of course, he gets possession, Martha obliges with " The last rose of summer," and the young man's fate is sealed. Toward the end of the second verse he strikes in harmoniously, and there follows a love-duet, tender and spirited, which would doubtless receive the praise it deserves were it attributed to a better-esteemed composer.

They are noisily interrupted by Plunket with the saucy Julia in his grasp. That lively young woman seems to have led him a dance all round the house, upsetting the furniture, breaking the crockery, spilling the wine ; now, however, he has her fast and—— But here the clock obligingly strikes twelve, and with perfect propriety the young men leave the girls to themselves, after an amicable " Good-night ! " quartet.

The Lady Harriet and her companion both agree that, come what may, they must get out of it and at once—but how ? There is a stealthy tap at the window—Sir Tristan to the rescue ! He has a carriage waiting outside, and the three drive off before their ill-used masters get wind of their intentions. Lionel is in despair at the loss of his Martha, but the irate Plunket vows he will have the law on them, and the neighbours, roused by the noise, and tempted by the offer of a reward, set out at once in pursuit of the fair runaways.

Act III. Sufficient time has elapsed for the young people to have reflected well upon their recent adventure, and we are now to see its effect upon the heart of each. Plunket, on whom the curtain rises, seems, as we should expect, his usual robust self; we find him drinking with some jolly farmers under the trees in Richmond Park, where the Queen and her Court go a-hunting to-day.

[His drinking song in praise of good old ale—though the Italian version, wishing to be ultra-English, calls it porter—is well worthy of notice ; it is far less noisy than such things are apt to be, and attracts by a certain Mozartian simplicity.]

The hunting-chorus which follows is largely in the hands of a bevy of charming young Dianas with their bows and arrows and Cupid's darts. When our once merry little Nancy (' Julia ' now no longer) enters pensively to an *andante* in the minor key, we feel that here is something amiss ; however, her aria, *Esser mesto il mio cor*, speaks of nothing worse than what we might call a ' pleasing pain,' and soon passes into a gay polka to remind us that, in spite of its Queen Anne label, *Martha* belongs emphatically to the age when that rather plebeian measure was all the fashion.

But here is Plunket bent on making trouble ; he has recognized this smart young woman as the runaway ' Julia,' and would insist on her returning with him to work out her time in his service. This, of course, she has no intention of doing ; she promptly summonses the fair huntresses to her aid, and with drawn bowstrings they drive the astonished young farmer off the stage. Now Lionel wanders on, the picture of a lovesick swain. After a few bars of " The last rose of summer," of fragrant memory, he sings the best-known air in the opera, *M'apparì tutt' amor* ; its universal popularity is now a thing of the past, though " Emma Parry," as it was once affectionately referred to, is still a favourite, we believe, in certain circles.

The lady of his heart is not long in appearing, but to his passionate avowals she dare not respond ; although absence has taught her how much she loves him, she cannot bring herself to stoop to one whom she believes to be so far beneath her. Stung by her contemptuous reply, Lionel attempts to assert his rights as her lawful master, a piece of folly which leads to his arrest by Sir Tristan's orders. The musical interest culminates in a melodious and well-built quintet, *Ah! chè a te perdoni Iddio*, and the announcement of the Queen's approach gives Lionel the opportunity of placing in her hands, through Plunket's agency, the ring which is to end all his troubles.

Act IV. This is one of those last Acts in which much has to be done in too short a space, and the music suffers in consequence. Lionel's troubles, it would seem, are by no means over ; the ring, it is true, has worked a great improvement in his fortunes—it has proved him to be the son and heir of the late Earl of Derby, whose title and estate he now inherits. But he is unable to realize his position—his mistress's coldness, nay, her treachery as he conceives it, has turned his brain. Poor Lady Harriet, too, is quite distracted ; her love for Lionel has naturally increased now that she is free to indulge it, and she is torn with remorse when she sees the sad effects of her former cruelty.

Such is the situation when the two are brought together again in the long duet with which this scene is chiefly concerned. Lady Harriet hopes to restore the young man's reason by an open avowal of her affection, but the result is very different from what she had expected. Lionel's darkened mind is obsessed by one idea only, his mistress's heartless conduct. She pleads repentance, implores forgiveness, in vain—he is obdurate—even " The last rose of summer " fails to move him, even her frank offer of her hand in marriage. Lionel only loads her with reproaches, and rushes from the stage, leaving the poor lady tearful, humbled, but still in love.

The *dénouement* is as happy as it is unexpected. By a change of scene we find ourselves in a part of Lady Harriet's private grounds where a merry throng are doing their best to reproduce an exact presentment of the Richmond Mop Fair in Act I. Here are the chattering wenches waiting to be hired, here are the farmers and their wives, here is the sheriff with the contracts ready for signing. And here, gently led on by the faithful Plunket, comes our sad lover, wasting in despair. The well-remembered spectacle, the familiar sounds that greet him, work like a spell through heart and brain; the evil spirit is banished and Lionel is himself once more. This time the Lady Harriet's wit has served her well—she stands expectant of her reward. The noisy chorus are silent, while Plunket, assuming the part of the sheriff, strolls up to the once haughty beauty : " Well, my girl, and what can *you* do ? " Not much, it seems—and yet enough ! the only service she can render is that of love, to one master only, her Lionel—and to him while life shall last. Lionel needs no further hint ; he cares not whether her name be Martha or Harriet, so long as he may hold her in his arms. Meanwhile Plunket has no difficulty in engaging Nancy on similar terms ; all join in a hearty rendering of " The last rose of summer," and we leave the theatre with that agreeable melody lingering in our memory.

DER FLIEGENDE HOLLÄNDER

Words and Music by WAGNER.
Dresden, 1843; *London,* 1870; *New York,* 1877.

THE 2nd January, 1843, is the most portentous date in the history of modern opera—it marks the production, at Dresden, of *Der fliegende Holländer,* and in this work the real Wagner emerges for the first time. Henceforth the reign of Italian 'opera' is threatened, the very word is discredited, and 'music-drama' is shortly to be the accepted term in musical circles.

The overture alone must have been an unmistakable herald of the coming change ; who that had ears to hear could fail to realize that this was something entirely new —a new atmosphere, new horizons, a new-created world ? As the opera unfolds we are conscious that the composer is still bound by the fetters of many old conventions— there are set pieces, inflexible melodies that distort the textual meaning, concessions to the singers—yet the work throughout is felt to be pulsing with new life-blood. Again and again we see the working of the two great principles which underlie all that is valuable in Wagner's subsequent reforms, and which he enunciates so plainly with reference to his *Tristan und Isolde* : (1) that the mere melody must in all cases be subservient to the words, must be prescribed by the tissue of the text ; and (2) that the substratum, the basis of everything, is to be found in the orchestral music.

The amazing developments of Wagner's genius in his later works have naturally thrown this early opera into the background—it is performed only too rarely at the present day; yet it contains moments of sheer inspiration which are unsurpassed by anything the master ever wrote, and it is permissible to suppose that, for the sake of these, *The Flying Dutchman* may still be acceptable to a future generation no longer patient of the cumbersome machinery of *The Ring*.

The story of *Der fliegende Holländer* is based on the age-long legend of the Wandering Jew, or rather on Heine's variant of it, from which Wagner's libretto was directly adapted. In both versions the central figure of the legend is condemned, for some transgression, to bear the burden of this mortal life for countless generations—to wander, an outcast on earth, until the end of time. The Wandering Jew had mocked the Saviour on his way to crucifixion; to the later story a more trivial and fantastic turn is given. A Dutch sea-captain, prevented by adverse winds from rounding the Cape, swears a fearful oath that he will not give in though he has to sail the seas for evermore; Satan hears, and condemns the wretched man to the fate he had so rashly invoked—the sea shall be his place of torment until the Judgment Day.

To this motive, common to both stories, Heine added a new element, on which Wagner was quick to seize— the redeeming power of a woman's love. Once in seven years the Dutchman was allowed to come to land in the search for a woman who would be faithful unto death. This idea was one of Wagner's most constant obsessions; it finds its happiest expression in *Tannhäuser*, and students of *The Ring* will know how large a part it plays in the psychology of that elaborate structure. In *The Dutchman* it is the dominating force of the plot, assuming dimensions which somewhat disturb the proportion of the drama and the probability of its incidents. Nevertheless,

Wagner has given us a libretto of absorbing dramatic interest, of swift action, and well-balanced situations, in which the two chief characters at least are no mere stage-puppets, but living, passionate creatures, with power to move our deepest sympathies.

The symphonic poem which forms the overture presents a magnificent impression of a vessel storm-tossed upon an angry sea; we hear the whistling of the wind through the cordage of the straining ship, the wild cries of the sailors at their strenuous work, and always the tumultuous voice of the ocean:

> The hiss and roll of the rising, the crash of the falling wave.

From all this din and turmoil two arresting and well-contrasted themes emerge—the grim curse-motive attendant upon the Dutchman, and the suave and lovely melody which typifies Senta's devotion, the love that is faithful unto death. In this respect the overture has affinity with that of *Tannhäuser*, where the theme of the Pilgrims' Chorus struggles with the wild insistence of the Venusberg music and eventually triumphs, as does the Senta motive in this, the earlier, opera.

Act I. From a rockbound shore we look out over a wide expanse of stormy sea; foul weather off the coast of Norway has driven Daland, a sea-captain on his homeward voyage, to seek shelter in a little bay some miles distant from his own port. His ship lies anchored close to land; her captain has gone ashore to get his bearings, while the sailors shout and sing as they haul at the ropes. Daland comes on board, and, satisfied that the storm is passing, sends his crew below to take some rest, and retires to his cabin, leaving the ship in the steersman's care. The young sailor, overworn by long watches, tries to fight off sleep with a song, *Durch Gewitter und Sturm,* a lovely piece of spontaneous melody, comparable to the young shepherd's song in *Tannhäuser*, "Dame Holda came from the dark hillside." Before the second verse is ended he is asleep. The storm rolls up again, the air grows darker and more eerie; the curse-motive is heard in the orchestra, and a ship looms out of the mist, the sails blood-red, the masts as black as night. She casts anchor close to Daland's vessel; in silence and without a sound the spectral seamen furl the sails; her captain, the Flying Dutchman, goes ashore. Once more the term of seven years is ended—once more begins the hopeless quest for the maiden whose love shall bring the wanderer rest at last. In the long declamatory scena, *Wie oft im Meeres tiefsten Schlund*, he tells of his never-ceasing search for death. No seas will drown him, no natural force, no human hand, can end his misery. And yet one hope remains—even the Accursed One's torment must end when earth itself shall pass away.

> Day of destruction ! Judgment Day !
> When shall thy morning dawn for me ?
> Thou trumpet, sound the crash of doom
> At whose dread blast the stars shall flee !
> When at the last the dead shall rise,
> Then death shall close my weary eyes.
> Ye planets, fall from heaven's dome !
> Endless oblivion, take me home ! [1]

And from the hold of the phantom vessel comes the echo, in tones of unutterable anguish :

> Endless oblivion, take us home !

Daland now comes up from his cabin, to find the steersman asleep and the strange vessel anchored within call of his own. To his loud hail the Dutchman answers

[1] These extracts are taken, by kind permission, from the English version by Paul England, published by Messrs Adolph Fürstner, Berlin, W.10 (copyright, 1895, by Adolph Fürstner).

only after a long silence, but the two are soon on friendly terms. In one of those overlong and tedious duets into which Wagner was so often betrayed, Daland explains his situation, and the Dutchman, learning that his home is near at hand, begs the favour of his hospitality if only for a single night ; furthermore, on hearing that Daland has a daughter he at once proposes for her hand. In order to further this strange proposal he bids his men bring from his ship a chest of jewels, of such splendour and in such profusion that the dazzled father is ready to consent to whatever the stranger may demand. The storm is over now ; the sweet south wind springs up ; Daland will hoist the sails at once and make for home. The Dutchman, for the sake of his o'erwearied crew, pleads for a few hours' delay ; he will follow soon. In joyful mood the Norwegian sailors put out once more to sea, raising their voices all together in the steersman's tender song of the homecoming :

> On the wings of the storm, from distant lands,
> Belovèd, home I fly !
> From the billows that break on southern strands,
> Belovèd, here am I !
> Dear maiden, bless the good south wind
> That hurries me home to thee !
> Blow, blow, ye breezes, warm and kind ;
> My true love doth wait for me !

Act II. The orchestral prelude to this Act is little more than a repetition of the melody we have just heard from the sailors at the end of Act I. To the audience of 1843 this must have seemed a piece of audacious unconventionality—yet no happier way of linking the two Acts could be imagined. The song tells of the seaman's longing for the girl he has left behind him, and the curtain now rises on a group of these very maidens, who sit at home and dream of their absent sweethearts' return. The scene is the great hall in Daland's house, where the girls are seated at their spinning, under the watchful eye of old Mary, who keeps the house in perfect order. Fresh and homely is the ditty they are singing as the wheels fly round—*Summ' und brumm', mein gutes Rädchen* :

> Twirl and whirl, my spindle, gaily !
>   Merry, merry wheel, spin on !
> For the flax must dwindle daily
>   Till our winter's task be done.
> My lover sails the ocean foam,
> And thinks of her who sits at home.
> Then fly, good spindle, fast and free—
> Ah ! couldst thou blow him home to me !

Dame Mary urges them to greater diligence ; the men will soon be home with their pockets full of money—no one like a sailor to pick up the good red gold !—and it is the busiest spinster who gets the finest present.

There is one, however, who does not spin. Senta, the daughter of the house, sits apart and in another world ; on the wall toward which her chair is turned hangs a portrait on which her eyes and all her thoughts are fixed. It is a face that moves to pity and terror, a face pallid and drawn with pain—the hungry lips, the sunken eyes with their hopeless appeal, framed in a tangle of long, black hair—the face of a doomed and haunted man. From childhood Senta has known that picture on the wall ; too early did she learn the story attached to it, the legend of the Flying Dutchman. The horror, the pity of it, have filled her soul ; the presence of the picture in her father's house leads her to imagine that some member of her family ages ago may have betrayed the unhappy man by breaking troth with him ; she has become obsessed by one idea, that she herself was born to be the maiden faithful unto death who shall deliver the Dutchman from the curse of existence.

Sunk in such musings, Senta can have no share in the happy business, the lively chatter, of those round her. Old Mary scolds her, and the maidens tease : fie ! to fall in love with a picture, and that, too, when she has a lover of her own ! What will Erik say when he finds it out ? Why, he will shoot his rival—from the wall ! So the tittering chaff goes on, till Senta can bear it no longer ; she begs them to stop the whirring wheels for a time; perhaps Mary will relate once more the woeful legend of the picture on the wall. But Mary bridles indignantly. The Flying Dutchman ! Heaven forbid that she should meddle with any such wickedness ! Then Senta herself will sing the ballad. The maidens leave their spinning and gather round her ; only Mary keeps her place and still spins on ; but by the end of the first verse she too is carried away by the passion which the young girl puts into the piteous narrative, and her wheel stands idle. The restless tides of ocean, the voices of the storm, are heard in the orchestra as Senta begins the ballad of the Flying Dutchman, *Traft ihr das Schiff im Meere an.*

> Say, hast thou seen the phantom ship,
> Its blood-red sails, its ebon mast,
> Upon the deck the ghostly man,
> His long hair streaming to the blast ?
> Hui !—so pipes the wind !—yo-ho-hey !
> Hui !—how shrill it sings !—yo-ho-hey !
> Like an arrow the ship flieth on, never resting for aye !

Then comes the delicious refrain heard already in the overture as the motive of faithful love :

> Yet might a woman's hand the doomèd man deliver,
> Could he but find on earth one heart that loves for ever.
> Ah, where and when, pallid wand'rer, wilt thou meet her ?
> Pray ye with me, that heaven may send her to him soon !

> The wind was wild, the sea was wroth,
>   As once he strove to clear the bay ;
> The baffled seaman swore an oath :
>   " I will not rest till Judgment Day ! "
>   And Satan heard
>   The fatal word—
> He is doomed o'er the ocean to roam, never resting for aye !

As the song proceeds Senta's excitement increases, until toward the end of the third verse she sinks back exhausted in her chair, and the girls, with hushed voices, take up the refrain :

> Ah, weary wanderer, where is she that shall deliver ?
> When wilt thou find the maid whose love shall last for ever ?

Like one inspired, Senta springs to her feet, and gives the answer :

> Mine be the faithful love that shall redeem him !
> Yea, though for him my life be given,
> Through me shall he find grace with heaven !

[Senta's *aria*, as a combination of dramatic intensity and melodic beauty against the richly wrought orchestral background, is something altogether new in opera. The slow movement with which each stanza ends foretells clearly the great melodist who was to give us the Prize Song and its companion pieces in *The Mastersingers*. On the other hand, the immaturity of Wagner's judgment at this period is nowhere more apparent than in the short conventional *cadenza* with which Senta closes her final outburst ; so accustomed has the listener become to absolute dramatic sincerity in the music of this opera that this slight concession to vocalistic tradition strikes us with almost painful surprise.]

Mary and her companions are aghast at Senta's wild outburst ; not less horrified is Erik, who enters in time to hear her last utterance. But the news he brings of the arrival of Daland's ship turns their thoughts in another direction; the girls are beside themselves with excitement, and would be flying off at once to the quay, but Mary insists on their staying at home to help in her lavish preparations for the hungry seamen who will soon be clamouring for food and drink. The bustling chorus (*presto possibile*) *Das Schiffvolk kommt mit leeren Magen* is a very acceptable little comedy interlude at this point.

The duet which follows between Senta and Erik can hardly be said to have much musical value; Erik, the tenor, the timid lover, is but a shadowy figure, for whom Wagner was content to write conventional music. Dramatically, however, the scene is an interesting experiment. Erik, never too sure of Senta's affection, and troubled by her fanciful devotion to the portrait on the wall, urges her to hurry on their wedding while her father is at home. Senta is little inclined to listen to his pleadings—her sympathy is wholly with the Ghostly Man. She leads Erik to the portrait, and bids him contemplate the awful suffering written there. " What are *your* sufferings matched with his ? " she cries. Her lover, in deep despondency, is moved to tell her of a dream he had last night; and here we have an excellent example of Wagner's power of dramatic invention. Senta, leaning back in her armchair, with closed eyes, passes (as Wagner puts it) " into a magnetic sleep, in which she seems to live in the dream which Erik relates." He tells how in his sleep he had seen a ship come sailing in; how two men came ashore, the one her father, the other—ah ! Senta sees him too, his long, black cloak, his face so deathly pale ! She stirs and speaks in her trance while Erik tells how, as the two men approached the house, he saw Senta come out to greet her father, but fall instead at the stranger's feet !

SENTA [*speaking in her trance*]. He raised me up !
ERIK.   Upon his breast,
As in a happy dream, you lay.
Your burning lips to his were pressed.
SENTA. And then——
ERIK.   With him you sailed away !

Senta, now fully awake, springs to her feet, a wild-eyed
prophetess of doom :

For me he calls ! To him I go !
His fate is mine, for weal or woe !

In horror and despair Erik rushes from the room.
Senta sinks into a reverie ; with her eyes upon the picture
she sings very softly the refrain of the Ballad. Then the
door opens, and there before her stands the Flying Dutchman—no picture, but a living man. He advances slowly
into the room ; Senta, after one loud cry, stands rooted
to the spot ; Daland remains by the door, unheeded,
until he forces himself upon his daughter's notice. He is
naturally in a merry mood, and full of his plans for the
advantageous match he is bent on making between the
two. He acquaints Senta at once with the stranger's
proposal, shows her rings and bracelets as a foretaste of
the wealth that may be hers, and hopes that the next day
will see them safely married. As neither Senta nor the
Dutchman have spoken a word as yet, but remain motionless, gazing fixedly on each other, Daland concludes that
they wish to be alone, and leaves the room in some vexation. The scene that follows is frankly tedious in action.
Still motionless and on opposite sides of the stage, they
have a long duet, and the Dutchman a solo, both of
which are treated as ' asides.' Not till the situation has
become intolerable do they move at last toward each
other, at the section *Wirst du des Vaters Wahl nicht
schelten.*

Senta is now assured that the dream of her life is near its fulfilment; hope flames up once more in the Wanderer's breast, and the two link their destinies in one for evermore.

Daland makes a welcome re-entry; the orchestra hints of the feast which the returned sailors are impatiently expecting; their captain is delighted to find that he will be able to add to the general gaiety by the announcement of his daughter's betrothal, and a short trio brings the Act to a cheerful ending.

Act III. For the undeniable dullness of much of Act II the Act before us makes rich amends; it is full of colour and movement; the interest, whether dramatic or musical, never flags.

The scene shows us a little bay with the two ships at anchor under the rugged cliff and Daland's house near the shore. It is a starry night; the Norwegian vessel is gaily illuminated for the expected feast, and the sailors are all on deck, singing and dancing; but the other shows no light: no form is seen: no sound is heard. Before the rise of the curtain the orchestra has given us part of the rousing Sailors' Chorus, "Steersman, leave the watch!"; it is a joy to hear it again in all its full sonorousness as the seamen stamp it out upon the deck.

From Daland's house come the maidens with store of wine and food for both the crews; they go first to the Dutchmen's ship and hail them from the shore—no light is shown, no sound is heard—there is a long, uncanny silence. It may be that the storm-tossed mariners are still asleep—the girls challenge them in a cheery dance measure, the Norwegians joining in with mock seriousness:

> 'Tis waste of breath! The men are dead!
> They have no need for wine or bread;
> They sing no song, they make no sign;
> In all their ship no light doth shine.

For a little while the lively interchange goes on, the sailors growing more and more hilarious, the maidens more uneasy; their loudest call is answered only by a longer silence than before, and in no dramatic work do we remember a silence so impressive. Their spirit fails them ; truly it seems as if these men were dead ! Overcome by a feeling of unaccountable horror (in which the audience can hardly help sharing), they turn away from the ship of death, leave their baskets with the Norwegian sailors, and hurry back to the house. The men, on the other hand, have been growing ever noisier in their mirth ; now that they are well supplied with wine and good cheer their jollity breaks loose ; they clank their wine-cups, roar a mighty chorus, and shout a challenge to their neighbours in the darkened ship.

And the challenge is answered. For some time the 'cellos and basses in the orchestra have been hinting at the growing unrest of ocean and the rising of the storm-wind ; the Sailors' Chorus is ended ; the dance is just beginning, but is stopped by a terrific crash in the orchestra, and the voices of fiends rather than men give out the curse-motive on a wild " Jo-ho-hoe ! Jo-ho-ho-hoe ! " All eyes are turned to the Phantom Ship, where a blue light flares at the mast-head, revealing for the first time the forms and faces of the spectral crew. Around their ship the sea is in wild commotion, the tempest howls and whistles through the rigging, in horrible contrast to the calm which prevails elsewhere. Higher and shriller than the wind ring the fiend-like voices as they defy the storm, and jeer at their accursed captain's idle quest.

The Norwegian sailors, at first struck dumb by what they see and hear, try to gain fresh courage by a renewal of their jovial song, straining their voices in a vain attempt to drown the pandemonium from the neighbouring vessel ;

but gradually overcome by terror they leave the deck, making the sign of the Cross as they go below. A wild burst of fiendish laughter seems the end of everything— the storm ceases, the sea is calm again ; darkness and silence once more resume their reign over the doomed ship. Thus ends a scene which for tense dramatic interest, for truth of musical expression, has rarely been equalled ; never has the device of contrast been more effectively employed ; as for the element of supernatural horror, the scene of the Wolf's Glen in Weber's *Der Freischütz* had hitherto been the standard—we have only to compare that scene with the present to realize what new worlds Wagner had already conquered.

With the entrance of the miserable Erik we sink to a much lower plane—indeed, Wagner's musical treatment of this character would almost suggest that he was, at times, of the same opinion as his friend von Bülow, who declared a tenor to be "not a man, but a disease [*eine Krankheit*]." In this case, however, he is very necessary to the drama, which now hurries to its close.

The broken-hearted Erik has learnt from Senta that she can never be his ; as they come from the house together he is reminding her that not so long ago she had promised to be his for ever ; Senta is inclined to dispute this, but Erik makes out a fairly good case for his assertion in the anæmic solo *Willst jenes Tags du nicht dich mehr entsinnen*.

Alas! The Dutchman, who has approached them un- seen, hears enough to convince him that Senta has been false to her former lover—then how can he hope she will prove true to him ? Once more he sees his hope of salva- tion vanish : once more the ocean claims him for its own. To sea ! To sea ! With a despairing cry, "Senta ! fare- well ! Lost, lost for evermore !" he turns his face seaward, and pipes the order to his men to hoist the sails. Senta clings to him, and swears he is mistaken, but she has yet to learn the whole truth from his lips. It is compassion for her that bids him leave her: to swear eternal truth to him, and then to break that oath, would mean that she must share his awful fate—" Lost, lost for evermore ! " That oath she has not yet sworn before Almighty God, so she may yet escape. Tearing himself away, the Dutchman hastens aboard his ship, while the curse-motive is already heard as the horrible crew haul at the ropes. Daland and Mary rush from the house and try to drag Senta back, but with the strength of madness she breaks from them and mounts the highest cliff ; with arms outstretched toward the Dutchman's ship she cries :

Behold me ! faithful unto death !

Immediately the Dutchman's ship with its howling crew sinks beneath a boiling sea; but beyond the whirl-pool and the tossing waves are seen the figures of Senta and the Flying Dutchman, united now for evermore, and soaring heavenward in the red light of the rising sun.

TANNHÄUSER

Words and Music by WAGNER.
Dresden, 1845; *New York*, 1859; *London*, 1876.

OF all Wagner's operas *Tannhäuser* is the one best known to the general musical public, as distinguished from the regular opera-goer; for forty years the overture has been a favourite stock piece with every orchestra in the world, the two vocal numbers *Dich, theure Halle* and *O du mein holder Abendstern* have been done to death in the concert-room, while the famous March and the Pilgrims' Chorus have even found their way into instruction-books. It must be confessed that these extracts (with the exception of the overture) are but slightly imbued with the true essence of Wagner—the thorough Wagnerian, indeed, is apt to deplore their existence; but they have done incalculable service by inducing countless thousands to make themselves acquainted with an opera which, with the possible exception of *Die Meistersinger*, enjoys a more solid popularity than any other of the composer's works. One chief reason for this is, beyond doubt, the attractive nature of the almost flawless libretto; it deals with what we might call Wagner's favourite theme, a woman's devotion, and the redeeming power of love. The story has all the advantage of a picturesque mediæval setting, and is unfolded in a perfectly natural sequence of events, without gaps or obscurities; there are numerous massive *ensembles* and scenes of spectacular splendour, for which the music makes noble provision; and, finally, in the purely lyrical passages, Wagner's verses are well worthy of the lovely melodies to which he has allied them.

The interesting nature of the plot and the sympathetic appeal of the chief characters may be gathered from the following synopsis : [1]

"Among the Singers attached to the Court of Hermann, Landgrave of Thuringia, at the beginning of the thirteenth century, were Tannhäuser and Wolfram, both of knightly rank. Both were in love with Elizabeth, the Landgrave's niece, whose heart secretly inclined to Tannhäuser. A year before the action of the drama begins, Tannhäuser, in a fit of anger and unrest, had left the Landgrave's castle on the Wartburg. Wandering on the slopes of the Hörselberg, or the Hill of Venus, in the recesses of which the goddess held her Court, he had fallen to her wiles, and for a whole year had dwelt at her side, bound fast by all the sensual pleasures that her power could command. Wearying at length of this unnatural existence, and moved by the memories of his earthly life, he contrives to break the spell and escape from her thrall. On waking from his trance, he finds himself in a valley in front of the Wartburg, the Landgrave Hermann's castle. Here he is discovered by the Landgrave and his nobles, and is persuaded to rejoin the Court by Wolfram's assurance that Elizabeth still loves him.

" To celebrate his return, the Landgrave lets proclaim a Tournament of Song, to which especial dignity is given by the promise that Elizabeth herself shall award the prize. The theme proposed to the assembled singers is the Nature of Love. Tannhäuser, in the course of his song, is brought again under the unholy sway of Venus, and after wildly chanting the praises of sensual love,

[1] This synopsis and the subsequent quotations are given by kind permission of Messrs Boosey and Co.

boasts that he himself has dwelt in Venus' Hill. The nobles, incensed at this outrage, draw their swords on Tannhäuser and are about to kill him, when Elizabeth throws herself in front of him and pleads for his life, in order that he may yet work out his redemption. The Landgrave consents, on the condition that Tannhäuser shall leave the country and go on a pilgrimage of penance. Crushed with remorse, he sets out for Rome. Elizabeth, left desolate, though tenderly guarded by Wolfram, watches anxiously day by day for the return of the Pilgrims in whose company Tannhäuser has departed. At length they come—but he is not among them. Broken-hearted, she withdraws from the world, to spend her life in prayers for his salvation.

"Tannhäuser at length comes back from Rome. To Wolfram he relates the story of his pilgrimage, and the failure of his appeal to the Pope; sooner shall green leaves grow on the Papal Staff (such was the doom pronounced) than he, Tannhäuser, shall find forgiveness. Mad with despair, he seeks once more the entrance to the Hill of Venus, and the goddess herself comes forth, to lure him in, while Wolfram struggles to prevent his going. At this moment a funeral chant is heard from the Wartburg and a procession descends, bearing the body of Elizabeth. Venus and her train are vanquished, and disappear. At the same time a band of pilgrims enter the valley, bringing tidings from Rome of the miracle that has been wrought—the Pope's Staff has put forth green leaves. Elizabeth's prayers have been heard. With a last cry, 'Holy Elizabeth, pray for me!' the ransomed Tannhäuser falls dead beside her bier."

There is no overture which sets forth so plainly, so succinctly, the drama subsequently to be unfolded as does the overture to *Tannhäuser*. There are two main themes, two broad and striking melodies in admirable contrast—the solemn chant of the Pilgrims and the bold, trenchant song of Tannhäuser in praise of Venus ; in addition to these, we have a medley of ' motives ' from the Venusberg revels, a wild orgy of sensuous excitement, which is finally quenched by the growing solemnity of the Pilgrims' Chorus. In this wonderful tone-picture we apprehend clearly the old struggle between " Sacred and Profane Love," in which the former triumphs—and this, briefly, is the argument of the drama.

Act I. The first Scene, known as ' The Bacchanal,' exists in two different forms—the original version produced at Dresden, 1845, and the Paris production of 1861. For the latter, Wagner, in order to comply with the inexorable traditions of the *Grand Opéra*, wrote a quantity of additional ballet-music, and greatly elaborated his original scheme ; when this version is given, the curtain rises while the overture is still in progress, and there is no break in the continuity. In this country, however, the older form is usually adhered to ; the overture is brought to a formal close, and the ballet is confined to very moderate dimensions.

Scene 1. We are in the Hill of Venus, the Court of the Queen of Love, and the abode of all sensual pleasures. Around a blue lake stretching to the back of the stage are grottoes, groves, and wooded slopes, peopled with nymphs and fauns, dryads and satyrs, disposed in amorous couples. The whole scene is bathed in a rosy light, while a Bacchic dance goes on, rising at times to furious disorder. From the far end of the lake is heard the sirens' lovely song :

> Dream through the hours
> Here in these bowers,
> Till on your slumbers
> Bright visions thronging
> Fill you with rapture,
> Calm every longing.

A sense of languor steals over all—the dancers slacken ; a dense mist rolls down the heights and hides the general scene, thus concentrating our attention on the figures of Venus and Tannhäuser in the foreground, the goddess reclining on a couch, with her arms around the neck of the kneeling man. Tannhäuser is in no mood to answer her caresses ; he is wearied of her soft ways, of all the endless pleasures her realm can offer ; he longs for the old familiar joys of earth—in his ears is ever a sound of bells from village steeples. Venus questions him anxiously— what is it he lacks ? " The sunshine, the moonlight, the kindly stars of heaven ! The grass that clothes the meadows—the nightingale, that sings when May is blooming ! Ah—am I doomed never to see them more ? " The goddess reproaches him for his ingratitude—how has she failed him ? He replies in the great lyric outburst *Dir tön' ich Lob*—one of the two chief themes of the overture. Nay, the Queen of Love has not failed him, she has been only too bounteous in her favours ; it is the weakness of his own mortal nature which makes him turn from pleasures such as only immortals can long endure :

> To scenes of earth I long to flee !
> Ah, Queen and Goddess, set me free !

Venus' answer is to put forth even more powerful enchantments than before. The soft, sensuous music of the Bacchanal stirs again in the orchestra—the climax of voluptuous excitement has not yet been reached ; in strains of exquisite seductiveness she invites him to still greater blisses :

> Belovèd, come ! See yonder bower
> With rosy vapours perfumed sweet ;
> A god might rest for ever blest
> In such a fragrant, cool retreat !

With festal joy we'll mark our bond's renewing,
Love's raptures to their farthest bounds pursuing.
Shrink not till her most secret rites are done !
Come ! and with love's own goddess mingle into one !

And from far away is heard again the Sirens' Chorus : " Dream through the hours ! "

For the third time, and with ever-increasing ardour, Tannhäuser repeats his song in Venus' praise ; but his resolve is taken—to earth he must return ! Venus, baffled, rises in rage and despair : " Go then," she cries, " madman and traitor ! After long years of friendless wandering on earth, outcast and broken, thou wilt return to me, craving for pardon at my hands ! But of this be sure— Heaven's pardon thou wilt never find ! For thee there is no salvation ! "

" Heaven's pardon ! " cries the knight. " Yes ! that indeed I hope to find—through the Blessed Mary's intercession ! " At the invocation of that name of power, the goddess, with a cry of anguish, vanishes, and the whole scene is for a moment plunged in darkness.

Scene II. When the stage is again visible, Tannhäuser seems not to have changed his position, but the scene around him is changed indeed. Instead of the unnatural glow and glamour of the secret cave, we have the green earth flooded with sunshine, and the clear blue of heaven over us ; instead of the wild, voluptuous music and the rush of frenzied dancers, the sound of sheep-bells and the solitary figure of a young shepherd piping from a rocky height. We are in a lovely valley of the Wartburg, with the castle soaring in the background, and the Hörselberg, the Hill of Venus, seen dimly in the distance. In the foreground is a shrine and image of the Blessed Virgin.

The young shepherd has a delicious unaccompanied song, *Frau Holda kam aus dem Berg hervor*, the signifi-

cance of which is not generally understood. In old
Teutonic mythology Holda is the beneficent Goddess of
the Spring with all its regenerating powers ; Goddess of
Love is she too, but far removed from that Venus "whose
habitation is in the dark places of the earth and whose
favours are a curse." The shepherd's song, then, expresses " a pure and natural delight in the manifestation
of the Great Power which Tannhäuser apprehended only
in its corruption."

> Queen Holda came from the warm hillside
>   To roam where flowers were springing ;
> Sweet airs were wafted far and wide—
>   Ah ! sweetly the birds were singing !
> A soft dream on my eyelids lay,
> And as I woke at break of day
>   The sun shone bright around me.
>
> .   .   .   .
>
> Now on my pipe I merrily play,
> For May is here, the lovely May !

But the shepherd's pleasant piping soon gives way to
graver sounds, the solemn chant of a band of Pilgrims who
are seen descending from the Wartburg. Their song is
not the triumphant Pilgrims' Chorus heard in the overture, but a humble prayer for guidance :

> To thee I turn, O Saviour blest,
> In Thee the Pilgrim's hope doth rest ;
> And thou, O Virgin, pure and sweet,
> In mercy guide the Pilgrim's feet !

The shepherd boy waves them a greeting as he goes his
way : " God speed to Rome ! Pray for my sinful soul's
salvation ! " Tannhäuser, deeply moved, sinks in prayer
before the shrine ; with contrite heart he follows the
penitential words of the chant :

> Borne down beneath this load of sin,
>   In heavy chains my soul is lying,
> Nor peace nor rest I seek to win,
>   But gladly walk in pain and sighing.

Shaken with sobs, the knight lies prostrate on the ground as the song of the Pilgrims dies away.

A different music now comes from the heights, the music of the chase, horn answering horn in various keys, as a party of green-clad huntsmen make their way down from the Wartburg ; it is the Landgrave and his minstrel-knights, Tannhäuser's old companions. The noise of distant and approaching horns is like a fresh burst of sunshine, and prepares us for a *finale*, cheerful, vigorous, and animated in the highest degree.

It is long since Tannhäuser, in a fit of anger, had forsaken the Landgrave's Court, and all are glad to welcome back their most brilliant singer. But it is Wolfram, his dearest friend in former times, who takes the lead here ; he is the first to recognize the kneeling figure, and when Tannhäuser, who has not yet shaken off the evil influences of his late experience, declines their invitation to return to his fellows, and begs them to leave him to his lonely fate, it is Wolfram who finds a way to win him back.

In the old days the two comrades had both been suitors for the hand of Elizabeth, the Landgrave's niece, who was accustomed to grace with her presence the singers' contests in the great Hall of Song in the Wartburg ; it was known that her heart had inclined to Tannhäuser, and now Wolfram, with noble unselfishness, tells his friend how, after his departure, the maiden had grown pale and listless, and withdrawn herself altogether from the minstrels' gatherings ; only Tannhäuser's return, he says, could bring back the colour to Elizabeth's cheek, and its former glory to the Hall of Song. [The lovely melody of this narration, *Wär's Zauber, wär' es reine Macht*, is repeated by the orchestra and the men's voices with fine effect.]

The mention of Elizabeth's name works an instant change in Tannhäuser ; the evil spell is now entirely lifted, pure love once more resumes its sway, and his way lies open to that earthly Paradise from which he has so long been exiled. He breaks out in a jubilant song of thankfulness : *Ha ! jetzt erkenne ich sie wieder !*

> Now once again thy charm comes o'er me,
>   Thou wondrous world from which I fled !
> How fair thy meadows gleam before me,
>   How bright the boundless skies outspread !
> 'Tis spring ! A thousand tuneful voices
>   My lightened soul to gladness stir,
> Enraptured all my heart rejoices
>   And cries aloud : " To her ! To her ! "

The Landgrave and his minstrel-knights join a lusty septet, to which the horns soon lend their music ; more huntsmen crowd the stage with hounds and horses, and the curtain falls on a typical presentment of the picturesque out-of-door life of the Middle Ages.

Act II. The Minstrels' Hall in the Wartburg, with windows overlooking the valley of the previous Scene. Almost the whole of the Act is taken up with the splendid Tournament of Song which the Landgrave has commanded in order to celebrate Tannhäuser's return to the scene of his former triumphs ; the three opening numbers, while necessary to the action, can hardly be said to have any great musical interest, although one of them, " Elizabeth's Greeting," as it is usually called, has been done to death on the concert platform more ruthlessly perhaps than any other Wagnerian excerpt. The scene is empty when the curtain rises, but Elizabeth soon makes an ecstatic entry with arms extended in greeting to the " Dear Hall of Song " (*Dich, theure Halle*) where she had spent so many happy hours. Her rhapsody of joy and thanksgiving for Tannhäuser's return is scarcely ended when that knight, escorted by the unselfish Wolfram, appears in the gallery, and hurries down to cast himself impetuously at Elizabeth's feet. He wins from the young girl a frank confession of her love in the passage *Der Sänger klugen Weise*, and they join in a long-drawn out duet, *Gepriesen sei die Stunde*, inevitably reminiscent of the *allegro* of Agathe's great scene in Weber's *Der Freischütz*. Tannhäuser goes off in an ecstasy of new-awakened happiness, stopping on the way to embrace the long-suffering Wolfram, who has been the means of restoring him to life and love.

The Landgrave now appears, and after some words of tender encouragement to his blushing niece—"My guardian, my second father!" she calls him—escorts her to her place on the high daïs from which they are to watch the brilliant pageant which now begins. To the strains of the famous March the company assembles; glittering knight and gorgeous lady in long succession pass, with due obeisance, before the Presence, and are escorted to their seats, until the whole hall is filled with the flower of Thuringia, and a full-throated chorus, *Freudig begrüssen wir die edle Halle*, goes up in praise of Landgrave Hermann, noblest patron of the glorious art of song.

When all are seated, the competing singers, six in number, enter, and are ushered by four pages to their places. The Landgrave now rises, and, after a courteous reference to Tannhäuser's return, announces the subject on which the minstrels are to exercise their art: Love is the theme, its nature and begetting. The victor is free to name his own reward, and Elizabeth's gracious bestowal will enhance the value of the prize. And so the contest opens. Order of precedence is determined by lot; six scrolls, each containing the style and title of one of the minstrels, are handed to Elizabeth; she draws one, and the pages call out the first name: "Wolfram of Eschinbach, begin thou!"

Although Wolfram's solo, *Blick' ich umher*, has little of the melodious charm of the famous "Star of Eve" in Act III, it resembles it in the vague mediæval allegory of the words ; Elizabeth is his

> One bright star that shineth
> Lone in her splendour, though the rest be fair ;

there is also a silver fountain leaping heavenward, and that is love ; but star and fountain are equally unapproachable, for the devout lover may only worship from afar.

> Oh, ne'er may I profane that well's pure water,
> Nor stain with impious hand that silver flood !
> In lowly devotion I kneel before it,
> Contented there to shed my heart's last blood.

Toward the end of the song Tannhäuser has shown some not unnatural signs of impatience, and now rises, half in protest. He, too, knows that fountain and does it homage ; but not for him is Wolfram's cold restraint— he must approach and taste it.

> In fullest draughts I drink of rapture
> Where never doubt or dearth prevails,
> For none can quench that fount immortal,
> Which, like my longing, never fails.
> So, that my thirst may last for ever,
> Drink I these waters day by day.

This, declares Tannhäuser, is "love's most perfect way." Elizabeth, under the spell of her beloved's voice, thinks so too ; she begins to applaud, but is checked by the chilly silence of all around her ; it is plain that trouble is brewing. Walther von der Vogelweide (the poet whom that other Walter in *The Mastersingers* acknow- ledged as his teacher) rises in support of Wolfram ; continuing the imagery of the two previous songs, he administers a grave rebuke to Tannhäuser :

> The holy fount that Wolfram honours,
>   I, too, have watched its waters flow;
> But what its sacred stream concealeth,
>   That, Heinrich, thou canst never know!
> Then, for thy guidance, let me teach thee,
>   That holy fount is virtue's shrine.
>
> .   .   .   .   .
>
> Wouldst thou possess its charm, yet not destroy it,
> Then must thy soul, and not thy sense, enjoy it.

Tannhäuser is merely irritated by such cold-blooded moralizing: "Thou doest love a grievous wrong," he declares;

> The world itself would fall in ruin
> Were men to heed thy frigid song.

Far different is his own ideal of love; the stars of heaven we may regard with awe-struck reverence:

> But that which seems to crave caresses,
> Which to our heart and sense appeals,
> And, in our own familiar likeness,
> Into our bosom gently steals,
> Let us enjoy with fullest pleasure,
> For by enjoyment love I measure!

During this song the orchestra portrays clearly the dangerous excitement that is already rising in Tannhäuser's breast and influencing those around him. The rugged Biterolf, oldest of the minstrel knights, leaps angrily from his seat and pours forth his indignation upon the frivolous blasphemer, who answers him with scorn and insult. The nobles side eagerly with Biterolf, and an actual fray seems imminent, when Wolfram restores calm by a melodious appeal to the Star of Love to guide their judgment, *Dir, hohe Liebe*. But by this time Tannhäuser is once more completely under the influence of his evil past; scarcely allowing Wolfram to finish, he rises in wildest ecstasy and sings the praises of the heathen goddess in the very strains with which her sensuous charms had inspired him in her own unhallowed cave.

> Hail, gracious goddess ! Fount of every pleasure !
> Thy mighty power shall still be sung by me !

Then, as a last outrage, in the face of all that noble and God-fearing company, he flings the fearful challenge :

> Faint-hearted ! would ye taste love's keenest raptures,
> Away ! swift to the Hill of Venus haste !

The assembly breaks up in horror and confusion ; the knights and minstrels gather round the Landgrave in excited consultation ; the ladies leave the hall—all but Elizabeth, who, like the rest, has risen, and, shaken with emotion, supports herself against a pillar of the throne. At the other extremity of the stage stands Tannhäuser, a solitary figure, still gloating over the unholy visions he had conjured up. The Landgrave and his courtiers decide on instant vengeance ; Tannhäuser, who, by his own confession, has leagued himself with the Powers of Evil, is no longer fit to live. All, even Wolfram, draw their swords and are closing round the doomed man when, to their utter amazement, Elizabeth rushes forward to his rescue. "Back! back! from him ! " she cries, and takes her stand in front of her fallen idol, a perfect picture of heroic love :

> Strike here ! I care not—if it be your will !
> What were the deepest wound your swords could give me
> Matched with the deadly thrust that he hath dealt my heart !

Astonished, horror-struck, they can only suppose the unhappy girl to have lost her reason ; again they close in upon their victim ; but Elizabeth, strong in faith, in love, in spotless purity, controls their fury—she speaks like one inspired :

> Who, then, are ye, that ye should be his judges ?
> Would ye destroy his only hope of heaven ?
> Do ye not know God loves the sinner too ?

Why should they seek his death? He has done *them*
no harm! But let them think what he has done to *her*—

> the maid, whose lovely spring-time
> Is blighted, ne'er to bloom again.

Yet she can forgive him, pity him, pray for him. In a strain
of infinite tenderness, *Ich fleh' für ihn,* she pours forth her
appeal :

> I plead for him! Let not his life be taken!
> By long repentance let his soul be tried,
> Till faith returning shall new hope awaken—
> Even for him Christ, our Redeemer, died!

Such love as hers is sure of victory ; anger softens, desire
for vengeance dies away—it is the voice of Heaven that
they hear. A calmer spirit spreads among them—Tannhäuser alone is in the throes of a fearful agitation : " Woe,
woe is me for mine offences ! " cries the unhappy man,
torn with remorse and near to despair. For him there
is no present balm of healing, no hope of earthly pardon ;
only one way remains, and that the Landgrave shows
him : " We thrust thee from our Court, thou wretched,
sin-polluted man! With us thou canst no longer look
for shelter ! Yet, though we reject thee, one hope still
is thine. Hear, then, what thou shalt do ! "

The orchestra here gives out the theme of the Penitent
Pilgrims in Act I ; another such band, the Landgrave
relates, are even now in the valley, on their way to Rome ;
Tannhäuser must join them, in the hope of working out
his own salvation.

> To Rome thou now must journey
>   In lowly pilgrim's dress,
> There kneel in dust and ashes,
>   And all thy guilt confess.
> Beseech him who hath power
>   Through God to pardon sin,
> But never turn thou homeward
>   If thou no pardon win !

In a massive and elaborate *finale* the conductor must exercise all his powers of control if, through a full orchestra and an excited and high-pitched male chorus, we are to hear the two solo voices which dominate the situation —Tannhäuser's poignant cries of contrition, and, above all, the broad melody in which Elizabeth offers her life, her all, to Heaven, if only her beloved may find salvation. As if in answer to her prayer the Pilgrims' Hymn is heard in the valley far below—

> O blessèd who in faith endure !
> Their sin shall find redemption sure !

Even Tannhäuser's face is lit up with a glow of newly kindled hope ; he hastens to join the train of penitents, while all the rest call after him, in the words of the young shepherd in the first Act—

> To Rome ! God speed ! To Rome !

Act III. The orchestral introduction, labelled "Tannhäuser's Pilgrimage," is built up of four principal themes. With two of these we are familiar, the chant of the Penitent Pilgrims, and Elizabeth's appeal, " I plead for him " ; to these are added two new motives, one in throbbing phrases of broken semiquavers which well express Tannhäuser's contrite heart, his " tears and heavy sighing "—the other a broad ecclesiastical melody in six-four time, symbolical of the pomp and ritual of the Vatican. The grave and sombre atmosphere thus created is thrice disturbed by the rapid upward rush of whirring violins, with which we are familiar from the overture, suggesting the tumult of earthly passions ever striving for the mastery. It would be difficult to imagine a more complete epitome of the experiences of the penitent whose return from Rome we are expecting.

The curtain rises on the lovely valley we remember at the end of the first Act. At the Virgin's shrine where Tannhäuser then knelt, Elizabeth lies prostrate in prayer. It is late autumn, and the evening is fast closing in.

Wolfram is seen descending by a woodland path, but stops half-way at the sight of Elizabeth—each evening at the same hour he finds her there :

> The wound deep in her breast still burning,
> For him she prays with ceaseless yearning,
> Pleading with Heaven by night and day.
> O perfect love, that nought can slay !

Long indeed has seemed the time since Tannhäuser left her in the spring of the year ; all through the summer she has possessed her soul in patience, but now the fall of the leaf tells her that the return of the Pilgrims is close at hand ; each day raises her hopes and renews her fears —will he return with them ?

Scarcely has Wolfram ended his soliloquy when he hears the sound of voices chanting far away :

> It is the joyful chorus
> That tells of happy souls by grace absolved.

Elizabeth, too, hears it and takes her stand where she can listen and watch. As the sounds draw nearer we recognize the opening theme of the overture, the noble song of hope and love triumphant, now heard for the first time in full choral splendour as the singers come in sight.

> The grace of God to the sinner is given,
> He too shall dwell with the blessed in heaven,
> Nor death nor hell can him dismay,
> Therefore we'll praise our God alway !

Weary, bowed, and travel-stained, but with faces radiant with joy, the Pilgrims crowd upon the scene—

Elizabeth scans each group as it passes, with painful and ever-growing anxiety. Alas! the face she looks for is not there—henceforth she is to look no more on earthly things. When the Pilgrims' Song has died away, the broken-hearted maid falls on her knees and to the Virgin-Mother a virgin's prayer ascends:

> Let me but share thy sweet protection
> And humbly kneel before thy throne,
> Not for myself a boon to win,
> Only to plead for his great sin.

When at last she rouses from her trance-like state, Wolfram approaches in the hope of accompanying her homeward. Elizabeth makes a courteous gesture of thanks, but gently shakes her head and points to heaven, henceforth her only care. Slowly she climbs the winding path that leads upward to the Wartburg; Wolfram watches her until she is lost to sight among the trees. He too seems to pass into Elizabeth's visionary region; after preluding softly for some time upon his harp, he sings the famous " Star of Eve," of which the widespread popularity is due, in a great measure, to the atmosphere of vague ' mysticism ' that surrounds it.

> Like death's grim shadow, darkness round me hovers;
> A misty veil the sombre valley covers;
> The spirit that would soar to yonder height
> Doth shrink in dread before that awful flight.
>
> There shinest thou, the fairest star in heaven,
> Whose gentle beams to mortal eyes are given;
> Before thy radiance night's dim terrors fail,
> For thou dost point my pathway through the vale.
>
> O pure and tender star of eve,
> Sweet is the comfort thou dost give!
> This faithful heart's unheeded sigh
> Bear to her when she shall pass thee by—
> When, borne aloft on angel pinions,
> Her soul shall enter heaven's dominions.

[The above, though not a literal translation, fairly renders the spirit of the original words, the meaning of which is by no means too clear. The actual evening star has just risen over the heights of the Wartburg, and to it Wolfram addresses his romance, at the same time identifying it with the " Star of Love " of which he has already sung, and also with Elizabeth herself, " the fairest star in heaven." In the last six words he seems to foretell the approaching release of her spirit from its earthly prison, and its flight to heaven :

> This faithful heart's unheeded sigh
> Bear to her *when she shall pass thee by.*]

Wolfram's musings are interrupted by the entrance of a wild figure in tattered dress, supporting himself painfully on a pilgrim's staff ; he is horrified to recognize Tannhäuser, whose life is forfeit should he be found here, his guilt still unforgiven—and this man's looks speak not of peace and pardon. But Tannhäuser is beyond all such consideration—his one object in returning is to find once more the entrance to the Hill of Venus, the only refuge left for such as he.

Wolfram questions him. Yes—he has made the pilgrimage to Rome, the sincerest penitent of them all, outdoing his fellows in acts of mortification :

> When through the green and pleasant meads they wandered,
> On stones and thorns I trod with naked feet ;
> When others sought the fountain's cooling waters,
> I only drank the summer's parching heat.

At Rome he, like the others, did penance in the dust.

> A thousand souls confessed their guilt, and shriven,
> A thousand joyful pilgrims went their way.

But Tannhäuser was not among them—for guilt such

as his there was no forgiveness. These were the awful terms in which the Holy Father had pronounced his doom :

> Since thou in Venus' Hill hast dwelt
> Thy soul is lost beyond recall.
> As on this staff that here I hold
> Never again a leaf shall grow,
> So from the fiery pangs of hell
> Redemption thou can'st never know.

Mad with despair he had fled from Rome and hurried back, longing once more to taste those unhallowed joys which are now his only solace. In spite of Wolfram's horrified remonstrance, Tannhäuser proceeds to invoke the goddess in the very strains which she had used in Act I to bind him closer to her side, " Beloved, come ! See yonder bower." The wild music of the Bacchanal is heard in the orchestra, the old seductive themes are repeated, the Sirens' Song, the dance of nymphs and satyrs. Now the scene is filled with wreaths of rosy mist, through which the forms of the hellish revellers are dimly discerned. At last Venus herself is clearly seen, in her most voluptuous attitude, eager to welcome back her truant lover, who listens greedily to the honied voice he so well remembers.

> Say, does the cruel world reject thee ?
> Then shall my loving arms protect thee !

A violent struggle now begins between Tannhäuser and Wolfram, who seeks by force to drag him away from the awful peril. But Tannhäuser's resolve is taken :

> My soul can never find salvation,
> So be her love my consolation !

Venus redoubles her allurements and seems sure of her

triumph, when Wolfram, as on a former occasion, employs once more the word of power : " Elizabeth ! "

The music of that name on Wolfram's lips seems to break the spell of evil ; with a cry of despair the goddess vanishes ; Tannhäuser, freed for ever from her power, turns with a new rapture in his face to Wolfram, as the sound of pious voices is heard descending from the Wartburg ; Wolfram explains their meaning to him in the solemn words :

> Thine angel pleads for thee at God's right hand !
> Her prayer is heard ! Heinrich, thou art forgiven !

By this time the magical vapours have dispersed, to make way for the ruddy blaze of torches, as a funeral train, escorting the body of Elizabeth, winds slowly toward the valley. A great burst of song proclaims the triumph of her whose mighty love was faithful unto death, whose patient suffering and ceaseless prayer have won salvation for the man she loved.

> Oh blessed soul, that hath out-soared
> This pious virgin's earthly frame !
> Thine is the faithful's just reward,
> Joys that the saints alone can claim.

Tannhäuser's strength is nearly spent—he lies exhausted in the arms of Wolfram, who, as the procession passes, bids them set down the bier ; to this he leads the dying man, who sinks gently down beside the dead Elizabeth, his arms extended across her body : " Blessed Elizabeth, pray for me ! "—and with the words he dies.

The valley is flooded with the red light of morning as a belated train of pilgrims comes in sight, jubilant with the news they bring from Rome. God's mercy is over all His works ! After Tannhäuser's departure from the Holy

City, the miracle, too great for mortal man to credit, had actually happened :

The withered staff the Pope did bear
Hath blown in leafage fresh and fair ;
So he whom toils of hell did bind,
Mercy and pardon yet shall find.

With God all things are possible—and the opera closes as it began with the great choral melody which speaks of pity and pardon, infinite and eternal.

LOHENGRIN

Words and Music by WAGNER.
Weimar, 1850 ; *New York,* 1871 ; *London,* 1875.

WAGNER had finished *Tannhäuser* in 1844 ; the following year he started work on *Lohengrin*, and the opera was completed in 1847. But although the two works are separated by such a short interval of time, *Lohengrin* shows an enormous advance on its predecessor. Wagner's genius was maturing rapidly, and in this work we can distinguish most of the chief characteristics of his later style.

The story is the very old one of the Mysterious Lover whose name must not be known, the vow of obedience exacted from the Beloved, and the disaster that ensues from her breaking of that vow at the prompting of jealous advisers.

Act I takes place on the banks of the Scheldt, near Antwerp. King Henry is seated under the Judgment Oak, surrounded by his Saxon nobles. He is the one historical character in the piece, being that Henry who was called ' The Fowler,' and became celebrated for his successful wars against the wild tribes of the Hungarians. Opposite him are the nobles of Brabant, headed by Frederick of Telramund and his wife Ortrud. Henry has come to summon the Brabantine levies to join him in his proposed campaign against the Hungarians. But he finds there is a dispute to be settled first—Frederick explains it. The late Duke of Brabant had appointed Frederick guardian of his children, Elsa and Gottfried ; one day Elsa returned alone from the forest, where she had been wandering with her brother, with a tale of how she had lost him in the wood. Further search failed to discover the missing boy, and Frederick now accuses Elsa of fratricide, and claims the dukedom for himself and Ortrud. The King is horrified at this indictment, and demands that Elsa shall be summoned to answer it. She comes timidly forward, but is at first too much overcome to speak. When she finds her voice it is not to defend herself, but to describe a vision she has seen of a knight in shining armour who was sent by Heaven in answer to her prayers.

The great song generally known as "Elsa's Dream" is justly famous. Opening with a feeling of quiet and restraint, the music gradually grows richer as Elsa's excitement increases, till at last, kindling to ecstasy, she stakes all on her faith in Providence, and hurls her challenge at Frederick :

> That Knight be my defender !
> He shall my champion be !

But Frederick is unmoved—he honestly believes in the justice of his cause, and is prepared to uphold it in single combat against any knight. Let Elsa produce her champion ! At the King's command the trumpets are sounded—twice—but no one appears. Already the judgment of Heaven seems to have been given against her, and she has fallen on her knees in fervent prayer, when in the far distance, visible only to those by the river bank, a wonderful sight is seen. A knight appears, in silver armour, as in Elsa's dream, and standing in a boat drawn by a swan. Rapidly he approaches and at length steps ashore amid the acclamations of the astonished people. Dismissing the swan with a few gentle words of farewell, he makes his obeisance to the King, and announces that he has been sent by God to defend a slandered maiden.

Then, turning to Elsa, he offers himself as her champion. Should she accept him and should he conquer in the ensuing combat, he will be suitor for her hand as well. But let her understand clearly—she must trust him absolutely and, whatever befalls, she must never ask his name.

To these proposals, and the condition that goes with them, Elsa gladly gives her assent. The lists are prepared, the King makes an impressive appeal to God to defend the right, the people echoing his words, and the fight begins. It is of short duration; Lohengrin soon fells Frederick to the earth. His victory is hailed by a shout from the people and an ecstatic song of rapture from Elsa, and all unite in a somewhat conventional *finale*, singing the praises of the victor. Ortrud joins in with threats of vengeance, and even Frederick so far recovers himself as to bewail his defeat in lusty tones.

Act II. The citadel of Antwerp; at the back are the men's apartments, on the left are the women's; on the right is the Cathedral. It is deep night, and in the darkness we can hardly distinguish the figures of Ortrud and Frederick, seated on the Cathedral steps and listening in bitterness of heart to the sounds of revelry proceeding from the men's quarters. The scene that follows is wholly admirable and is a worthy foretaste of Wagner's later triumphs. To fierce and sombre music Frederick upbraids Ortrud with being the cause of his downfall—it was her definite statement that Elsa was guilty which let him into levelling his accusation and thereby to that disastrous fight. Now he is a ruined man, his honour lost, himself an outcast in the land he had hoped to rule. Ortrud has been proved false by the judgment of God. "God!" cries Ortrud. "No, it was not by His help that Lohengrin's victory was won; on the contrary, it was by the power of sorcery." Even now it is not too late for them to repair their shattered fortunes. If they can only work on the impressionable Elsa and induce her to ask Lohengrin the fatal question, the spell will be broken. And failing that, there is still another hope. Those whose might is drawn from sorcery lose their strength if a portion of their body, be it ever so small, is cut from them. Could they contrive that Lohengrin should receive the slightest wound, his magic power would be destroyed. Frederick is doubtful at first, but Ortrud ends by convincing him.

Here there comes a change in the music, as though a cloud were passing from the face of the moon. Elsa appears on the balcony above them, and all oblivious of their presence whispers to the night the secret of her love, in the lovely number known as "Elsa's Song to the Breezes." At sight of her, Ortrud hastily bids Frederick withdraw, and herself calls Elsa by name. It does not take her long to work on the girl's sympathy and persuade her to descend and admit her. Freely she forgives Ortrud all the wrongs she has suffered—she will win her pardon, and Frederick's too, from Lohengrin and the King. The crafty Ortrud is full of humble thanks, but, even as she pours out her gratitude, she begins her task of poisoning the young girl's mind. How can she repay Elsa ? Never ! But at least she can be near to support her when trouble comes. For come it will ! The magic which brought Lohengrin to her aid will some day take him from her in the same way. As the two women go in together Frederick emerges from his hiding-place, and in a short monologue rejoices in his wife's success. Then, as day begins to dawn, he conceals himself again behind a buttress of the Cathedral.

Signs of life soon begin to show themselves in the citadel, and the nobles and people gradually assemble for the forthcoming ceremony, the marriage of Elsa and Lohengrin. After a chorus a herald appears and announces the King's decree. Frederick is banished and Lohengrin shall rule in his stead as Guardian of Brabant; his wedding with Elsa is to be celebrated immediately. Another chorus follows, in the course of which it happens that four of Frederick's old adherents find themselves near the buttress. Frederick shows himself, tells them he will soon prove Lohengrin an imposter, and invokes their aid. The episode is over in a moment, and Frederick retires once more, just as Elsa and her train appear from the castle on the way to the Cathedral. But an interruption occurs. Elsa has reached the very steps of the sacred building when Ortrud comes forward and confronts her. Publicly she taunts her with neither knowing the name of her husband-to-be, nor the source of his supernatural power. Lohengrin appears with the King, and reduces Ortrud to silence with a few sharp and contemptuous words. But now Frederick reveals himself, and directly challenges Lohengrin. If he is truly sent by God let him reveal his name! Lohengrin scornfully refuses—his worth is well known, for he has proved it by his deeds. The people assure him of their confidence, but in the tumult Frederick and Ortrud have found their way to Elsa's side and are whispering their slanders in her ears, and again Lohengrin is forced to rebuke them before he turns with his bride and enters the Cathedral.

Act III opens with an orchestral Introduction which is one of the finest things in the work as well as one of the most popular. After this " superb, full-blooded epithalamium " (to quote Mr Ernest Newman) the curtain rises on the bridal chamber. Lohengrin is led in by the men at one door, Elsa by the women at the other, to the strains of the Bridal March. It is difficult to praise this number, however one may wish to do so. One can sympathize with Wagner's desire for simplicity here, but for once his instinct is at fault, and he has only succeeded in being banal. The poverty of the piece is the more apparent owing to its being placed between the magnificent introduction just referred to and a love-scene which, in spite of certain weaknesses, is a worthy predecessor to those in *Siegfried* and *Tristan*.

At first no shadow mars the rapture of the pair. It is only when Lohengrin caressingly murmurs Elsa's name that the first signs of the approaching tragedy are seen. Elsa complains that she is unable to utter her husband's name in reply, and in spite of all Lohengrin's attempts to calm her, or to change the subject, her agitation steadily increases ; Ortrud's poison has done its work. In vain he assures her that his secret is no shameful one—his race and station are among the noblest. This only adds to her alarm. If he has given up all this for her he may some day be tempted to return to it. In a hysterical vision she sees the swan approaching down the river, drawing the fatal boat. All remonstrance is useless, and in an access of terror she breaks her vow and utters the forbidden question : " Whence comest thou ? Where is thy home ? Tell me thy name ! "

Hardly are the irrevocable words spoken when Frederick rushes in with drawn sword, accompanied by his four associates. Elsa has just time to hand her husband his sword before they are upon him. With a single blow he strikes Frederick dead. The other four, seeing their leader fall, give up the fight and sink on their knees. He bids them take up the body and bear it to the King. Then summoning Elsa's ladies he instructs them to attend to their mistress, who has fainted. Let them prepare her also to appear before her sovereign.

The scene quickly changes to the banks of the Scheldt
as seen in Act I. In the early dawn the nobles and their
retinues are slowly gathering. The King himself arrives
and greets the assembled army. But he misses its leader:
Lohengrin is absent. At this moment the four conspirators enter with the shrouded body of Frederick. They
are followed almost immediately by Elsa, pale with fear,
and almost fainting. Finally a general stir heralds the
approach of Lohengrin. He comes forward, clad in full
armour, and in answer to the acclamations of King and
people replies shortly that he cannot lead them forth to
victory. Briefly he recounts the circumstances of Frederick's death, and receives their assurance that he was
justified in slaying him. Then sorrowfully he reveals
how Elsa, fallen a victim to the plots of Ortrud, has
broken her vow and demanded to know his name and
origin. With that demand he must now comply. To
the strains of solemn music, mostly based on the Grail-
motive, he tells of the Castle of Montsalvat and the wondrous cup it holds ; of the Knights of the Grail, who,
invincible under its protection, go forth to distant lands
to fight for God and the right, and of how their might
depends upon their keeping secret their name and origin—
once that is known, straightway they must return home.
Such a knight is he. It was the Grail that sent him, and,
obedient to its laws, he must now go back to Montsalvat.
" My father Parsifal reigns there in glory ; his knight am
I, and Lohengrin my name ! "

This narrative, with its splendid music, is as familiar on
the concert platform as on the stage. His story told,
Lohengrin returns to Elsa and gently reproaches her for
her lack of faith. She begs him to remain and forgive
her, for without him life to her will be impossible. The
King and the people second her petition : let Lohengrin

stay and lead them forth to battle. But the knight is adamant—he must not heed their prayers.

The swan is seen approaching. He greets it sorrowfully, and lingers to take yet one more farewell of Elsa. Could she but have remained one year faithful to her oath, then by the power of the Grail he could have restored to her her brother now held in enchantment.

He is going sadly to the bank when suddenly Ortrud appears, with an air of triumph. Yes, Lohengrin must go indeed, but let the foolish Elsa learn who it is that in the form of a swan is dragging him away. It is her brother Gottfried, turned into this shape by Ortrud's own enchantments! But the departing knight has heard. He falls on his knees in prayer, and the dove of the Grail hovers over him. The swan sinks, and in its place there rises a beautiful youth, who comes gravely forward and makes obeisance to the King. It is Gottfried of Brabant, and he hastens to his sister's side. Ortrud falls with a shriek, while Elsa, momentarily forgetful of her own trouble, welcomes her long-lost brother. Suddenly she remembers Lohengrin, and turns to the bank; but he is already far away upstream, standing in his boat that is now drawn by the holy dove. With a stricken cry, " My husband ! " she falls lifeless in her brother's arms.

The Prelude to *Lohengrin* is Wagner at his best. It is constructed on a single theme, that of the Grail. This is first heard *pianissimo* on the violins alone, in their highest register, the effect being ethereal in the extreme. Slowly as it draws nearer the vision gains clearness and solidity; the violins are joined first by the wood-wind, and next by the horns, 'cellos, and basses; lastly the brass takes up the theme *fortissimo*—the radiance is overwhelming. But immediately it begins to fade, the instruments are gradually withdrawn, and the piece ends in the remote atmosphere of the commencement. It is a beautiful epitome of the whole opera.

The music of *Lohengrin* as a whole shows us Wagner in a state of transition. He seldom achieves the richness and sustained inspiration of the works of his full maturity, although at times he comes very near to doing so (notably in the Prelude, the scene between Ortrud and Frederick in Act II, the Introduction to Act III, and the love-scene that follows). Nor has he yet completely succeeded in freeing himself from the conventionalities of the type of opera which it was his ambition to supplant (the very use of the words ' Romantic Opera ' in the title, in place of the later 'Music-drama,' is significant in this connexion). The bad old tradition is reflected in the amount of chorus work, which is out of all proportion to the dramatic importance of the chorus, and is a serious blemish, especially as the music for these concerted pieces is sometimes (though not always) of an almost perfunctory kind. The *finale* to Act I is a case in point. The whole cast, principals and chorus, join in an elaborate and lengthy *ensemble*, although no one has anything of real importance to say, either dramatically or musically, and the singers are soon reduced to the old and wretched device of repeating their words over and over again in order to keep going at all. We notice, too, here and in other places, a certain rhythmic squareness, a clumsy rigidity of phrase, which seriously interferes with the flow of the music. This weakness is, however, far less obvious in *Lohengrin* than in any of Wagner's previous works, and there are long stretches that are completely free from it. But perhaps the most remarkable thing about the opera is the treatment of the orchestra. Here a tremendous advance has been made. The old dummy accompaniment has been finally exorcised, and in its place we see already the beginnings of that wonderful wordless commentary that delights us in *Tristan* and *The Ring*. Occasionally the instruments fade into the background for a moment, becoming a mere support for the voices, but far more often they are playing independent and interesting parts of their own. The *leit-motifs*, too, are more numerous and more characteristic than in any previous work; there is one for the Grail, one for Lohengrin, one for the question Elsa must not ask, and several more besides. The composer has not yet developed them into the marvellous system of his later years, but the elements of that system have at any rate been isolated. *Lohengrin*, in fact, contains practically all the constituents of Wagner's mature style; the parts have been assembled and the first tentative model of the future ' Music-drama ' has been constructed. But the machine does not yet run quite smoothly; certain improvements of detail are necessary, and the general standard of the workmanship must be of a still higher order before complete success can be achieved. Wagner realized this, and for the next few years he wrote no music of importance, devoting himself to literary work, while his great conception was slowly ripening in his mind. When, in 1852, he set to work on *The Rhinegold*, the rich results of the long period of gestation were immediately apparent, and with the completion of that work in 1854 the creation of the new art-form was definitely accomplished.

TRISTAN UND ISOLDE

Words and Music by WAGNER.
Munich, 1865 ; *London,* 1882 ; *New York,* 1886.

THE tale of the unhappy loves of Tristan and Isolde is one of the great stories of the world. Whence it came it is hard to say, but it was a well-known and popular subject among the singers and poets of the Middle Ages. Sir Thomas Malory devotes to it a large part of his *Morte d'Arthur*, and in modern times it has been treated in verse by Matthew Arnold, Tennyson, and Swinburne. Debussy is said to have used it as the basis of an opera (hitherto unpublished) that he left incomplete at his death, and as recently as 1924 it reappeared again as *The Queen of Cornwall*, a play written by our veteran author Thomas Hardy, and set to music by Rutland Boughton.

Wagner's version differs from all these in being much simpler. The original legend covers a considerable period of time and includes a large number of characters, and modern writers, while exercising their right of selection, have used the pruning-knife with moderation. Not so Wagner. He had been at work for some years on *The Ring*, weaving and reweaving those intricate threads, and now he was tired of complication. He was still an exile, too, and there seemed little chance of persuading anyone to produce his Tetralogy, even if he succeeded in finishing it. The longing to cut himself free, to let the keen, fresh wind of a single strong emotion blow through him and kindle the spark of his genius to a flame again, grew ever stronger. Already he had cast his eyes on the story of

Tristan and Isolde and seen in it the one strong motive that he was looking for. But something was still needed to drive him to the decisive step, and this was eventually provided by a curious incident. It was in the summer of 1857 that he received a visit one morning at his house at Zurich from a stranger who turned out to be an emissary from the Emperor of Brazil. The Emperor desired him to write an opera for the theatre at Rio, and offered him his own terms. Wagner was surprised, no doubt, but he accepted the commission, laid aside the unfinished score of *Siegfried* and set to work. By the time the new opera was ready in 1859 the Brazilian proposal had evaporated into thin air, but it may be doubted whether the composer wasted much time in vain lamentations. He had written *Tristan and Isolde* more to satisfy an inner need of his being than for any other reason. Performance might be delayed, but the score was there, and he knew it was his masterpiece.

Just as there are people who can be loved or hated but never ignored, so there are works of art that it is impossible to pass by with a polite indifference. *Tristan and Isolde* is one of these. It owes its magnetic power to a happy combination of qualities; not only is Wagner's inspiration more sustained here than in any other of his works, not only is his mastery of his medium complete and absolute, but there flows through these pages a singleness of purpose, an intense concentration of thought on a single idea, that are surely unique in operatic music. The composer has but one theme here, the passionate love that sweeps his two principal characters to ruin and death. Before the surge of this immense force everything else has to give way. The story has been lopped of everything but its bare essentials by a ruthless hand whose one object was to make of it a fit channel for the conveyance of this fiery flood. And magnificently he has succeeded. There is no break in *Tristan*, no digression. From the first note to the moment when the curtain falls at the end of the Third Act it is all of a piece. In the whole of nature there is nothing with which to compare it, save the sea; there, and there only, as one watches the waves ceaselessly breaking on a rock-bound coast, does one find the same restlessness, the same infinite variety, and the same inflexible purpose.

With the very beginning of the Prelude Wagner goes straight to the heart of his subject. Out of the silence of the darkened theatre there float the yearning notes of the 'cellos; above them a bitter-sweet discord on the wood-wind dissolves into a sigh. It is the very voice of desire made audible, and it gathers strength as the music proceeds, till at length a climax is reached in which the pent-up forces seem to exhaust themselves. But as the storm of passion dies away the same troubled harmonies emerge once again and persist till the rising of the curtain.

They are a fit emblem of the emotions raging in Isolde's bosom. There she lies upon a couch, attended by her lady, Brangäne, who vainly endeavours to calm the storm of anger and resentment by which her mistress is over-whelmed. The scene is on the deck of a ship—the ship that is bearing the Irish Princess to King Mark of Cornwall as his promised bride—but the two women are alone in " a tent-like apartment " that has been erected to shield them from the eyes of the crew. We hear the song of a sailor from the mast above. Isolde imagines that it contains a slighting reference to herself and breaks out into a fit of rage which Brangäne is powerless to control. But her outburst soon exhausts her, she cries for air, and, the curtain being flung back, Tristan and his friend and follower, Kurwenal, stand revealed among the sailors.

Isolde regards Tristan gloomily, while the music harping on the love-*motif* betrays the inward trend of her thoughts. Presently she speaks : why does he not approach her ? Ah, well she knows the reason ! Loving her as he does, he dares not face her now that he is bearing her away to a loveless marriage. But as his future Queen she can command him, and she sends Brangäne to bid him present himself before her.

Tristan's evasive answers compel the girl to lay emphasis on the strict imperative which the message contains. This rouses the faithful Kurwenal, and in rough words he tells her that his master owes obedience to no Irish Princess.

Brangäne can only return to her mistress, close the curtains, and report the failure of her mission. Isolde's stroke has failed ; it has only served to make clear the ignominy of her position. Now she will tell Brangäne how it has all come about.

Not so long ago Morold, Ireland's bravest knight and Isolde's betrothed, was sent to Cornwall to collect the tribute which Mark had failed to pay. He was slain in battle by Tristan and his head sent insolently back in place of the tax he had come for. But Tristan did not emerge scathless from the encounter. Sorely stricken he sought the aid of Isolde, whose skill in the art of healing was well known, concealing his identity under the name of ' Tantris.' She soon saw through his disguise, and her first impulse was to slay him and avenge Morold. But, touched by his helplessness, and also (though she does not admit it) smitten with love, she spared him, healed his wounds, and allowed him to return home. This is how he repays her ! This is his knightly honour ! He reappears in Ireland as envoy of a victorious Cornwall to claim her as bride for the elderly King Mark ! And

Ireland, helpless before Tristan's might, must needs submit. Why did she hesitate when his life lay in her hands? It is her own disgrace that her weakness has compassed !

Again Brangäne endeavours to soothe her. Cornwall, after all, is a goodly kingdom—and should King Mark prove cold, there is a spell that will bind him to her. Isolde, roused by this reference to her mother's magic arts, bids Brangäne bring her a certain casket that contains various potions. Yes, this holds the solution to her difficulties ! But it is not the love-draught she selects. Vengeance is what she desires, vengeance for Morold, vengeance for her own injuries—the poison-draught alone will serve her need !

Cries from the sailors indicate that their destination is near, and Kurwenal appears to bid Isolde prepare for the landing. She sends him back with a fresh message for Tristan : she will not prepare for the landing nor let him lead her to King Mark unless he now presents himself and craves her forgiveness for the slight she feels he has put upon her. Alone again with Brangäne, she bids the reluctant girl prepare the fatal potion. Her instructions are scarcely given when Kurwenal returns and announces, " Sir Tristan ! "

Tristan enters, to music whose repressed, concentrated force is eloquently expressive of the intense self-control that he is exerting. Isolde tells him why she has sent for him. Blood lies between them—the blood of Morold. To her falls the task of vengeance. The knight in answer draws his sword, and, holding it by the blade, quietly offers it to her. Let her spirit not fail her a second time. But this is not what she wants. She tells him to sheathe his weapon. She may not slay King Mark's most valiant servant. Let them drink atonement. He has guessed what lies behind this proposal, but he accepts death as the only way out of the intolerable situation. Seizing the cup which Brangäne brings forward he drinks deep. Isolde does likewise.

But Brangäne, shrinking from her mistress's awful command, has disobeyed. It is not the poison-draught that she has prepared, but the love-potion! Tristan and Isolde stand silent, awaiting death.

But soon the spell begins to work. Reluctantly, but irresistibly, they are drawn toward one another; a moment later they are in each other's arms. Oblivious to the shouts of the sailors, who have cast anchor and are now momentarily expecting the arrival of the King, they join in a song of rapture. Brangäne puts Isolde's cloak around her mistress as she falls on Tristan's breast. Kurwenal enters and goes to Tristan. The curtain falls with the lovers still lost in each other and the trumpets blaring forth their welcome to Mark.

Act II. The bulk of the Second Act consists of the glorious duet which forms the glowing centre-piece of the whole work. This defies any attempt at description in cold prose, but the events which surround it must be briefly narrated. An impassioned Prelude, in which the strains of the love-*motif* are blended with others depicting the calm beauty of the summer night, prepares us for the scene that follows. The stage represents the garden of the royal castle; on the left one sees the exterior of Isolde's chamber, over the door of which a blazing torch is fixed, for it is night. The King has arranged a hunting party, moved thereto by the knight Melot, and to the sound of horns the hunters canter by. Brangäne at the door watches them pass. Soon she is joined by Isolde, and together they listen to the notes of the receding horns, which are gradually swallowed up in the murmurs of the fragrant night.

Isolde, who has seized the opportunity of Mark's absence to arrange a meeting with Tristan, exhibits signs of the utmost impatience; she longs to summon her lover, and it is with the greatest difficulty that Brangäne restrains her till the hunters have got well away into the forest. The girl is uneasy : let Isolde beware of Melot ! This midnight hunt may be a device of his to entrap Tristan and the Queen.

But Isolde derides her suspicions, proclaims her complete confidence, and after a rapturous pæan in praise of Love, seizes the torch from the door and hurls it to the ground, where it is extinguished.

This is the signal for Tristan. In terrible excitement she awaits him. When he does not immediately appear she takes her scarf in her hand and waves it with ever-increasing urging. At length she catches sight of him and then, as he enters, rushes toward him and falls into his arms. After the frantic rapture of their first embrace the turmoil in the orchestra subsides and there follows that wonderful outpouring of lyric ecstasy, unique and supreme even among Wagner's works—the love-duet. Throughout its multitude of varying moods there runs the crimson thread of passion, unifying and colouring everything, while the orchestra, full-throated, untiring, exultant, envelops all in such a flood of inspired melody as the world has not heard the like of before or since. From time to time the voice of Brangäne is heard from the tower above, whither she has gone to watch, warning them that the night is swiftly passing and dawn draws near. But this does not interrupt the flow of the music. At length, in an elation that grows ever greater, they rise from the flowery bank on which they have sunk, and now, as the crisis approaches, their exaltation reaches a pitch at which the world seems to fall away, and they are left alone in a brimming, pulsating universe of pure emotion.

It is here, at the very climax of their ecstasy, that disaster overtakes them, sudden and overwhelming. Brangäne shrieks, Kurwenal rushes in with drawn sword crying, " Save yourself, Tristan ! " and in a moment the stage is full of armed men. The hunt has returned! In the grey light of dawn Melot, delighted with the success of his plot, turns to Mark for thanks.

But Mark is overcome with grief. It is not so much the faithlessness of his Queen that wounds him as the thought that it is Tristan, the friend whom he has regarded as the very soul of honour, who has betrayed him. With sad dignity he reproaches him. How has it happened ? What fearful spell is at work ? Tristan, whose demeanour has expressed increasing shame, raises sympathetic eyes to his King. But he may not answer his question. His resolve taken, he turns to Isolde. To a wonderful echo of the love-music he asks her, dare she accompany him to the dim region of night whither he is going, where no cold dawn breaks the everlasting gloom. In perfect trust she signifies her readiness to follow him whither he will. Suddenly he addresses Melot and taunts him with his treachery. Swords are quickly drawn and Tristan rushes at his enemy. But as he gets within reach he deliberately lowers his guard, allowing Melot's blade to pierce his breast, and falls back into the arms of Kurwenal.

Act III takes us to Careol on the coast of Brittany. Tristan lies sorely wounded and unconscious in the garden of his ancestral castle, watched over by the devoted Kurwenal. Everything around breathes an atmosphere of decay, for the place has been left uncared for during its master's long absence in Cornwall, and is now falling into ruin. The beautiful and pathetic Prelude contains a new version of the love-*motif*, gloomy and sad, expressive of the fate that has overtaken Tristan. In the distance are heard the notes of the shepherd's pipe playing a wild and haunting *ranz des vaches*. The player appears and asks Kurwenal for news of his master. It is little enough that he can tell him—Tristan is still unconscious. But no sooner has the shepherd departed than the sick man stirs and opens his eyes—he asks where he is and how he came there. Kurwenal tells him : he is in Careol, whither the speaker himself has brought him. And now a messenger has gone to Cornwall—soon he will return, and with him Isolde. She it was who cured the wound that Morold inflicted ; her skill will suffice this time also. At the mention of Isolde, Tristan rouses himself from his lethargy. The sad notes of the shepherd's pipe check for a moment his growing excitement, but soon it rises again, till at last the memory of the fatal draught causes him to break out into terrible cursings, at the end of which he falls back, unconscious once more.

For a moment Kurwenal fears he is dead. But his heart still beats—he revives in a calmer mood ; a soothing vision of Isolde floats before his fevered imagination. Then, his agitation returning, he seems to see the ship approaching with his love on board. Kurwenal is holding him down by force when again the pipe is heard. But this time it is a new and joyous strain that we hear—the ship has been sighted ! Still half delirious, Tristan cries out with growing vehemence. Kurwenal is sent off to help Isolde ashore, and once more the music surges toward a climax. It is reached as Isolde hastens breathlessly in. Tristan, who, risen from his couch, has been staggering wildly about the stage, falls into her arms and sinks slowly to the ground. Opening his dying eyes, still filled with

unquestionable longing, he murmurs the one word
" Isolde ! " and expires. Despairingly she endeavours to
revive him, but in vain, and at length, realizing that he
has passed beyond the reach alike of her skill and of her
love, she falls senseless on his body.

At this juncture the shepherd arrives in a state of great
alarm. He tells Kurwenal (who has entered during the
scene just described) that another ship is fast approaching.
Kurwenal casts a look seaward, and, uttering a fearful
oath, summons all to help him defend the castle. It is
Mark and Melot who are upon them. A moment later
Brangäne's voice is heard, and Melot appears in the gate-
way—with a shout of rage Kurwenal hurls himself upon
him and strikes him down. But Mark and his men are
close behind, and Kurwenal, fighting furiously to the last,
is overborne. Mortally wounded, he staggers back and
falls. He has just strength enough to crawl to Tristan's
body and kiss his dead hand before his spirit follows that
of his beloved master.

Mark gazes around him. He has heard the whole story
now, and, rejoicing to know that Tristan was not deliberately guilty, but rather the victim of forces outside his
control, he has come with forgiveness in his heart, inspired
by a noble wish to unite the lovers at last. But he has
come too late. Tristan is dead.

And now Isolde, who has remained unconscious of
everything that has been going on around her, raises her
head and looks at her lover. To her clouded eyes he
seems to live again, and on a final flood of passionate
adoration and surrender her soul, too, floats out to whatever lies beyond. It is the matchless *Liebestod*, crowning
this drama of love with the sublime majesty of death.

Wagner was conscious that in *Tristan and Isolde* he
had risen to heights which it was unlikely any man

could reach twice in a lifetime. It was as magnificent an embodiment of his ideal as he was likely to achieve, and by it he took his stand. If judgment is to be passed on him, this is the work that must represent his case. There can be little hesitation about the verdict. Even the critics are almost unanimous. Weaknesses indeed they have claimed to discover in this as in all other products of human endeavour, and these we can leave them to discuss. But for us and for them the opera remains the supreme expression of a mind that saw more clearly and felt more deeply than it is given to other men to see and feel. Had Wagner written nothing else than this it would be sufficient to ensure his immortality. For Beauty does not grow old, and as long as music has power to move the hearts of men so long will *Tristan and Isolde* survive to bear witness to the mighty genius of its creator.

DIE MEISTERSINGER VON NÜRNBERG

Words and Music by WAGNER.
Munich, 1868 ; *London,* 1882 ; *New York,* 1885.

THE genial character of *The Mastersingers* gives it a unique position among Wagner's works. Putting aside his philosophic symbolism and all his mythological paraphernalia, he is content to wander happily about the streets of 16th-century Nuremberg, enjoying the freshness of the air and taking life as he finds it. No doubt Mr Ernest Newman is right in attributing this change of attitude to a natural reaction from the somewhat hectic passion of *Tristan,* but a further explanation may be found in the composer's altered circumstances. It was while he was at work upon *The Mastersingers* that the ban of exile, which had so long embittered his life, was raised, and by the time the opera was finished in 1867 he was already basking in the favour of his new and generous patron, the King of Bavaria.

Happiness is notoriously popular, and it is little wonder this sunny masterpiece secured for itself a speedy production and an enduring reputation. A masterpiece it certainly is, a gem of such pure water and dazzling lustre that even in the Wagnerian treasure-house there is none to match it, save *Tristan* alone. It is needless to enter into a sterile discussion of the relative merits of these two works—of either of them we may say with Hans Sachs,

> Yet what could gauge its greatness ?
> A measure no mortal hath seen.

The very completeness of both achievements renders comparison impossible.

But alike though they are in sureness of execution and imaginative splendour, they are poles apart in almost every other respect. We feel the difference with the very first phrase of the Prelude to *The Mastersingers*, which creates an atmosphere whose grateful freshness never comes to revive the passion-laden hearts of the immortal lovers. It is an entirely new country that we are exploring now, and by the time the curtain rises on the Church of St Catherine in Nuremberg we have already breathed a plentiful supply of this exhilarating air into our lungs, and are ready and eager for the adventure.

Immediately in front of us we see the open space of the choir of the church, while on the left is the end of the nave with the last few rows of seats. In one of these (for a service is in progress) sits Eva, the daughter of Pogner the goldsmith, with her maid Magdalene, while leaning against a pillar at some distance away is Walther von Stolzing, a young knight, whose ardent glances quickly betray the secret of his heart. The congregation are singing a Chorale to the accompaniment of the organ, while the knight's perturbation is admirably conveyed by the orchestra, which fills the long pauses between the lines of the hymn with eager phrases, including some fragmentary hints of the immortal Prize Song. The ceremony ended, the congregation begins to disperse. Walther succeeds in intercepting Eva, an excuse is found for getting rid of Magdalene for a moment, and during her absence the knight asks his question : Is Eva betrothed ? But Magdalene has already returned and it is she that makes answer, Eva interrupting her at intervals :

> MAG. The answer you would have, Sir Knight,
> No single word can give aright.

> For though betrothed is Eva held——
> EVA. No man hath yet the bridegroom beheld !
> MAG. None knows in truth the bridegroom's name,
> Until to-morrow shall sound his fame,
> When a Mastersinger the prize hath won——
> EVA. And him the bride herself will crown !

Walther is a stranger to Nuremberg, and this reply naturally leaves him more bewildered than ever. But now there enters David, a young apprentice in love with Magdalene, and to him is entrusted the task of enlightening the knight. Magdalene hurries Eva away, and the stage is filled by a crowd of apprentices who have come to prepare for the meeting of the Mastersingers. David, too, settles down to his business of explaining to Walther what a Mastersinger is and how the coveted distinction may be gained. Music in Nuremberg has become encrusted with a mass of rules, many of them absurdly pedantic, a knowledge of which is indispensable to anyone aspiring to the title of Mastersinger. As Walther knows nothing of all this, his informant goes into voluble detail, and a most entertaining dialogue ensues. David himself is apprenticed to Hans Sachs, the shoemaker, who teaches him cobbling and music at the same time, and his description of the technique of the Mastersinger's art is not made simpler by his frequent digressions on the subject of shoemaking. Long before he has finished our minds are in a whirl, and we heartily sympathize with Walther's despair at ever grasping the endless list of rules and formulas. There comes a time, however, when even David's eloquence is exhausted, and with a polite expression of goodwill he turns to help his fellows at their work.

It is midsummer eve and the Mastersingers are meeting in the church to make arrangements for the morrow's festival and to decide who shall be qualified to compete for the singer's prize. The nave of the church is cur-

tained off, benches are placed in position for the Mastersingers, a raised chair for the singer, and the ' Marker's '
cabinet is erected in the centre of the floor.   This last is
a curious structure, in which the Marker (or Judge) is to
sit hidden from all eyes while the examination is in progress.

Meanwhile two Mastersingers have come in—Pogner,
Eva's father, and Beckmesser, the elderly town clerk.
Beckmesser is a bachelor, and we soon gather that he has
pretensions to Eva's hand.   But his conversation with
Pogner is interrupted by Walther, who greets the goldsmith as an old friend, and announces that he has come to
compete for the prize.   Pogner is surprised and delighted,
and undertakes to introduce him to the other Mastersingers, who now begin to arrive.   Soon the muster is
complete; the Mastersinger Kothner calls the roll, and
the meeting proceeds to business.   Pogner begs leave to
make an important announcement, and, rising to his feet,
explains his project for the festival.   Being a rich man,
and filled with a desire to honour the art he loves and to
rebut the charge of avarice that has been levelled against
the burghers of the town, he has decided to offer as a
prize for the contest of song his daughter Eva in marriage,
together with the inheritance of all his possessions.   The
Masters receive his words with acclamation, but his
qualification that the successful candidate must also win
the maiden's favour gives rise to a discussion, Beckmesser
maintaining that the prize should depend on something
less fickle than a girl's fancy.   However, this objection is
overruled, as also is Hans Sachs' plea that the people
and not the Masters should be the judges of the contest,
and eventually Pogner's terms are agreed to.

The goldsmith now formally introduces Walther as an
aspirant for admission to the Guild, and in spite of the
protests of Beckmesser, who scents a dangerous rival, his

birth and standing are approved and he is allowed to enter for the preliminary test. Questions as to his teacher and the school at which he has studied elicit from him a lovely song of three stanzas, *Am stillen Herd*, in which he tells us that his teacher was Walther von der Vogelweide (a historical personage, some of whose poetic work still survives) and his school the school of nature. This strikes the Masters as very unorthodox, but they decide to allow him to sing his song. Beckmesser takes his place in the Marker's cabinet, the rules to be observed are read out, and the knight unwillingly seats himself in the singer's chair. The result, of course, is a foregone conclusion. The song, *Fanget an !* in praise of Love and Spring, is as fine an example as can be found of Wagner's lyrical gift, but it pays little regard to the laws of the Mastersingers, and gives Beckmesser all the opportunities he desires to vent his spite. Soon he is heard angrily scratching on the Marker's slate and doubtless his temper is not improved by the sly hit at the beginning of the second verse :

> Deep hid in thorny cover,
>   Consumed by wrath and hate,
> When now his reign is over,
>   Old Winter lies in wait.

He emerges from the cabinet, holds up the slate, all covered with chalk marks, and protests that the farce has gone far enough. The other Masters, who have been completely bewildered by the novel music, are of the same opinion. Sachs alone supports the singer and demands that he be heard to the end, but Beckmesser makes an angry retort and the proceedings speedily develop into an unseemly wrangle. Acting on a hint from Sachs (" Sing but to make the Marker sore ") Walther finishes his song, but his voice is scarcely heard in the rising clamour. At last the apprentices start dancing and singing round the Marker's cabinet and the meeting breaks up in confusion. Sachs alone remains awhile, lost in thought. Then he, too, leaves the stage.

Act II. It is evening in Nuremberg, and the apprentices are heard singing as they put up the shutters of their masters' houses. David is performing this duty for Sachs' home, a modest dwelling on the left of the stage with an elder-tree in front of it. On the right is Pogner's more pretentious abode, shaded by a lime-tree. Between the two a narrow street runs toward the back, and we have to imagine another one running at right angles to it across the proscenium. From Pogner's house there emerges Magdalene. She questions David eagerly about the morning's doings, only to retire disconsolately on hearing of Walther's failure. A moment later Sachs arrives, and he and David go into the house together, leaving the stage clear for Pogner and Eva, who come down the street on their return from an evening stroll. A short dialogue reveals that Pogner is somewhat doubtful of the wisdom of his project for the festival, but the goldsmith soon disappears through his own door, leaving Eva to speak for a moment with Magdalene. As soon as the girl hears the news of Walther she makes up her mind to seek further information from Sachs ; but for the moment she goes indoors with her maid. Meanwhile Sachs has reappeared at his own door; David brings him his stool, table, and tools, that he may taste the evening air as he works, and is dismissed to bed.

Sachs arranges his materials, but he cannot work. Always there is running through his mind a lovely phrase from the song Walther sang in the morning, and leaning back he breaks into his famous monologue, *Wie duftet doch der Flieder*.

Secretly and gravely in the gathering darkness he gives utterance to his longing for beauty, his sense of the inadequacy of his own artistic efforts, and his realization of the true genius with which capricious Fortune has endowed the careless, untutored knight. No sooner has he finished than Eva appears once more. She desires to learn the details of Walther's failure, but the wise shoemaker is not easily drawn, and she has to employ all her arts of seduction to coax the story out of him. The pathos of the scene lies in the fact that Sachs, who is a widower, is himself in love with Eva. He knows that she is not for him, and guessing how things stand between her and Walther he has schooled himself to an attitude of generous renunciation. But though his will is firm it cannot prevent his heart being wrung during this intimate conversation. Wagner has risen to the occasion, and his music here strikes a chord of delicate tenderness that we hardly find elsewhere in his work. But, moved though he is, Sachs does not lose his head. He allows himself to be cajoled into giving an account of the morning's doings, but cunningly pretends a hostility to the knight that he is far from feeling, and thus betrays Eva into a fit of anger that confirms his suspicions as to the true state of her affections. Her mission accomplished, the girl crosses the street once more, but is delayed at her own door by Magdalene, who informs her that Beckmesser is coming shortly to serenade her. Eva suggests that Magdalene should take her place, but before they have time to develop a plan footsteps are heard and Walther himself comes up the alley. Eva is soon in his arms, and in a brief but exquisite duet they declare their love. She agrees to fly with him at once, and is just returning to the house for suitable clothing when again there is an interruption. This time it is the Night Watchman on his round, and the girl has barely time to draw her lover behind the lime-tree and to disappear herself through Pogner's open door before he arrives, blows a blast on his absurd, discordant cow-horn, and goes on his way.

During all this Sachs had been sitting at his doorway, concealed from the lovers by the door itself. He has heard everything, and though he wishes them well he heartily disapproves of the proposed elopement, and sets himself to prevent it. Taking his lamp into the house he opens a shutter on the ground floor and brightly illuminates the alley in the middle of the stage just as Eva, who has returned in Magdalene's dress, is about to pass down it with Walther. Fearful of being observed the two draw back, and while they are hesitating fate again intervenes in the person of Beckmesser, who approaches, playing on his lute, by the very route they wish to take. They have no choice but to conceal themselves once more behind the lime-tree, where they remain throughout the forthcoming scene.

Beckmesser reaches Pogner's house, and having placed himself before Eva's window is about to begin his serenade when Sachs, who is now back in his doorway once more, strikes a resounding blow with his hammer and starts bellowing a cobblers' song at the top of his voice, *Jerum!* *Jerum!* His theme is Adam and Eve being driven shoe-less from Eden, but the frequent recurrence of the name of Eva increases the anxiety of the lovers, while the whole song throws Beckmesser into a frenzy of rage. Knowing nothing of the evening's doings he supposes Eva to be at her window, and is desperately afraid of her mistaking Sachs' voice for his own. Deciding, however, that it is a case for diplomacy he comes up to the cobbler and bids him good-evening. Sachs pretends that he now observes his fellow-Master for the first time, tells him that he is working hard to have his (Beckmesser's) shoes ready for the festival, and goes on singing louder than ever. This is the moment that Magdalene chooses to appear at the window in her mistress's garments, and the sight of her causes the frantic Beckmesser to redouble his efforts to induce Sachs to stop. For some time he fails to produce the least impression, but at last he hits on an ingenious idea. He has composed his song for the festival, he says, and would be grateful for the cobbler's criticism. Sachs considers for a moment, and then declares that though he will readily hear the song, he must be allowed to cobble at the same time. This produces a deadlock, until Sachs makes the brilliant suggestion that Beckmesser should give him a lesson in the duties of a Marker : he will listen and mark the faults by a blow of his hammer. In despair the unhappy man agrees, but he has hardly got through a bar of his futile serenade before the sound of the hammer interrupts him. He tries to ignore it, but Sachs finds plenty to criticize, and soon he is brought to a standstill, and turns on the amateur Marker with a flood of angry recrimination. Still, remembering the figure at the window, he dare not waste time, and soon the serenade proceeds once more, to the irregular accompaniment of noisy hammer blows from Sachs and furious asides from the singer. The shoes are finished long before the song, and their maker lifts up his own voice in a pæan of triumph, while Beckmesser sings even louder to drown the din. At last the law-abiding Nurembergers can stand it no longer. One neighbour after another throws open his window and shouts to them to stop. David is awakened among the rest, looks out, and seeing his Magdalene being serenaded by Beckmesser rushes down into the street with a stick and administers a sound cudgelling.

By this time the neighbours also have reached the

scene and are soon joined by journeymen and apprentices
from all parts of the city who have been attracted by the
growing clamour.   Seeing David and Beckmesser at blows
the rest fall to, and within a few moments there is a street
fight in full swing.   Everyone is shouting at once, and
the volume of sound is increased by the women who by
now are watching at their windows.   The uproar is at
its height when suddenly several things happen simultaneously.   Walther comes forward from the lime-tree,
sword in hand and with Eva clinging to him, resolved
to cut his way through the crowd.   Sachs, seeing this,
makes a successful sally, catches Walther's arm, and
pushes Eva in at the door of Pogner's house, where her
father receives her under the impression that she is
Magdalene.   A well-aimed kick from Sachs deals effectively with David, and, still keeping a tight hold on Walther, the shoemaker follows his apprentice in at his door.
The few seconds that this manœuvre has occupied have
been well employed by the women in pouring quantities
of cold water from the windows on the heads of the
combatants below.   Just as the flood descends a very
loud blast on the cow-horn announces the imminent return
of the Night Watchman.   A sudden panic ensues, the
mob melts as quickly as it collected, doors and windows
are closed, and even the discomfited Beckmesser manages
to limp away.   The Watchman finds nothing but an
empty street with silent shuttered houses, whose pointed
roofs are just touched by the silvery light of the rising
moon.

   Act III.   The grave, expressive phrase which opens the
Introduction to the final Act makes it immediately clear
that the mood of uproarious merriment that culminated
in the street fight has given place to a more serene atmosphere.   It is the *leit-motif* associated with Hans Sachs,

and admirably suggests the poetic side of the Master's
nature. A sudden change to the major key brings in the
tune of the solemn chorale that we hear later in the Act,
while snatches of the Cobbling Song remind us of previous
events, though even this is now coloured by the prevailing
thoughtfulness.

The rise of the curtain discloses Sachs in his living-room,
seated by the window absorbed in a book. It is morning
—the morning of the festival—and David appearing from
the street with a basket full of flowers, ribbons, and dainties, is obviously intending to enjoy the general holiday.
His naïve apology for his escapade of the night before gets
no reply for some time, but when at last his master rouses
himself and speaks, his voice has an unwonted gentleness.
He bids David sing to him, and the lad stands up and
dutifully repeats his lesson. He sings of St John baptiz-
ing in Jordan, of the German woman who brought her
child to him to be christened by his name, and of how
that name was changed in Germany from Johannes to
Hans. A thought strikes him : " Hans ? Hans ? Why,
Master ! 'tis your name-day too ! " Eagerly he offers
the contents of his basket. Sachs is touched ; he refuses
the gift, which will be better appreciated by the giver,
but sends the boy off to get himself ready for the festival.
David joyfully departs, and Sachs loses himself once
more in his thoughts. " Mad ! mad ! everyone's mad ! "
he murmurs, and there follows another great soliloquy,
Wahn, Wahn !—a piece of writing so true, so tender, so
expressive of the warm heart and wise head that are
combined in the character of the shoemaker, that it easily
and naturally takes its place among the greatest things in
all opera. Musings on the spirit of mischief give way to
a lyrical outburst of pride in his native Nuremberg. Yet
even to this peaceful spot trouble has found its way :

reminiscences of the night's doings bring an episode that
has the delicacy of dew at sunrise, and then finally he
pulls himself together :

> But now has dawned Midsummer day !
> We'll see now how Hans Sachs intends
> Turning this madness to his ends,
> That good may come of it. . . .
> For work hath never virtue in it
> Unless someone that's mad begin it !

And now a door opens and Walther enters and greets
his host.   Their attitude makes it clear that the two have
reached a perfect understanding.   Presently the young
man's casual reference to a dream he has had " of beauty
rare," and his reluctance to speak of it lest it fade, brings
words full of wisdom from the shoemaker :

> My friend, just that is poet's work ;
> To find in dreams what meanings lurk. . . .
> Perchance your dream may show the way
> To win the Masters' prize to-day.

It is some time before this wise counsel prevails with
the young knight, still raw from his rejection by the
Guild on the previous day.   But Sachs is persistent and
gets his way at last.   The end of the discussion is worth
quoting :

> WALTHER. Through all the rules that you have taught
> Meseems the dream hath come to naught.
> SACHS.   The poet's art, then, try betimes ;
> Lost words are often found in rhymes.
> WALTHER. Then 'twere no dream, but poet's art.
> SACHS.   Good friends are they, ne'er far apart.
> WALTHER. But how by rules shall I begin ?
> SACHS.   First make your rules and keep them then.
> Think only on your vision's beauty,
> To guide you well shall be my duty.

He draws paper and ink toward him and prepares to
write what he hears, while Walther, convinced at last, pours

out the first lovely strain of the Prize Song, *Morgenlich leuchtend in rosigem Schein*. Prompted by his mentor, he matches it with a second, somewhat similar, and rounds off the whole with a rapturous ' after-song ' which wins generous approbation. Sachs elicits a second verse as well, but wisely refrains from pressing his demands for a third when the singer shows signs of restiveness. Master and pupil retire together to prepare for the festival, leaving the stage clear for the next comer. This is no other than Beckmesser, who hobbles in, still aching from the effects of David's stick, and finding the shop empty limps uneasily round, till suddenly his eyes fall on Sachs' copy of the Prize Song, which has been left on the table. He scans it hastily and then puts it in his pocket. So Sachs has been writing a trial song! He suspects a plot, and accuses the shoemaker, who now reappears from the inner room, of intending to enter for the contest of song and of having contrived the events of the previous night in order to discredit a dangerous rival. At first Sachs is puzzled by this outburst, but soon he notices the absence of the paper and puts two and two together. He meets Beckmesser's charge by a counter-accusation of theft, and then takes his breath away by offering him the song as a gift. Beckmesser well knows the value of Sachs' work, but at first he fears a trap. However, when the shoemaker promises to refrain from singing the song himself and to keep the secret of its authorship, suspicion and spite gradually give place to confidence and friendship in the town clerk's bosom, and eventually he departs jubilant, while Sachs looks after him with a thoughtful smile. He is not alarmed : he knows that Beckmesser's limitations will effectually prevent him from turning his good fortune to a profitable issue.

The sight of Eva diverts his mind into a new channel.

He knows what has brought her and is not deceived when she excuses her visit by complaining that her shoes do not fit. A charming episode follows : Sachs places her foot on a stool in order to discover just where the shoe pinches, and it is in this situation that they are found by Walther when he appears. Enraptured anew by Eva's beauty as she stands radiant in her festival finery he bursts spontaneously into the third verse of the Prize Song. Overcome by this and by the presence of her lover the girl falls weeping on Sachs' breast while Walther clasps him by the hand. It is more than he can bear, and turning moodily away he eases himself by singing a verse more of his Cobbling Song in a voice that is gruff with emotion. But Eva has at last seen into her old friend's heart, and tearing herself away from Walther she impulsively pours out her gratitude to the man to whom she owes her happiness. Yet, even as she speaks, her passion masters her again ; gratitude gives way to the demands of a stronger feeling, and soon she is singing the praises of Love in a splendid outburst of ecstasy. The music, too, touches an oddly familiar chord, until presently the words of Sachs show whither it is that our steps have wandered :

> My child,
> Of Tristan and Isolde a grievous tale I know ;
> Hans Sachs is wise and would not endure King Marke's woe.
> To find the man before too late
> I sought—else that had been my fate.

In these few words lies the motive that has guided the shoemaker's actions, and the full depths of his generous nature are revealed. But now come David from his room and Magdalene from the street, and he puts aside his troubles that nothing may mar the happiness of the others. Drawing all around him he proceeds to 'christen' the newly created Prize Song. The scene culminates in the celebrated quintet, *Selig wie die Sonne*, which crowns it with a garland of incomparable beauty.

The curtain descends for a while, and the orchestra conducts us to the scene of the festival, an open meadow on the banks of the Pegnitz, with a raised platform on one side for the Mastersingers. When the stage becomes visible many of the people have already arrived, and the crowd is continually increased by the constant stream of journeymen and apprentices who advance in processions, guild by guild. The appearance of a boat-load of girls is naturally the signal for a dance, a merry interlude that is soon, however, cut short by the herald announcing the approach of the Mastersingers. Their procession comes slowly forward with Pogner and Eva in the midst, and the members take their places on the platform.

The proceedings open with a solemn hymn, the words of which are by the historical Hans Sachs, on whom Wagner's character is based, while the tune is the one we have already heard at the beginning of the Act. Sachs rises to his feet, and after acknowledging the acclamations of the crowd in a voice that trembles with emotion proceeds to set out the conditions of the contest. Then with a private word of encouragement for Pogner and a more enigmatic utterance for Beckmesser, he calls for the trial to begin.

As it happens, it is Beckmesser who has to sing first. No sooner has he begun than it becomes evident that Sachs has not misjudged his man. Beckmesser has utterly failed to grasp the song he tries to render, his memory forsakes him, and he only brings forth a stream of unintelligible balderdash. His efforts are received with shouts of mockery, and in a fury he rushes to Sachs, accuses him publicly of having written the song to bring about his discomfiture, and disappears in the crowd. Sachs picks up the fatal paper that Beckmesser has thrown down, and proceeds to explain. The song is not by him ; such an achievement would be beyond him—as to its beauty, it must be properly sung before that can be appreciated. Beckmesser has proved his incompetence, and Sachs now summons anyone who may be able to stand forth and give the music the performance it deserves. Walther immediately steps forward amid the applause of the people, and a hush of excitement falls as he mounts the singers' platform. For the first few bars of the song several Mastersingers are busily engaged in scanning the paper which Sachs has passed to them, hoping to catch the singer tripping, but the spell of the melody quickly makes itself felt, and the 'score' is put aside. This is just as well, for the new version has several points of difference from the old, and though the changes are all improvements the detection of them might have given rise to difficulties. Long before the song is over it is plain that Sachs' stroke has succeeded, and at its conclusion the Mastersingers rise in a body and acknowledge the singer's right to the victor's wreath, which Eva shyly places on his brow. Once more the crowd hail Sachs as their chosen leader, while Pogner advances to invest Walther with the rank and insignia of a Mastersinger. But the knight petulantly refuses the honour, and it is left to Sachs to smooth away this last difficulty. He does so in his final oration, a musical masterpiece of amazing vigour and contrapuntal skill. The Prize Song and the theme of the Mastersingers are mingled in the music to symbolize the union of genius and tradition to which he urges that the efforts of all should be directed. We pass from climax to climax, the people join in to swell the chorus, and our last view of the stage shows us Hans Sachs receiving the homage of the folk he loves so well, their idol and their friend.

There is no doubt that *The Mastersingers* owes a great deal of its success to its plot, in which Wagner reveals a happy gift for comedy of which his other works give us no suspicion. The play is full of incident, and the action is so varied that it is safe to say that no other composer could have possibly welded the material into a satisfactory whole. Few people realize that the opera, if played without cuts, is considerably longer than *Tristan*. We become so absorbed in following the intricacies of the story presented to us in a series of ingenious and well-constructed situations that we lose count of the passage of time. Such a mass of detail would have ruined a more serious work, but here where the subject is comedy it is perfectly in place. Indeed, a more ideal libretto scarcely exists. The central idea of a contest of song offers unique opportunities to the composer, and the superb melodies and choruses that enchant our ears with each successive climax are not extraneous, but born out of the imperious demands of the drama itself.

And certainly Wagner has scattered his tunes with an ungrudging hand! Pogner's address and Walther's two songs in Act I; Sachs' monologue, his duet with Eva, and his Cobbling Song in Act II; and the Introduction, Sachs' second monologue, the Prize Song, the quintet, and numerous other things in Act III—all these selections enjoy a well-deserved popularity in the concert-hall, though lack of space renders it necessary to dismiss them here with a mere mention. Something, however, must be said of the Prelude. So compact and well-balanced is it that as a piece of orchestral music pure and simple it can stand beside the symphonies of Beethoven and Brahms, and yet at the same time it contains the very essence of the opera that is to follow. With the magnificent opening theme the sturdy Mastersingers rise up full

of life and character and march in procession to the tune
that is presently given out on the brass. The treatment
of this section, diatonic, and full of ingenious counter-
point, suggests the old 16th-century fraternity with its
traditional ideals, without a trace of any troublesome
archaisms. But now the harmony assumes a richer and
more subtle colouring, and a phrase or two taken from the
Prize Song form the basis of a movement that has for its
subject Walther and his love for Eva. Again we return
to the Mastersingers' theme, which now appears in a light
and impertinent version, as though to remind us of the
apprentices, the Mastersingers of the future. And then,
as the music rises toward its climax, the supreme touch is
added by the master-hand : the *motif* of the Mastersingers is played simultaneously with the Prize Song (in
anticipation of the conclusion of the opera). Here is the
lesson Wagner desired to teach. Tradition is good and
innovation is good, but it is in the blend of the two that
Art reaches its highest manifestations. That this was the
composer's own view is manifest from every page of the
score, even if he had not given it such convincing expression in the mouth of the greatest of his characters, Hans
Sachs. It is, of course, Hans who is the real hero of the
piece, beside whom Eva appears a rather colourless young
woman and Walther fades into little more than a lay
figure. About the shoemaker-poet himself, the man who
has looked life in the face and borne his burden uncom-
plainingly, there can be no two opinions. Lohengrin,
Wotan, Siegfried, Tristan, Parsifal—the mighty creations
of Wagner's genius—pass in stately review before the eyes
of our imagination ; but Hans Sachs dominates them all,
just as he dominates the Nurembergers of the opera, by
right of his mellow, gentle wisdom, and his triumphant
humanity.

DER RING DES NIBELUNGEN

Words and Music by WAGNER.

1. DAS RHEINGOLD.   3. SIEGFRIED.
2. DIE WALKÜRE.   4. GÖTTERDÄMMERUNG.

First complete production, Bayreuth, 1876; *London,* 1882;
New York, 1889.

(" *Das Rheingold* " *was produced at Munich in* 1869, *and*
" *Die Walküre* " *at Munich in* 1870.)

*T*HE RING OF THE NIBELUNG is not only
one of the greatest of all musical works, it is also
the longest, dwarfing by comparison any other
single conception that the genius of a musician has
ever sought to express with the aid of the art of sound.
It consists of three complete operas and a Prologue,
providing between them more than twelve hours' music,
and it includes, besides its own complicated plot, side-
lights and reflections on most of the things that occupied
Wagner's busy mind from the time when, in 1848, he
first occupied himself with the story of the hero Siegfried,
to that day in 1874 which saw the completion of *The
Dusk of the Gods*. To do full justice to such a monument
of industry (to call it by no higher name) would require
many volumes. Here it will be impossible even to allude
to many of the interesting questions that are involved. But
it would be unpardonable in a book of this kind to pass over
such a masterpiece in complete silence. The bare outline
of the story at least must be given; any who would probe
deeper must refer to other works on the subject.[1]

---

[1] The general reader cannot do better than consult Mr Ernest Newman's *Wagner* (" The Music of the Masters " series). If after reading
this he is still eager for information, he will find at the end of Mr Newman's book a bibliography that should satisfy all his requirements.

Those who have never considered the workings of a great creative mind, who picture Beethoven spending an afternoon in his study writing sonata after sonata, and who fondly imagine that a work like *The Ring* sprang complete in every detail from the mind of its maker, like Athene from the head of Zeus, would do well to pause a moment and examine the facts. It was in 1848, as already stated, that Wagner, still an official at the Dresden Court, first devoted his attention seriously to the Nibelung legends. He wrote the libretto of an opera entitled *Siegfried's Death*, and probably sketched a good deal of the music. Then followed the political troubles that led to his ignominious flight from Germany, and it was as an exile in Zurich that he took up the subject again three years later. Finding that the story of Siegfried's death required a vast amount of explanatory matter which it was difficult to incorporate in the drama, he solved the problem by writing the poem of " Young Siegfried." But still there was much that remained obscure, and the poems of " The Valkyrie " and " The Rhinegold " followed, in that order. Having thus written his tetralogy from the end backward he naturally found that " Young Siegfried " and " Siegfried's Death " required modification, and so they were recast and appeared eventually under the titles of *Siegfried* and *The Dusk of the Gods*. And now that the enormous libretto was completed he set to work upon the music, and by 1857 *The Rhinegold*, *The Valkyrie*, and the first half of *Siegfried* were finished. At this point, however, there came a break. Wagner was beginning to lose heart. He was still an exile from Germany, and the prospects of the ban upon him being raised appeared as remote as ever. *Tannhäuser* and *Lohengrin* were slow in winning their way to the hearts of the public, the chief obstacles to their success being the novelty of their style, the seriousness of their aim, and their great length. If this was true of these earlier works, what would be the fate of the immense tetralogy, even supposing the composer ever brought his labours to a successful issue ? The new work was far more novel, far more profound, than anything that had hitherto come from his pen, and he realized only too well how small were the chances that these ' silent scores ' would ever be brought to a hearing. Would he not do better to abandon the whole thing and take up some more practicable project ? The story of how these vague thoughts were crystallized by the coming of an envoy from the Emperor of Brazil is told in the chapter on *Tristan and Isolde.* The unfinished score of *The Ring* was laid aside, and it was not till 1869, more than ten years later, that he took it up again. The intervening period had been eventful in more ways than one ; musically it had seen the creation of *Tristan and Isolde* and *The Mastersingers,* in the practical affairs of life it had witnessed the composer's return to Germany and the wonderful piece of luck that had come to him in the whole-hearted support accorded him by Ludwig, King of Bavaria. There was no limit to the enthusiasm of this eccentric monarch, which included, among other things, the building of a theatre at Bayreuth specially to meet the requirements of *The Ring.* Now, at last, the path to a production seemed clear, and Wagner returned eagerly to his neglected score. *Siegfried* was finished in 1871, and in 1874 the completion of *The Dusk of the Gods* put the crown on the whole edifice. The foundation-stone of the Bayreuth theatre had been laid on the 22nd of May, 1872, and the building was, as it were, consecrated by the first performance of the entire *Ring* cycle, which took place under the baton of Richter on the 13th, 14th, 16th, and 17th of August, 1876.

It will be seen from this short sketch that the composition of *The Ring of the Nibelung* was spread over a period that extended to more than a third of its author's lifetime. When we consider that this was also the period of his greatest creative activity and that a large part of that activity was spent on this very work, we shall not be surprised to find it packed with ideas, allegories, and philosophic reflections to a degree unusual even with this most philosophic of composers. It is not within the design of this book to discuss these matters or to add yet another to the many attempts that have been made to harmonize the inconsistencies that appear from time to time. It will be sufficient to point out that such inconsistencies, blemishes though they are, are very natural. In the course of twenty-five years a man modifies his ideas upon most subjects. The mature Wagner who completed *The Dusk of the Gods* was a very different man from the wild revolutionary who had first conceived the outlines of " Siegfried's Death." To eliminate all the incompatibilities would have involved rewriting the work entirely, a task from which the composer very naturally shrank. A more serious defect is the result of the haphazard order in which the libretti were completed. Each opera, it must be remembered, was intended originally to explain itself without the aid of a predecessor, and we consequently find in *The Valkyrie, Siegfried*, and *The Dusk of the Gods* many long sections devoted to the recapitulation of previous happenings with which we are already familiar from the earlier operas. Now that we have the complete tetralogy before us these sections are often extremely tedious and, doubtless, a further revision of the work would have led to their curtailment or excision. Against these defects we must set the breadth and power of the general conception, the sureness and ease of the execution, and the astonishing sense of progression that is preserved throughout. Above all there is the marvellous music. These things must be put to the credit side of the account. But before attempting to strike a balance we will turn for a while to the plot.

THE RHINEGOLD

The Rhinegold, which Wagner desires us to regard as a Prologue to the other three dramas, opens with one of the most imaginative scenes in the whole realm of opera. The orchestral Prelude is constructed on the simplest possible lines, being founded entirely on a single chord. A deep note on the horn, followed by chords on other low-pitched instruments, creates an impression of pregnant darkness, out of which is born a theme full of beauty and romance. The ebb and flow of this, and the ever-increasing agitation in the accompaniment, culminate in the rise of the curtain, which shows us the three Rhine Maidens swimming in the dark waters, immediately above the bed of the Rhine. Their lovely song is interrupted by the appearance of Alberich, the Nibelung dwarf, who has climbed hither from his home in the bowels of the earth. The Rhine Maidens easily elude his clumsy attempts to catch them and are going on to fool him to the top of his bent when a ray of sunlight from above strikes through the water on to the summit of a rocky pinnacle where a dull gleam betrays the presence of the magic Rhinegold. The maidens, swimming joyously around, sing of its powers ; how, when fashioned into a ring, it will give to its owner the lordship of the world, but only he who forswears for ever the delights of love will hold the spell that will enable him to work the stubborn metal. Alberich has listened attentively, and now with hideous eagerness he scrambles up the pinnacle and seizes the gold. With a great oath he abjures love for ever, and disappears with his prize into the depths whence he came. The curtain descends on the horror-struck cries of the Rhine Maidens.

It rises again on " an open space on a mountain height." Wotan, the father of the gods, is sleeping, his wife Fricka by his side. The dawning day lights up the glittering towers of Valhalla, the great castle seen in the back-ground, which the giants have just completed for Wotan and the other gods. It soon transpires that the giants have not laboured without hope of reward : Freia, the goddess of youth and beauty, is the price that Wotan has agreed to pay. No sooner is he awake than Fricka reminds him of this rash promise. Wotan is relying on Loki, the god of fire and deceit, to extricate him from his difficulty, but Loki has not yet put in an appearance, and meanwhile Freia rushes on in full flight from the giants, Fasolt and Fafner, who arrive a moment later. Fasolt checks Wotan's attempts to evade the issue with the stern reminder that the god's power depends upon his keeping faith, and Freia's doom seems imminent, when at last Loki is seen approaching. Resourceful as ever, the fire-god tells the story of Alberich's rape of the gold, of the Ring that he has fashioned, and of the power of the Ring. The giants catch at the bait and offer to release Freia if Wotan can secure the prize and give it to them in exchange. Meanwhile she must remain with them as a hostage. Gloom and old age descend on the gods as the goddess of youth departs in the hands of the giants, and Wotan in desperation summons Loki to aid him in an attempt to steal the gold from Alberich.

This very ungodlike enterprise he successfully carries through in the grotesque scene that follows. Under the guidance of Loki he enters a cleft in the ground and begins his downward journey to Nibelheim. The orchestra gives a vivid picture of the progress of the celestial robbers till at last the clanging of innumerable anvils announces their arrival in the home of Alberich and the dwarfs.

Alberich has created sad confusion in Nibelheim through the power of the Ring, which he has used to enslave the dwarfs, compelling them to dig for him the precious metal and work it into ornaments. We see him first in converse with his brother Mime, the most cunning of the smiths. Mime has wrought for him a strangely fashioned helmet, the ' Tarnhelm,' that confers on its wearer many gifts, including invisibility, and the power to transform himself into any shape he likes. Alberich snatches it from him, and, disappearing suddenly by its help, gives him a sound whipping for his pains and goes off. Mime is still rubbing his back when the gods enter. Soon Alberich returns, driving before him his unwilling slaves, each of whom is loaded with some piece of gold or silver jewellery. They deposit their burdens in a heap, and then, obedient to the spell of the Ring, depart to fresh tasks under the supervision of Mime. Loki engages Alberich in conversation. The suspicions of the dwarf are allayed by the open admiration of his visitor, and presently he consents to satisfy Loki's curiosity about the powers of the Tarnhelm. He transforms himself first into a dragon, then into a toad. This is the moment Loki has been waiting for. A quick word to his companion and Wotan's foot is upon the crouching thing. Loki snatches the Tarnhelm from his head, and Alberich reappears in his own shape. Swiftly they bind him and carry him off by the way they came.

The final scene takes place in the upper regions once more. Alberich is compelled by his captors to give up his treasure. Summoned once more by the Ring, the Nibelungs appear from the cleft, make a pile of the hoard, and swiftly depart again. Loki throws the Tarnhelm on to the heap, and finally Wotan wrenches the Ring itself from the finger of his prisoner, in spite of the dwarf's anguished protests. Then, and only then, do they untie him. Alberich raises himself in impotent fury; he can still curse his oppressors :

Am I now free ? Really free ?
Then listen, friends, to my freedom's first salute !
As at first by curse 'twas reached, henceforth cursed be this Ring !
Gold which gave me measureless might, now may its magic deal each
    owner death !
No man shall e'er own it in mirth, and to gladden no life shall its lustre
    gleam !
May care consume each several possessor, and envy gnaw him who
    feareth it not !
All shall lust after its delights, but none shall employ them to profit him !
To its master giving no gain, aye, the murderer's brand it shall bring !
To death he is fated, fear on him shall feed :
Though long he live, shall he languish each day,
The treasure's lord and the treasure's slave !
Till within my hand I in triumph once more behold it !

So, stirred by the hardest need, the Nibelung blesses his Ring :
I give it thee, guard it with care !
But my curse canst thou not flee ! [1]

With this frightful invocation of that strange power behind the gods called by the Hindus ' Brahma,' and by the Greeks ' Nemesis,' he disappears into the cleft.

Wotan is only just in time. The gods have hardly reassembled when Fasolt and Fafner return for their wages, bearing Freia with them. The gold is ready, but the giants will not be content till the pile is high enough to hide Freia from their sight. The hoard is heaped up, but even so it hardly suffices, and the giants,

[1] These extracts from the English version of *The Ring* are made by kind permission of Messrs Schott and Co.

who in truth care little for the treasure, desiring only
the Tarnhelm and the Ring, refuse to be satisfied till
the last fruits of Wotan's raid are added to the spoil.
The Tarnhelm is willingly relinquished, but Wotan flatly
refuses to part with the Ring till Erda, the primeval
earth-goddess, appears and solemnly warns him that to
retain it will only bring disaster and death to the gods.
Awed by her words, he yields : the Ring is added to the
heap and Freia is released. But immediately the curse
of Alberich begins to work. The giants fall out over the
division of the loot and Fafner strikes Fasolt dead with a
blow of his staff. While he calmly makes off with the
booty the gods stand horror-struck, dismayed at the web
of evil that fate is weaving round them. Donner is the
first to recover. Crying that he is sick of the gloom he
mounts a crag and, swinging his hammer, summons the
forces of the storm. The mists collect round him, completely hiding him from sight, till his hammer is heard
falling on the rock with a crash. Immediately there is a
flash of lightning and a terrific peal of thunder, the darkness is rent asunder, and behold ! a rainbow bridge
stretching across the valley to the castle. Full of mutual
congratulations, the gods prepare to cross to their new
and glorious home, Wotan especially feeling well satisfied
with the issue of the day's work. But they are not to
depart without a warning that the trouble is not yet
over. The Ring in Fafner's hands is still a mighty power
of evil, and with it goes the awful curse of Alberich.
Wotan's own position, depending, as it does, on equity
and fair dealing, has been gravely compromised by his
surrender to Fafner of the Ring, the lawful property of
the Rhine Maidens. And so, as the dignified procession
moves across the bridge in triumph, there are wafted from
the waters below the voices of the maidens calling for

the return of their gold and crying out on the injustice of the gods.

THE VALKYRIE

Shortly before the end of *The Rhinegold* the orchestra announces very emphatically a new and striking *motif*, a phrase that we shall soon hear again associated with the magic sword. Its statement here is Wagner's method—a rather clumsy one—of telling us that there have arisen in Wotan's mind the outlines of a scheme by which he may free himself from the toils that threaten to destroy him. This plan he has begun to put into execution during the long interval that separates the close of *The Rhinegold* from the opening of *The Valkyrie*. To begin with, he has paid a long visit to Erda, who besides imparting much good counsel has borne him nine daughters, the Valkyries. These now roam over the world on their winged steeds ; after every battle they collect the bodies of the slain warriors and carry them over their saddle-bows to feast with the gods in Valhalla. Thus Wotan is gathering an army with which to face the hostile powers by which he is surrounded.

But this is not enough. There can be no peace for him until the terrible Ring is returned to the Rhine Maidens ; only when that is done will its power and that of the curse that rests upon it be destroyed. He may not himself steal it nor take it in fight ; he has given it to the giants as part of the ransom for Freia, and to take it from Fafner now would mean the abrogation of one of his own laws, those laws that are graven in runes on the shaft of his all-powerful spear, and which are the source of his own strength. But what if someone else, without his assistance, were to do the deed for him ? With this idea in his mind he descends to earth as Wälse, a warrior, and proceeds to bring into existence the race of Wälsungs. Wedding a mortal woman he has by her a son and a daughter, Siegmund and Sieglinde. Sieglinde is carried off one day by enemies while her menfolk are away, and married against her will to Hunding the Black. Some time later Siegmund loses his father also. The two are separated in the forest, and Siegmund's search for the missing Wälse leads only to the discovery of a discarded wolfskin. Wotan has returned to his own place. Siegmund leads for some time the life of an Ishmaelite, his hand against every man and every man's hand against him.

Act I. In championing a distressed maiden Siegmund is outnumbered and overwhelmed by her enemies, and at last, his sword broken, compelled to seek safety in flight. Night falls. Stumbling on through the darkness he is overtaken by a terrific storm, graphically depicted in the orchestral Prelude to *The Valkyrie*. At length he spies a forest dwelling. Completely spent, he staggers in and falls almost unconscious by the hearth. The living-room of the hut is empty when he arrives, but soon Sieglinde —for it is to Hunding's house that he has unwittingly come—enters from the back. Seeing an exhausted and wounded man she attends to his needs. The brother and sister do not recognize one another, but their mutual interest is obvious by the time Hunding returns home. The laws of hospitality are sacred, but the host is suspicious of his unexpected guest and asks his name and story. Siegmund for his part is equally distrustful, and, though he tells his tale truly, he speaks of himself as ' Wehwalt ' and his father as ' Wolfe.' Unfortunately, however, Hunding is allied to those with whom Siegmund fought during the day. The Wälsung's words betray this fact, and Hunding sternly tells him that in the morning they must meet in arms, although for the night his enemy is

safe under his roof.   He then retires with his wife, and
Siegmund is left alone.

The light from the dying fire falls upon the great tree
whose trunk forms the main support of the hut.   Something appears to glitter in the wood, something the nature
of which is revealed by the frequent recurrence of the
Sword *motif* in the orchestra, but Siegmund is heedless,
lost in gloomy reflection.   He is aroused by the return
of Sieglinde—moved by sympathy for the outcast, she
has come to help him in his difficulties, having drugged
her husband with a sleeping-draught.   She tells him of
how at her marriage-feast a stranger appeared, none knew
whence (though the orchestra informs us that it was
Wotan).   He carried a sword which he struck to the hilt
in a tree, saying that none but the strongest should draw
it forth.   Siegmund takes heart again, and there follows
a rapturous duet, one of the most lovely things in the
whole tetralogy.   Suddenly in the midst of it the door
flies open and reveals the night without.   The storm has
passed and the forest is bathed in moonlight.   Startled
at the noise made by the door Sieglinde exclaims, " Who
went ? "   Siegmund replies :

> No one went—but one has come !
> Laughing the Spring enters the hall !
> Winter storms have waned in the moon of May,
> With tender radiance sparkles the Spring ;
> On balmy breezes, light and lovely,
> Weaving wonders on he floats.
> O'er wood and meadow wafts his breathing,
> Widely open laughs his eye :
> In blithesome song of birds resounds his voice,
> Sweetest fragrance breathes he forth :
> From his ardent blood breathe all joy-giving blossoms,
> Bud and shoot spring up by his might.
> With gentle weapons' charm he forces the world ;
> Winter and storm yield to his strong attack :
> Assailed by his hardy strokes now the doors are shattered
> That, fast and defiant, held us parted from him.

They fall into one another's arms. But something in her lover's voice stirs a vague recollection in Sieglinde. Explanations follow, and Siegmund's true origin is revealed; he is a Wälsung, as she is! In great exaltation he takes his stand before the tree and invokes the sword under the name of ' Needful.' Then with a mighty effort he draws it forth. Sieglinde hails him as lord and brother, and together they hasten away into the night.

This love-scene between brother and sister has brought upon Wagner a good deal of hostile criticism. No doubt the idea is repellent according to our modern notions ; but such marriages were common enough in primitive communities, and indeed survived for long among civilized peoples, as is evidenced by such notable instances as those of the Pharaohs of Egypt and the Incas of Peru.

Act II. Another tempestuous Prelude, suggestive first of the lovers and later of the Valkyries on their galloping horses, introduces us to a rocky place among the mountains. Wotan, fully armed, addresses his favourite daughter, Brünnhilde the Valkyrie, and bids her hasten to assist Siegmund in his forthcoming fight with Hunding. Brünnhilde obediently departs, leaping lightly from rock to rock and uttering her wild Valkyrie cry. Before she disappears she warns Wotan that she can see his wife Fricka approaching. Fricka has come in her capacity of goddess of marriage to demand vengeance on Siegmund for carrying off Hunding's wife. The argument is long and tedious—it soon appears that Wotan is getting the worst of it. Fricka points out that if he were to help Siegmund he would once more be flouting those laws that are the mainstay of his rule, and when he pleads that Siegmund is the saviour who will extricate them all from their difficulties by securing the Ring without any assistance from the gods, she replies that Wotan has already

rendered his assistance by providing him with the magic
sword and sending Brünnhilde to aid him in the battle.

Wotan is compelled to yield. Brünnhilde re-enters as
Fricka goes out, and he now turns to her. He pours his
troubles into her sympathetic ear in another scene of
considerable length, and eventually revokes his previous
commands. It is Hunding she must protect, not Siegmund.

Brünnhilde finds this new commission (which she feels
to be contrary to her father's real desires) extremely irk-
some, but Wotan breaks out in fearful wrath at the first
suggestion of disobedience, and finally leaves her with
strict injunctions to carry out his orders to the letter.
Sadly she retires to a cave at the back, where she conceals
herself to await Siegmund. Already he comes, and Sieglinde with him. The poor girl is worn out with hardship
and anxiety; Siegmund is quite unable to soothe her,
and after a hysterical outburst she falls senseless in his
arms. Seating himself on the ground he pillows her
head in his lap, and then bending over her presses a long
kiss on her forehead. On raising his eyes again he perceives Brünnhilde, who advances slowly toward him. The
musical and dramatic interest has flagged sadly in the
earlier part of the Act, but from this moment it revives
once more. Brünnhilde informs the Wälsung that she
has come to bid him to Valhalla, to Wotan, the gods, and
the heroes. Siegmund inquires whether Sieglinde is to
accompany him. "No," comes the reply,

> Here on earth must she still linger;
> Siegmund will find not Sieglinde there.

"Then," says Siegmund,

> Greet for me Valhalla, greet for me Wotan,
> Greet for me Wälse and all the heroes,
> Greet too the beauteous wish-maidens :—
> To them I follow thee not!

It is Brünnhilde's sad task to convince him that the choice does not lie in his hands. When this at last comes home to him and he realizes that even his magic sword will not avail him he draws the weapon in a mood of anguished despair. Even should it fail him against the foe it will at least serve for Sieglinde and his child that is to be:

> Two lives laugh to thee here :
> Take them, Needful, envious still !

At this Brünnhilde's resolution breaks down. Rather than witness such a tragedy she will disobey her father's commands. Calling to Siegmund that the decree is revoked, that he shall live and Hunding die, she rushes from the darkening stage. Overcome with joy, Siegmund kisses once more the sleeping Sieglinde and hurries himself into the gloom at the back, whence Hunding's horn-call can already be heard. Sieglinde awakes, and finds herself alone in the gathering storm. Hearing the angry voices of her husband and her lover she runs forward to separate them, but a fearful flash of lightning causes her to stagger back. By its gleam Siegmund and Hunding are seen in mortal combat. Brünnhilde appears hovering over Siegmund and protecting him with her shield, but just as he aims a mighty blow at Hunding there looms over the latter the form of Wotan, his redoubtable spear outstretched. Siegmund's sword is shattered on the spear, and Hunding plunges his weapon into his disarmed adversary's breast. The light goes out, and it is with difficulty that the eye follows Brünnhilde as she picks up the fragments of the broken sword, hurries to Sieglinde, and carries her off. Wotan is left alone with Hunding ; his rage and grief are terrible.

> Go hence, slave ! Kneel before Fricka :
> Tell her that Wotan's spear avenged what wrought her wrong.
> Go !—Go !

Hunding falls dead, and the god's anger is diverted into another channel:

> But Brünnhilde ! Woe to the guilty one !
> Dire wage shall she win for her crime,
> If my steed overtake her in flight !

Act III. The celebrated ' Ride of the Valkyries ' provides a terrific exordium for this Act. The storm is still raging, and above the turmoil of the elements can be heard the cries of the Valkyries, the sound of galloping hooves, and the frenzied whinnyings of the horses. The characteristic rhythm persists long after the curtain has risen, disclosing the Valkyries' Rock, a desolate mountain-top. One by one the Valkyries arrive at the rendezvous, riding from the back on their winged steeds, which they tether in a neighbouring wood. Brünnhilde alone is missing. At last they catch sight of her, riding furiously, and a moment or two later she staggers in, supporting Sieglinde. Her sisters are amazed to find a living woman with her instead of the dead body of Siegmund, but their amazement turns to dismay as she breathlessly tells her story and begs the loan of a horse that she and Sieglinde may continue their flight from Wotan, whose relentless pursuit is already indicated by a persistent rhythm in the orchestra. None of the others dares to brave the fury of the angry god, and Sieglinde herself intervenes, begging to be allowed to await the death she deserves and desires. But the dauntless Valkyrie holds to her resolve. She appeals to Sieglinde in the name of Siegmund's child who is presently to be born to her, and who, she prophesies, will become " the world's most glorious hero." Now courage is kindled in Sieglinde's breast, and, obeying Brünnhilde, she flies eastward to the forest. Thither Wotan seldom goes : he leaves it to Fafner, who, transformed by the Tarnhelm into a dragon, guards there the Ring and the Nibelung's hoard.

But Brünnhilde remains to face her father. Riding on the thunderstorm he has already reached the rock, and now he comes striding in. The Valkyries cower in terror before him, vainly endeavouring to shield their sister ; he knows well she is with them and imperiously commands her to come forth. Meekly she obeys, and stands before him to receive her sentence. In mingled anger and sorrow he delivers it :

> Outcast art thou from the clan of the gods :
> For broken is now our bond ;
> Henceforth from sight of my face art thou banned !
> He who wins thee robs thee of all !
> For here on the rock bound shalt thou be ;
> Defenceless in sleep liest thou locked :
> The man shall master the maid
> Who shall find her and wake her from her sleep.

At this savage decree all shake in horror. But Wotan cares nothing for the feeble protests of the eight Valkyries ; let them hasten from their doomed sister and never return, on pain of sharing her fate. Terrified they ride off, and Brünnhilde is alone with her father.

The concluding scene is matchless in its beauty and tenderness. Meekly but eloquently the Valkyrie pleads for mercy. She has disobeyed Wotan's spoken word, it is true, but in doing so she has fulfilled his dearest wish, and rescued Sieglinde, her child, and the broken sword. But the god is adamant, and seeing that her doom is irrevocable she makes a final appeal :

> By thy command enkindle a fire ;
> With flaming guardians girdle the fell ;
> To lick with tongue, to bite with tooth,
> The craven who rashly dareth
> To draw near the threatening rock !

Overcome by love and pity Wotan yields. It only

remains to put the sentence into execution. But before he does this he bids a tender adieu to his daughter :

> Farewell, thou valiant, glorious child !
> Thou once the holiest pride of my heart !
> Farewell !
>
> Thy brightly glittering eyes,
> That smiling oft I caressed, . . .
> On mortal more blessed once may they beam :
> On me, hapless immortal,
> Must they close now for ever.
> For so turns the god now from thee,
> So kisses thy godhead away.

Gently he kisses her eyes, and she sinks unconscious in his arms. He carries her carefully to the side of the stage, adjusts her helmet, and covers her with her great shield, while from the orchestra arise the strains of a celestial lullaby. Then, finally turning away, he summons Loki. Thrice with his spear he strikes the rock, and at the third stroke a flash of flame leaps forth which quickly spreads to a fiery ring, encircling the mountain-top. As he stretches out the spear to cast a final spell we hear on the brass the theme of Siegfried, prophetic of the awakening to come. And now all is accomplished, and the god slowly and reluctantly departs, leaving his daughter in utter loneliness to her long, fire-girt sleep.

SIEGFRIED

Act I. Sieglinde did not long survive her brother. She succeeded in escaping into the forest only to die in giving birth to her son, Siegfried. Eighteen or twenty years have now elapsed, during which the boy has been brought up by Mime, the Nibelung smith. We last saw Mime smarting under the lash of Alberich's whip in *The Rhinegold*; now he and Alberich both haunt the forest in which Fafner, transformed into a dragon, guards the Ring. Mime inhabits a cave that he has fitted up as a smithy, and it is in this gloomy dwelling that the first Act of *Siegfried* takes place. The dark Prelude contains references to the Ring and Rhinegold *motifs*, elements in the drama that have rather fallen into the background during *The Valkyrie*. But the most prominent themes are those of Mime's Meditation (two chords with a big drop between them) and the Nibelung Smith. Mime is evidently hard at work, and the object of his labours is revealed by a *pianissimo* reference to the Sword *motif*. Further explanation is provided by his opening soliloquy. In Siegfried he has found, he hopes, the champion who will slay Fafner and win for him the Ring. But for that deed a sword is required, and no sword that he can forge is strong enough to satisfy the young hero. There is indeed a blade that would serve— 'Needful,' Siegmund's weapon, the broken splinters of which he received from the dying Sieglinde. But these mighty fragments it is beyond his power to fashion anew.

A merry horn-call announces the advent of Siegfried. It is soon clear that the youth wastes no affection on the shifty dwarf who has nurtured him. He starts by scaring him out of his wits by means of a wild bear he has captured in the forest. Then, driving the beast away, he demands his sword. Mime timidly hands him the fruit of his labours, a weapon that Siegfried contemptuously smashes with a blow on the anvil. Then he turns to the Nibelung and questions him about his (Siegfried's) birth and parentage. The dwarf's attempts to persuade him that he is himself the hero's father Siegfried scornfully brushes aside. But the truth he will have, and he almost throttles Mime in his endeavour to force it out of him. He gets his way, and now at last he hears of Sieglinde. Mime withholds Siegmund's name, but the fragments of ' Needful' are produced as witness of the tale. Seeing them, Siegfried exclaims joyfully, " And now these fragments straight shalt thou forge me!" A moment later he rushes off to the forest again, leaving Mime to the one task that is beyond his skill.

The dwarf's gloomy broodings are interrupted by the appearance at the cave's mouth of ' the Wanderer,' an old man with a large hat that hangs down over one side of his face, thus hiding the fact that he has lost an eye. This, we soon discover, is Wotan. Mime roughly refuses his plea for shelter and bids him begone. But the stranger is not so easily disposed of, and seating himself by the hearth he wagers his head that he will answer any three questions that the Nibelung chooses to ask him. Having accomplished this he claims the right to question his host in return. This part of the libretto must have been written before Wagner had decided on the composition of the earlier operas. The game of question and answer takes a long time and tells us nothing that we do not already know, except the answer to the Wanderer's last question, " Who shall forge the splinters of the sword ? " Of this Mime is as ignorant as we are. He cries out in despair, but the Wanderer only rises from his seat and calmly prepares to go. At the cave's mouth he stops and replies to his own question :

> He who the force of fear ne'er felt,
> ' Needful ' shall he forge.
> Thy wily head ward from to-day !
> I leave it forfeit to him
> Who has never learned to fear.

And so with a smile he departs.

The interview has proved too much for Mime's nerves, and he gives way to a fit of hysterics, fancying that Fafner

himself is after him. When Siegfried returns he finds
him hiding behind the anvil. He takes some time to
recover, and then begins to speak of fear. But his talk
only puzzles Siegfried, who accepts with naïve curiosity
his offer to guide him to Fafner's den, there to learn
what fear means. But first the sword must be forged,
and Mime confesses that this is a task he cannot ac-
complish. With a scornful reproach Siegfried takes the
pieces from him :

> My father's blade yields but to me !
> By me forged be the sword !

From here to the end the music proceeds with the
utmost animation. Siegfried blows up the furnace and
files the pieces of the sword into small fragments. These
he melts in the fire, pours into a mould, and so gradually
makes a new weapon out of the original metal, accompanying each step of the process with a stirring song.
Mime sees that the sword will be forged, and even the
dragon, he feels, will be unable to withstand the might
of this boy ; the Ring itself will fall into Siegfried's
hands ! He sets about, therefore, to prepare a poisonous
brew. With this he will come forward as soon as the
dragon is dead ; the thirsty Siegfried will drink, and the
Ring will be his at last ! Siegfried pays little attention
to what Mime is doing—already his work at the forge is
nearing completion. Soon he puts the finishing touches,
and swinging the newly fashioned sword before him,
cries in triumph,

> Needful, Needful, conquering sword !
> Again to life have I woke thee !
> Dead layest thou in splinters here,
> Now shin'st thou defiant and fair. . . .
> See, Mime, thou smith :
> So sunders Siegfried's sword !

With a mighty blow he cleaves the anvil in two from top to bottom, and the curtain falls.

Act II. The curtain rises again on a clearing in the forest before Fafner's cave. A Prelude built mainly on the theme of the Giants—now distorted to represent Fafner in his dragon shape—and full of dark references to Alberich's curse, is a fit opening to the first scene. In a night of inky blackness Alberich keeps his tireless watch on the Ring and its grim guardian. The sudden rising of a storm and its equally sudden passing herald the approach of the Wanderer. Much of the dialogue that follows is superfluous for those who know the earlier operas, but the Wanderer breaks new ground when he tells Alberich of Fafner's imminent destruction at the hands of the young Siegfried. The Nibelung's thoughts fly at once to the Ring by which he still hopes to gain universal dominion, and, incidentally, vengeance on the lords of Valhalla. He even acts on the Wanderer's suggestion that he should awaken Fafner, warn him of his danger, and persuade him to deliver up the Ring. But the dragon is not to be frightened, and the Wanderer rides off on his storm-cloud, prophesying wonders to come. Alberich, too, vanishes into a cleft in the rocks, and now, as the dawn breaks, Siegfried, piloted by Mime, comes out into the clearing. Here, Mime tells him, shall he learn the meaning of fear. But Siegfried's loathing for Mime is unabated, and the dwarf's pratings of love and gratitude move him to scornful anger. Mime takes himself off to await the issue of the fight, muttering to himself,

> Fafner and Siegfried, Siegfried and Fafner :
> Would each the other might slay !

At this point there creep into the music the first strains of the lovely ' Forest Murmurs ' which have made the Act famous. To begin with, Siegfried's thoughts wander to his dead mother, and are expressed in a tender soliloquy. But soon he is attracted by the song of a forest bird. His attempts to imitate this on a reed are a grotesque failure, as he readily admits, but he can do better on the horn, and placing this instrument to his lips he plays a rousing call. The effect of this is to wake Fafner, and after an interchange of compliments the battle begins. Wagner would have been better advised to place the slaying of the dragon off the stage; the clumsy machinery of the theatre is bound to make it ridiculous. Happily it does not last long; 'Needful' is duly planted in the monster's heart, and he dies with a half-uttered warning to his conqueror left unfinished.

In withdrawing his sword from the dragon's body Siegfried receives a drop of the blood upon his hand. It burns like fire, and involuntarily he carries his hand to his lips. The result of swallowing the blood is that he finds he can understand the song of the birds, and the bird who sang to him before now tells him clearly of the Tarnhelm and the Ring. With a word of thanks he disappears into the cave to seek these treasures. During his absence there is a short but wildly grotesque scene between Mime and Alberich, the latter of whom has just issued from his cleft. But their wrangling leads to no bargain and is brought to an abrupt end by the return of the hero bearing with him the objects of their greed. Once more the bird takes a hand in the game. He warns Siegfried of Mime's treachery: let him but listen to the dwarf's words; the dragon's blood that he has drunk will enable him to detect their true intent beneath the veneer of deceit. Here the stagecraft is again at fault. To friendly and seductive music Mime announces in set terms his intention to poison Siegfried. The suggestion is that the dwarf really uses cajoling words, but that, owing to the spell of the blood, Siegfried can see through his treachery. The effect, however, is childlike in the extreme, and it is a relief when the young hero puts an end to the episode by striking off Mime's head with a blow of his sword. He throws the corpse into the cave and pushes the dragon's body in the same direction, completely blocking the entrance. He feels no remorse, but he is acutely conscious of his loneliness and appeals again to the bird. His resourceful friend is ready with an answer in this difficulty too, and Siegfried learns of Brünnhilde, and the Rock whose girdle of fire none shall cross but he who knows not fear. Shouting with joy he begs that the way be shown him. The bird flutters off with Siegfried eagerly following, his whole mind bent on this new adventure.

Act III. It has already been said that the composition of *The Ring* proceeded interruptedly till 1857, and by that time Wagner had completed the libretto of the whole tetralogy and the music as far as the middle of *Siegfried*. The story goes that the end of the scene describing the death of Fafner marks the actual point when he laid down his pen. If that is so he proved himself a true artist when he started work again in 1869. During the interval both *Tristan* and *The Mastersingers* had been brought to birth, and the composition of these works represented an enormous addition to his experience and musicianship. Yet the score of the Second Act of *Siegfried* shows no signs of the twelve years' break : the style of the last part of it differs in no way from that of the rest. But when we reach Act III we immediately become conscious of a riper mastery, a more matured ease in the treatment. The stormy Prelude, based on various elemental ideas, such as the theme of Erda, that of Wotan's Spear, the Waters of the Rhine, and the End of the Gods, is the work of a man who treads with a firmer step, a greater assurance, than heretofore. And this remains true of the rest of the Act in spite of the manifest weakness of part of the libretto. The first scene, for example, is mostly redundant, immensely powerful though it is musically. It is placed in a wild spot at the foot of the mountain whose summit is crowned by the Valkyries' Rock. The Wanderer is at first the only figure on the stage; by potent spells he summons Erda, that her wisdom may help him in his perplexities. But when she appears her answers are so evasive that they are of no use to him—he does most of the talking himself, but we learn little from him, except that he has become a disciple of Schopenhauer. Realizing that there is no way out of the tangle in which he is involved, and that the doom of the gods is inevitable, he has found peace in accepting the situation and himself willing that which he knows must be. Erda descends "to endless sleep" and the Wanderer quietly awaits the coming of Siegfried.

The young man, when he arrives, is troubled at the sudden departure of his bird, which flew off (as we hear from the Wanderer a little later) to save its life from the ravens that always accompany Wotan. Siegfried asks the Wanderer to tell him the way to the Rock, and at first it seems that the god will help him. But Mime has not succeeded in teaching his foster-child good manners, and his rude jests at the Wanderer's appearance awake the divine anger, till at length the hallowed spear is stretched out to bar the path. Siegfried is no whit dismayed and, drawing his sword, breaks the spear in two with a single blow, thus, though he knows it not, raising the spell that surrounds Brünnhilde. The Wanderer picks up the pieces of his weapon and saying quietly, " Fare on : I cannot withstand thee," suddenly disappears. Siegfried joyfully proceeds to where the growing light of the fire beckons him on the mountainside.

The scene is now changed. During the interval while the stage is hidden the orchestra plays a new and wilder version of the Fire music, through which we hear the theme of Siegfried and the call of his horn. The music rises to a climax and then dies down till the lovely strains of the Sleep theme tell us that the summit of the Rock has been reached. The curtain rises on the same scene as that at the end of *The Valkyrie*. Brünnhilde is asleep in the foreground.

No words can do justice to the magnificent music of this final portion of *Siegfried* ; the reader must hear it for himself. Siegfried approaches, and, seeing what he imagines to be an armed knight asleep, he raises the shield, looses the helmet, and cuts through with his sword the rings on both sides of the breast-plate. This reveals Brünnhilde in woman's dress, and now for the first time he learns what it is to be afraid. His attempts to waken her are unsuccessful, till at last he yields to the temptation to kiss her on the lips. The spell is broken and Brünnhilde sits up, greets the world once more, and then turns to ask the name of her deliverer. On hearing that it is Siegfried she bursts into a cry of rapture, and the two voices join in a full Italian cadence—the first in the work :

> O mother, hail, who gave thee thy birth !
> Hail, O Earth, that fostered thy life !
> Thine eye alone might behold me,
> Alone to thee might I wake.

A flow of music follows hardly less wonderful than the duet in *Tristan*, although totally different in character. Siegfried's growing passion alarms Brünnhilde, who vainly attempts to lead his thoughts into other channels.

Suddenly he embraces her. She flies terror-stricken to the other side of the stage :

> No god's touch have I felt !
> Low bent all heroes, greeting the maiden :
> Holy came she from Walhall.
> Woe's me ! Woe's me !

The effect of the abrupt transition from the love-music to the majestic Valhalla *motif* is tremendous. But Siegfried's ardour is unabated, and already the woman in Brünnhilde is driving out the goddess. For a moment the issue sways in the balance while in a kind of vision she sees the awful shadow of Alberich's curse. But the cloud departs as swiftly as it came, and she pours out her happiness in a lovely lyrical song beginning,

> Ever lived I, ever live I,
> Ever in sweet longing delight—
> Yet ever to make thee blest !

The principal melody of which was also used prominently by Wagner in the tender " Siegfried Idyll." [The " Siegfried Idyll " is a composition for a very small orchestra, written by Wagner and played by a few of his friends as a tribute to his wife Cosima on her birthday— the first after their son Siegfried was born. Almost all the tunes in it are taken from the opera *Siegfried*.] A moment later she surrenders utterly, and the work rises to its last climax on the wings of love triumphant as, oblivious of her lost divinity, of the curse hanging over them, of everything but Siegfried, she throws herself into his arms.

THE DUSK OF THE GODS

Act I. Night reigns on the Valkyries' Rock. Brünnhilde and Siegfried have sought repose in the cave at the back, and the orchestral opening of the opera tells us that the place is given over to the shadowy elemental powers. The three Norns (or Fates) sit spinning, winding the rope of Destiny. Their talk is of Wotan, his history, and his approaching fall through the agency of the Ring and Alberich's curse. Suddenly the rope breaks, and the three sisters descend to their mother Erda, their work for the world at an end.

Dawn begins to brighten the sky, and soon the sun rises, just as Brünnhilde and Siegfried enter from the cave. The joy of their newly won happiness finds vent in a duet no whit inferior to the one in *Siegfried*. Musically it serves to introduce to us three new *motifs* : the first of them, a strong, virile tune in march-time, is really nothing but a rhythmical metamorphosis of Siegfried's horn-call ; the second, a tender strain containing a typical Wagnerian ' turn,' represents Brünnhilde and the change that love has wrought in her ; the third is a cadence of singular beauty which recurs often in the course of the scene and of which considerable use is made hereafter. The lovers are radiant, but it is not their intention that their lives shall be spent in an endless idyll on this lonely Rock. There is work in the world for Siegfried to do ! But before they part Siegfried gives Brünnhilde, as a pledge of his undying love, the Ring. She in return gives him her horse, Grane. Grane's supernatural attributes have been lost with those of his mistress, but his own equine courage and strength still remain to him, and these are put at the service of his new master. At length the farewells are said, and Siegfried and Grane quickly disappear from us over the edge of the hill, though they are watched by Brünnhilde till the curtain falls. Even after this the orchestra carries us with the hero on his journey down through the fiery belt till at last he reaches the banks of the Rhine. Here we notice a change : the music loses its exuberant vitality and the sinister Ring *motif* falls on our ears with a presage of evil to come. At this moment the curtain rises once more. All that has happened hitherto is but a prelude to the main action of the drama, and the First Act proper opens in the Hall of the Gibichungs.

These, we soon learn, are a noble race whose home is on the banks of the Rhine. Gunther, their chief, is disclosed in council with his sister Gutrune and his half-brother Hagen. Hagen takes the lead in the conversation. Referring to the fact that Gunther and Gutrune are still unmarried, he announces that he knows of fit mates for both of them, and tells of Brünnhilde and Siegfried. With the history of these two he is clearly well acquainted, but he maintains a discreet silence about Siegfried's ascent of the Rock, and the wooing and winning of his bride. Gunther's enthusiasm is for a moment somewhat damped when he hears that the fire is an obstacle he can never surmount, but Hagen asserts that Siegfried can achieve what Gunther cannot, and urges that the Wälsung be induced to undertake the task by the offer of Gutrune's hand. Should her beauty fail to subdue the hero's heart, he knows of a potion that can be relied on in matters of this kind. Gunther and Gutrune have hardly agreed to the plan when Siegfried's horn announces his impending arrival. He is warmly greeted by the Gibichungs, but Gutrune seizes an early opportunity to steal away, returning presently with a draught in which she has mixed some of Hagen's potion. Siegfried takes the drinking-horn and, pledging Brünnhilde, puts it to his lips. The orchestra accompanies the toast with the broad Italian cadence we heard in the love-duet of *Siegfried*. But the phrase is never finished : it stops on the penultimate note as the powerful drug takes effect, and after a moment's hesitation resolves unexpectedly on the theme associated with Gutrune, on whose form the hero's eyes have suddenly fixed themselves. There is no further difficulty ; Brünnhilde is entirely blotted from Siegfried's memory, and he willingly undertakes to win her for Gunther if Gutrune be granted as guerdon of his toil. By the charm of the Tarnhelm, whose use he now for the first time learns from Hagen, he will deceive Brünnhilde into believing that he is Gunther. Gunther and he swear a bond of blood-brotherhood and set out immediately for the Valkyries' mountain. Gutrune watches their departure, and then retires to her chamber. Hagen is left alone, and in a short monologue he gives us the first inkling of his true designs. It is not love of his half-brother that has led him to contrive his plot. The Ring alone is his object and with this in his possession he hopes to wield a power that will make both Gunther and Siegfried his obedient slaves.

The curtain falls for a short time, but the music goes on and quickly transports us to the Valkyries' Rock once more. Brünnhilde's love-dream is broken by the well-remembered sounds of the Valkyries' ride, and soon her sister Waltraute stands before her. The scene that follows is often tedious, but it can be saved by a good Waltraute. Driven by despair, the Valkyrie has braved her father's wrath and come to the forbidden Rock. She brings dark tidings from Valhalla, where Wotan sits in silence among the assembled gods, awaiting the doom that he cannot escape. One hope alone remains : let Brünnhilde return the Ring to the Rhine Maidens—then will the curse and its effects be removed for ever ! It is in the hope of persuading her sister to make the sacrifice that Waltraute has now come. But as soon as Brünnhilde realizes that it is Siegfried's love-pledge that is in question she breaks out in scorn. Is her sister so mad as to think that her lover's gift is not more to her than Valhalla and all it contains ? All Waltraute's pleadings are useless, and in the end she is compelled to return without accomplishing her mission.

No sooner has she gone than the flames grow brighter. For a moment Brünnhilde idly wonders what this may mean ; then, guessing it is Siegfried returning, she springs up to greet him—only to recoil in dismay. Siegfried indeed it is, but Siegfried disguised by the Tarnhelm so as to resemble Gunther, and speaking in a feigned voice. Announcing that he is Gunther, the Gibichung, he tells her he has come to make her his bride. What follows is quickly told. Brünnhilde, terrified, seeks refuge in the power of the Ring ; but this avails nothing against its rightful owner. After a short struggle he tears it from her finger, and then bids his fainting victim lead him to her cave. The vanquished Brünnhilde can do nothing but comply, and with trembling steps she goes to the cave-mouth and disappears. Siegfried, left alone for a moment, draws his sword. Let it be witness that it is for his blood-brother alone that he has wooed! Keeping it still unsheathed he, too, vanishes into the cave.

Act II. The First Act of *The Dusk of the Gods* plays for about two hours if we include the Prelude. Act II is shorter, but it gives the exhausted hearer little respite, its seriousness being unrelieved by any suggestion of a lighter or more lyrical mood. In an open space on the shore, in front of the Gibichungs' Hall, sits Hagen. He has set himself to watch through the night for the return of Siegfried and Gunther, but weariness has overcome him, and now he sleeps, his form barely distinguishable in the general obscurity. His rest is troubled by evil dreams: he seems to see the figure of Alberich crouching at his feet, and to hold converse with this grim nocturnal visitor. Their voices come to us from the heart of the shadows, and we learn for the first time of Hagen's kinship with the Nibelung. " Sleep'st thou, Hagen, my son ? " whispers Alberich, and exhorts him to ceaseless vigilance and undying hate. Only so will he succeed in wresting the Ring from Siegfried and in gaining for his father and himself the heritage of the gods. For revenge on them Alberich is still burning, and his last thought as he disappears is to extract from Hagen an oath that he will exact this vengeance to the uttermost when the Ring is his.

The coming of day brings Siegfried with it. By the power of the Tarnhelm he has conveyed himself instantaneously from the Valkyries' Rock to the Hall of the Gibichungs, and now he cheerfully greets Hagen and calls for Gutrune. While Brünnhilde and Gunther are making by more toilsome methods the journey that he has so easily accomplished, he tells the story of how the bride was won. The tale of the doings on the Rock excites a passing pang of jealousy in Gutrune, but Siegfried easily allays her fears and goes on to speak of how in the morning he led Brünnhilde down the mountainside, and then, by the help of a fortunate mist, succeeded in changing places with Gunther without arousing her suspicion. Nothing remains to be done but prepare the wedding-feast, and he hastens with Gutrune into the Hall to speed the arrangements. Hagen, alone once more, puts a great cow-horn to his lips and blows a blast summoning the savage folk who follow Gunther's standard. From all sides they come with their rough weapons, and in a wild chorus demand wherefore they have been assembled. Hearing that it is a feast that is in prospect they burst into good-humoured laughter and accord a hearty welcome to Brünnhilde and Gunther, who at this moment reach the water's edge. Gunther leads his bride forward to meet Hagen, who has now been joined by Gutrune and Siegfried, and thus the Valkyrie finds herself confronted with her faithless lover. At first she is utterly bewildered, but soon, seeing the Ring on his finger, she begins to suspect something of the truth, and asks how it comes that the charm wrested from her by Gunther (as she believes) appears now on Siegfried's hand. This is more than Gunther can explain, and Brünnhilde, in an outburst of wild fury, calls for vengeance on them all for their treachery and especially on the traitorous Siegfried whose wife she swears she is.

By this time everyone is at cross-purposes. Brünnhilde believes that Siegfried, to gain Gutrune, has deliberately sacrificed his first love. Siegfried, forgetful of his previous happiness, knows only that he has been faithful to the truth reposed in him by Gunther. Gunther, for his part, is beginning to entertain grave doubts on this same point. Hagen alone knows the whole truth, and it is on his spear-point that Siegfried swears that he has kept faith, Brünnhilde that he has broken it. Among the whole company Siegfried alone maintains his cheerfulness. He assures Gunther that Brünnhilde's outburst signifies nothing but a fit of feminine petulance, and departs with Gutrune and the vassals to complete the preparations for the wedding. Hagen, alone with Brünnhilde and Gunther, cunningly works on their suspicions of Siegfried until at length a plot is hatched to murder him. Since none of them is strong enough to withstand him in fight he must die by a stab in the back from Hagen's spear, the weapon on which his false oath was sworn. With this plan of vengeance both Brünnhilde and Gunther declare themselves satisfied ; the wedding procession with Siegfried and Gutrune appears from the Hall and as they join it the curtain falls.

Act III. The Third Act opens with a series of horn-calls indicating that a hunt is in progress. The stage shows us a wild valley; through it flows the Rhine, on whose waters the three Rhine Maidens are seen swimming. They have occupied the long interval since we last saw them at the beginning of *The Rhinegold* in composing and learning a new and exquisite song, with which they now delight our ears. Presently Siegfried appears on the bank; in the course of the hunt he has got separated from the rest, and has reached this spot in search of his lost quarry. The Rhine Maidens offer to find it for him if he will give them in return the golden Ring on his finger. For a single moment he seems about to grant their request, but they make the mistake of threatening him with evils to come should he not comply with their wishes. At this he calmly returns the talisman to his finger; he cares little for the gold itself, and as for the curse of Alberich, of which he now hears for the first time, no one shall ever say that he has yielded from fear. The Rhine Maidens swim slowly away prophesying that this very day he shall be slain. Brünnhilde will inherit the Ring, to her will they go, and she will not refuse to grant them their own.

The lyric loveliness of this scene provides a most welcome relief from the general sombre mood of the drama, but now the appearance of the hunting-party brings us quickly to the tragic climax. They sit down to eat and rest: Gunther is sunk in gloomy brooding and Hagen preserves his usual grim aloofness. Siegfried beguiles the time with the tale of his adventures, and once more we hear of Mime, of the slaying of Fafner, and the winning of Tarnhelm and Ring. At this point Hagen drops the juice of a herb into Siegfried's drinking-horn. Suddenly and wonderfully there steal into the music the notes of the cadence from the love-scene at the beginning of the opera. The gates of Siegfried's memory have been opened ; he recalls once more the wooing and winning of Brünnhilde, and this story too he tells, quite unconscious of the emotion his words are arousing in the breast of Gunther. Hagen's moment has come. Two ravens fly up from a bush in the background ; he draws Siegfried's attention to these and then, when the hero's back is turned, plunges his traitor's spear deep into his body. Siegfried rushes at him, raising his shield as though to bring it down and overwhelm him ; but his strength fails him and he falls to the ground. Gunther is horrorstruck when he sees the execution of the plot to which he has himself been a party, but the wounded warrior claims all his attention, and Hagen is suffered to depart unchallenged. Siegfried's dying thoughts fly back to his vanished happiness. He imagines that he is still on the Valkyries' Rock with Brünnhilde in his arms, and he dies with her name on his lips.

The interval required to change the scene is occupied by the tremendous 'Death March,' a piece which shows us the composer's genius in its loftiest aspect. It consists in reality of little but a series of *leit-motifs*, thrown into slow march-rhythm and so arranged as to bring before the eyes of our imagination the whole course of Siegfried's life. It is by no means long, but the epic quality of the themes themselves combined with the incomparable majesty of their setting creates an impression that is never to be forgotten. At length, when the heroic mood has exhausted itself, the march ends with a short but infinitely pathetic reference to Brünnhilde.

The curtain rises again on a moonlight night in the Gibichungs' Hall. Gutrune is alone, for Brünnhilde has gone down to the river and the hunting-party has not yet returned. Anxiously she awaits her Siegfried. But it is Hagen who appears first, Hagen in the wildest of spirits at the success of his villainy; brutally he breaks the news, just as the procession of death arrives at the Hall. All is horror and confusion. Gutrune casts on Gunther the blame for Siegfried's murder; Gunther accuses Hagen, who defiantly admits the deed and claims as his reward the Ring. Gunther refuses to give up Gutrune's dower, as he calls it, swords are drawn, and soon Gunther lies dead on the ground. With a cry of " Mime, the Ring ! " Hagen approaches Siegfried's body, but the dead man's hand raises itself threateningly, and horrified at the portent his murderer cowers away. And now with firm step Brünnhilde is seen making her way through the terror-stricken crowd to the front of the stage. Henceforth the interest is focused entirely on her. She begins quietly but with immense dignity :

> Silence your sorrow's clamorous cry !
> Whom ye all have betrayed,
> For vengeance cometh his wife.
> Children heard I whining to their mother, because sweet milk
>   had been spilled :
> Yet heard I not lament that befitteth the highest hero's fame.

Gutrune interrupts her with a shower of reproaches, but Brünnhilde, who has learnt all from the Rhine Maidens, quells her with a few words that reveal the whole plot, and with a wail of dismay at Hagen's treachery Gutrune falls senseless. Brünnhilde turns to the vassals, imperiously bidding them prepare a pyre and lift the body thereon. Others she sends to bring Grane, her faithful horse. Now she turns to Siegfried's body, and in a gentler voice pronounces his epitaph :

Truer than his were oaths ne'er spoken ;
Faithful as he, none e'er held promise ;
Purer than his, love ne'er was plighted :
Yet oaths hath he scorned, bonds hath he broken,
The faithfullest love none so hath betrayed !
Know ye why this was ?
O ! ye, of vows the heavenly guardians,
Turn now your eyes on my grievous distress !
Behold your eternal disgrace !
To my plaint give ear, thou mighty god !
Through his most valiant deed, by thee so dearly desired,
Didst thou condemn him to endure the doom that on thee
    had fallen—
He, truest of all, must betray me, that wise a woman might
    grow !
Know I now thy need ?
All things, all things, all know I,
All to me is revealed.
Wings of thy ravens wave around me ;
With tidings long desired I send now thy messengers home,
Rest thou, rest thou, thou god !

She bends down and takes the Ring from Siegfried's finger :

My heritage yields now the hero.
Accursed charm ! Terrible Ring !
My hand grasps thee—and gives thee away.

Soon the Rhine Maidens shall have their gold again, cleansed by the waters from the curse. Let them preserve it pure henceforth. Placing the Ring on her finger, she takes from a vassal a burning brand :

Fly home, ye ravens ! . . .
To Brünnhilde's Rock first wing your flight.
There burneth Loki : straightway bid him to Wallhall !
For the end of godhood draweth now near.
So cast I the brand on Wallhall's glittering walls.

She flings the torch on the pyre, and turns again to greet Grane, who has been led in. Does he know whither they are going on this last ride, and to whom ?

Hei-a-jo-ho! Grane!
Give him thy greeting!
Siegfried! Siegfried! See!
Brünnhilde greets thee in bliss.

She has mounted her horse and now urges it into the flames, in which it disappears with its rider. The fire blazes up till the Hall itself is alight and parts of the building come crashing down. But at this moment the Rhine suddenly overflows its banks, extinguishing the flames. On the bosom of the flood are borne the Rhine Maidens, who are seen circling over the place where the pyre has been. Hagen, who has been watching events in growing alarm, dashes into the water with a cry of " Give back the Ring ! " But one of the Maidens already holds the talisman, and the other two encircle the murderer with their arms and drag him with them into the depths. Meanwhile a glow in the sky betokens a new and mightier portent. The awestruck watchers raise their eyes, and behold, heaven itself is aflame! The stately pile of Valhalla is clearly visible for a moment with the gods and heroes seated in the great Hall. Then the whole is lost in a seething ocean of fire. The doom is accomplished, the struggle of ages ended at last.

Such is the massive grandeur of the ' Death March ' that it seems impossible that the opera should continue without an anticlimax. But this last Scene takes us a step farther still. Wagner's genius rises easily on strong wings of inspiration and provides us with a *finale* that for sustained elevation of thought stands quite alone. The stagecraft may be clumsy and even childish, the poetry no more than second-rate, but these things matter little. It is the music that signifies, the music that, soaring above the petty limitations of the empyrean, grasps the whole universe in its invisible fingers. It is not a mere human tragedy that we have witnessed, it is the end of an Æon, of a dispensation, in which a whole heaven and earth have gone down in irretrievable catastrophe.

The music of *The Ring* shows, as has been already hinted, a steady progress throughout. *The Rhinegold* was the first opera that Wagner had written since *Lohengrin,* and in it we see the fruits of the years of thought that had intervened since the completion of the earlier work. The *leit-motif* system which is applied only tentatively in *Lohengrin* appears in its completeness in *The Rhinegold.* The only defect is a slight awkwardness in the handling of the *motifs,* which occasionally degenerate into little more than labels. But in this and other respects the treatment becomes steadily firmer as the great work proceeds, until we reach the supreme mastery of the Third Act of *Siegfried.* The level of *The Dusk of the Gods* is not so consistently high. Wagner was handicapped by a libretto written years before, when his experience was much less than it had now become. We notice, too, that the new themes that are here introduced (chiefly in connexion with the Gibichungs) are not always so distinctive as those with which we are already familiar, and a suspicion grows that some of the material for this opera has been taken straight from the old abandoned score of " Siegfried's Death." There is yet another point worth mentioning. The very number of the *motifs* constitutes a difficulty in *The Dusk of the Gods.* More than a hundred have been classified, and it is almost impossible for any of the characters to make a remark without evoking one of them. This *embarras de richesse* seriously interferes with the musical continuity, and there are times when we feel we are listening to something that is more like a catalogue of *motifs* than a connected work of art. On the other hand, the piece contains, as we have seen, moments of such stupendous power as to eclipse even the greatest things in the earlier scores.

Brünnhilde is surely the most glorious heroine in all opera. In Wagner's own work there is no one who can possibly be mentioned in the same breath with her, except, perhaps, Isolde—and Isolde is of the earth, earthy, compared to Brünnhilde. But the Valkyrie maiden is the only character in *The Ring* who really succeeds in arousing our sympathy, and, though we would do a great deal for her sake, it is surely too much to expect us to bear with all the large circle of her friends and relatives. A more exasperating collection of people it would be hard to find anywhere. Wotan, of course, is the worst offender : the length and prolixity of his egotistical discourses put him in a class by himself. But none of the party is really attractive. Which of us, for instance, would not gladly give one half of our worldly goods for an afternoon on the river with Brünnhilde, and as cheerfully surrender the other half to avoid the prospect of a round of golf with Siegfried ? Of the terribly complicated tangle in which all these people get involved it is sufficient to say that this is not the stuff that plays are made of. Even Wagner got tired of unravelling it at last, so he effectually put an end to the story by getting rid of all his characters, human and divine, in one universal cataclysm—a simple but not very satisfactory solution.

The plain truth is that most of us find the drama as such a dreadful bore. No one would dream of bothering with *The Ring* if it were not for the music that accompanies it. Those portions of it where " the play's the thing "—or worse, where the dialogue's the thing—leave us quite unmoved, but the moment the music assumes the chief place our interest revives regardless of the dramatic situation. Those parts of the work with which the concert hall has made us familiar seem sure of immortality. Time alone can show whether the rest is aught more than the mortal coil. But if this indeed be so, it is a future generation that will attend its obsequies ; upon us and upon our children the mighty shadow of the master still lies too heavily. We may criticize his work, but we dare not yet venture to tamper with it. The ultimate verdict we can be content to leave to posterity.

PARSIFAL

Words and Music by WAGNER.
Bayreuth, 1882 ; *New York*, 1903 ; *London*, 1912.

THE vicissitudes of *Parsifal*, Wagner's last great work, form one of the most interesting chapters in operatic history. Finished in January 1882, and produced on the 26th of July in the same year, it appeared at a time when the composer's reputation was fully established, and in the ordinary course of events would soon have found its way into all the principal opera houses of Europe and America. But this was not to be. The singular regulations by which it was protected forbade its performance at any other theatre save the Wagner theatre at Bayreuth (the scene of the original production) for a period of no less than thirty years. It thus became inaccessible, except in a few concert selections, to the musical world at large, and there quickly grew up round it a kind of legend, sedulously encouraged by the select band of pilgrims to Bayreuth, in the romantic light of which it soon came to be regarded as an almost supernatural revelation having little or nothing in common with ordinary operatic affairs. An unscrupulous impresario took advantage of the fact that the copyright did not include America to produce *Parsifal* in New York in 1903 ; but for the European public the veil of mystery was not lifted till the monopoly expired in 1912. Many of us can remember the excitement which this created and the thrill that went through Covent Garden Theatre on that memorable night as the violins took up the first strain of the Prelude and we settled ourselves to what was for most of us a new opera by Richard Wagner.

But though *Parsifal* had left its shrine and was here to be heard, seen, and criticized by everybody, the old atmosphere still clung about it. The absolute novelty of the subject as a theme for operatic treatment was itself an obstacle to the estimation of its real value, for there seemed at first to be no criterion by which it could be judged. It contained, moreover, certain elements that diverted attention from its æsthetic aspects, and the controversy which presently arose was as much concerned with religion and propriety as with the problems of music-drama. Even to-day the battle still rages fiercely as to whether or not the story of *Parsifal* is suitable for representation in the theatre, and in the midst of this fog of war it is difficult for the mere musician to see his way. But let us take heart. After all, one fog is much like another, and we may profit by the example of the prudent Londoner as he threads the murky thoroughfares of his smoke-shrouded city on a typical January afternoon. Being only concerned with the musical and dramatic side of the discussion let us keep strictly to the curb, refusing to be drawn into any digression, however enticing the prospect may appear.

Parsifal, then, is an opera based on the story of the Holy Grail. Its hero is the Sir Percival of Tennyson, and Wagner tells us of the adventures by which he rose to become the leader of the Knights of the Grail and guardian of the castle's treasure. The temptation to link the drama with *Lohengrin* is a strong one, but in reality the connexion is very slight. Lohengrin, it is true, claims Parsifal as his father, but there is no mention in *Parsifal* of Lohengrin, who could not have been born until long after the action of the play is finished. As to the music, the points in common are so few as to be negligible for our purpose.

The Prelude is constructed on the simplest possible lines and makes use of only three themes, all of them associated with the Grail. The first (usually labelled ' The Love-feast of the Knights ') is played four times, twice in the major, and twice in the minor. The second (familiar as ' The Dresden Amen ') represents the Grail itself. The third (announced on the trombone and subjected to considerable development) is the theme of Faith. A return to the ' Love-feast ' idea immediately precedes the rise of the curtain. This reveals a forest in the Grail's domain with a lake at the back. In the middle is a glade, on the floor of which the old hermit, Gurnemanz, and two esquires are lying asleep. Gurnemanz is awakened by a solemn call on the trombones ; he rouses the esquires, and the three kneel and offer up their morning prayer. This done, they hasten to prepare for their King, who will soon be coming to take his morning bath in the lake and whose advent is even now heralded by the arrival of two of his knights. But here there is a weird interruption : a woman comes hurriedly in, unkempt and with dark, piercing eyes. In her hand she holds a small vial which she presses on Gurnemanz, bidding him offer it to the King—for the King, as all know, is afflicted by a grievous wound which defies every attempt to heal it. The woman, whose name is Kundry, then throws herself exhausted on the ground, just as the litter that bears King Amfortas is carried in and set down on the stage. Amfortas has almost ceased to hope for a cure—herbs and balsams from far and wide have been tried in vain. There is, indeed, a prophecy that help will come at last, at the hands of some mysterious visitant, a simple soul,

> Made wise through pity,
> And pure in heart,

but he has given up speculating what this obscure saying

may signify. Gurnemanz offers him Kundry's vial, and
he turns painfully to thank her for it, but the strange
woman only bids him begone to his bath, and wearily he
gives the signal to proceed.

Kundry's behaviour has not inspired the esquires with
confidence, and as soon as the King has gone they begin
to abuse her openly, accusing her of bringing misfor-
tunes upon them all by her wickedness. But Gurnemanz
rebukes them, recalling the many occasions on which she
has loyally helped them. He falls into a mood of reminis-
cence, in which he gradually unfolds the whole story of
the Grail. The two treasures of the castle were the
sacred Cup from which Our Lord drank at the Last
Supper, and the Spear which pierced His side. These
were delivered in a vision to Titurel, Amfortas' father,
and it was he who built the castle to contain them and
enrolled the band of knights for their defence. Among
those who sought admission to the fraternity was Klingsor, but as he lacked the essential singleness of heart
Titurel would have none of him. Enraged by his rejection, Klingsor turned to the black arts and raised by the
power of sorcery a garden of fair women to lure the
knights to their undoing. In time Titurel grew old and
bequeathed his kingdom to his son, Amfortas. But
Amfortas proved no match for Klingsor ; he allowed
himself to be enticed away by a woman of wondrous
beauty, and in his absence Klingsor secured the Spear.
He even succeeded in wounding the King with the stolen
weapon, and it might have gone hard with him had
not Gurnemanz himself been drawn to the scene by his
master's cry. Amfortas' life was saved, but the wound,
as they know, had refused to heal. Meanwhile the Spear
remains in Klingsor's hands and the sorcerer is plotting
to obtain the Grail itself.

Gurnemanz has no sooner finished than an outcry is heard from the lake. A wounded swan flutters weakly in and sinks dying on the stage, an arrow in its breast. All wild life is sacred in the domain of the Grail, and it is not long before the esquires have caught and brought in the author of the outrage. It is a young lad whose mien shows him to be utterly unconscious of having done anything wrong; but he is not lacking in sensibility, and at Gurnemanz' grave reproof his naïve pride in his archery turns quickly to remorse. His eyes fill with tears, and impulsively he breaks his bow and throws away his arrows. Questions elicit the astonishing fact that he knows neither his father's name nor his own. His mother he has but lately left, and after wandering through many wild places has come at last all unknowing to the holy mountain. His narrative rouses unexpected interest in Kundry, who betrays also a surprising acquaintance with his history. Now she startles him with the grievous news that his mother is dead; at this he exhibits the deepest emotion and seems about to faint, but she revives him with water and then herself sinks down as though overcome with emotion, while the sinister theme of Enchantment winds sinuously through the tissue of the music.

At this point the curtain usually descends, and it is left to the orchestra to lead us to the Hall or Temple of the Grail, in which the second Scene takes place. Wagner, indeed, directs that the stage itself should move, and that the young man and Gurnemanz should be seen walking, with a shifting panorama as a background, till they reach the castle. But in performance this device is horribly clumsy and most producers wisely leave it out.

The music has now assumed a grave and stately character, and the deep tones of bells increase the general

feeling of solemnity. The Hall is empty when Gurnemanz and the boy first arrive, but it soon begins to fill
with knights, who enter in dignified procession and take
their places at tables ranged round the walls. It is the
hour of the sacred rite. Amfortas is borne in to a choral
accompaniment and assisted to a couch in front of the
draped altar at the back. And now, when all is ready,
there is heard from a recess behind Amfortas' couch
the voice of the aged Titurel, speaking as though from
the tomb. He bids his son reveal the Grail, the sight of
which alone keeps him alive. But with an agonized cry
the tortured Amfortas raises himself in vehement protest.
The blessed spectacle which is joy and peace to them
is torment unspeakable to him, the accursed, who must
stand and minister to them while his tainted blood flows
wildly through his veins till it escapes by the gaping wound.
His magnificent outburst concludes with a prayer for
pardon and death, and he sinks down exhausted. But his
madness passes with his strength, and presently, rallying
his forces, he bows to the inward call. The shrine is
uncovered, revealing a crystal Cup, while a sudden darkness fills the Hall. Soon a dazzling ray falls from above,
the sacred vessel glows with a soft light, and Amfortas
lifts and waves it slowly from side to side, thus consecrating the bread and wine. Then he replaces it once
more on the altar, the covering falls, and daylight slowly
returns. The knights and esquires raise their voices in a
solemn hymn while the consecrated elements are dis-
tributed; but Amfortas falls weakly back, and the move-
ments of his attendants show that the wound has broken
out afresh. Presently he is assisted to his litter and borne
slowly from the Hall, the knights following behind.

Of all this scene Gurnemanz and his companion have
been silent but attentive witnesses. At its conclusion the

lad is so overwhelmed that he can offer no reply to the hermit's questions, and irritated by his seeming stupidity the old man pushes him angrily from the Hall, while a voice from above repeats the prophecy of him who is to come—the simple soul " made wise through pity, and pure in heart." There is a lovely choral cadence and the curtain falls.

Act II. It is in a very different atmosphere that the Second Act opens. The Prelude paints for us a horror of deep darkness, through which the coils of the Enchantment *motif* are ceaselessly writhing. At intervals, too, there is heard a descending *arpeggio*, like a shout of fiendish laughter. The stage, when we see it, is wrapped in profound gloom, and it is only with great difficulty that we discern the interior of the keep of Klingsor's magic castle, strewn with the apparatus of sorcery. The magician himself can just be distinguished at one side—half hidden in wreaths of strange, blue vapour, he is invoking some presence from the depths below. It is Kundry whom he summons and who seems to rise slowly from the shadows, her eyes closed as though in sleep. Waking suddenly, she utters a terrible cry and then a wail of misery and fear. Klingsor taunts her with her devoted service to the Knights of the Grail, and we learn that it was she who under his mighty spell lured Amfortas to his ruin. Now he calls her to a new task. Between him and the Grail, the object of his foul ambition, he sees but one obstacle, the youth who is even now approaching the castle walls—let her but rob him of his purity and the battle is won. Kundry refuses, and then ensues a mighty conflict of wills. But Klingsor's magic is strong, and at last with a shriek she vanishes, to carry out his behests. Already from his window the sorcerer has watched the new enemy scale the ramparts and disperse the castle's defenders. The time for the real trial of strength has arrived.

Suddenly the whole tower seems to sink into the earth, Klingsor with it, and in its place appears an enchanted garden, filled with strange and lovely flowers. In it stands the young man, of whose ignominious ejection from the Hall of the Grail we were so lately witnesses. The contrast with the preceding Scene is complete, and it is heightened by the sudden irruption from all sides of groups of ' Flower-maidens,' clad in light, diaphanous garments. We need not follow these dainty creatures in their successive attitudes of fear, shyness, and ardour toward the comely stranger. He is willing enough to play with them, but he remains utterly unconscious of their efforts to seduce him. One of Klingsor's weapons has failed ; now he employs another, the strongest in his armoury.

From out of the foliage is heard the voice of Kundry, and soon her form becomes visible through an opening. It is a transformed Kundry that we behold, reclining luxuriously on a couch. Gone are the wild garb and penitent mien, and in their place we perceive rich silks, soft outlines, and an attitude of voluptuous charm. Her advent puts an immediate end to the fairy-like episode of the Flower-maidens. They disappear as swiftly as they came, so that the bewildered lad, looking round the empty stage, is moved to murmur, " Of all this did I now but dream ? " However, he has no time to waste in idle speculations—Kundry's first words have given him other food for thought. She has called him by his name, ' Parsifal,' and now she is telling him of his unknown history with an intimate familiarity that be-speaks a first-hand knowledge. He hears how his father was slain in battle, and how Heart-Sorrow (Herzeleid), his mother, reared him, far from the stormy ways of men. And then, too, he is reminded how he left her to languish and at last to die under a burden of grief too heavy to bear.

All this is part of a carefully laid plot. Parsifal is naturally moved by the tale, and it is while he is defence-less under the stress of emotion that Kundry, whispering that she comes to him as his mother's last gift, bends over him and presses a long kiss on his lips. For a moment her plan seems to have succeeded. But suddenly, with a loud cry, " Amfortas ! the Spear-wound ! " Parsifal starts up. That burning embrace and the pain it brings have shed a flood of light on his mind. He sees once more, as in a vision, the scene in the Hall of the Grail, and sees it for the first time with a full understanding of its significance. Kundry's attempts to lead his imagination back to thoughts of passion only serve to explain to him the exact nature of Amfortas' temptation, and he pushes her angrily away. But her resources are not yet ex-hausted, and she next appeals to his pity by telling him of the curse under which she labours. Back through the centuries her story takes her to that day, dim ages ago, when she watched a condemned Man staggering beneath His Cross on the road to Golgotha :

> Then laughed I !
> On me fell His look. . . .
> I seek Him now from world to world—
> Yet once more to behold Him.
> In darkest hour ween I that the hour is near,
> His eye on me doth rest;
> Then once more the accursed laugh outbreaketh,
> A sinner falls upon my bosom ! [1]

But now, at long last, she has found one who will

[1] These extracts from the English version are printed by kind permission of Messrs Schott and Co.

redeem her. Let her but for one hour bewail her sins upon his breast and all will be forgotten.

Parsifal, however, is by this time fully conscious of his mission and sees clearly how it is to be performed. He offers her not comfort but deliverance, and that is not to be achieved by indulgence in a guilty passion. To all her burning words he replies only with a stern rebuke and a request to be shown the way back to Amfortas. At that she turns on him with all the fury of thwarted desire, curses his homeward road which she swears he shall never find, and calls Klingsor to come to her assistance. The sorcerer appears on the battlements grasping the Holy Spear, which he hurls with an angry taunt at Parsifal's unprotected form. But the weapon miraculously changes its course and remains suspended in the air over the young man's head. Seizing it in his hand, " he swings it in the sign of the Cross. The castle falls as by an earthquake ; the garden withers to a desert ; the ground is scattered with faded flowers ; Kundry sinks down with a cry." Parsifal, turning to go, has but one word for the stricken woman,

> Thou knowest where thou canst meet with me again.

Act III. Once more we are in the domain of the Grail, close to Gurnemanz' hut, which is seen at the back of the stage. The pleasant freshness of spring is over the landscape, but there is no joy in the face of the hermit as he emerges from his door. A long time has elapsed since last we saw him, and he is now a very old man. His ear has caught the sound of groans, and, going to a thicket, he pulls aside the undergrowth and peers within. Then, bending forward, he pulls out the unconscious form of Kundry, stiff and cold. However, he is successful in his efforts to revive her, and presently she opens her eyes and sits up with a cry. She is dressed in the robe of a penitent, and the wildness has gone from her look. To the old man's inquiries she gives only two muttered words in reply, " Service ! Service ! "

There now appears striding slowly from the wood a man encased from head to foot in black armour, a lowered spear in his hand. He seems worn and weary, and at first vouchsafes no answer to Gurnemanz' welcome. But when the hermit tells him it is Good Friday morning he lays down his weapons, raises his vizor, and kneels in silent prayer. His face is now visible, and the old man recognizes him as Parsifal returned. His devotions over, the wanderer greets him and acquaints him briefly with his story : how, driven from his path by the power of Kundry's curse, he has roamed the world over and encountered innumerable perils in defence of the sacred weapon he carries. Even now he scarcely dare hope that his journey is near its end.

Gurnemanz is overcome with a transport of joy at the thought that the Spear is recovered. He assures Parsifal that it is indeed the Grail's domain that he has reached, and gives him in his turn an account of how the brotherhood has fared. It is a gloomy tale. In the vain hope of winning death by denying himself the sight of the holy Cup Amfortas has refused to perform his office. For long the Grail has lain in its shrine, unseen by mortal eyes, while the strength of its knights has languished and the aged Titurel passed sadly to his grave. The emotion caused by this news is more than Parsifal's exhausted body can bear, and he sinks to the ground supported in Gurnemanz's arms. Aided by Kundry, the old man refreshes him with water from the holy spring and washes away the stains of travel. Soon he recovers and asks to be taken to Amfortas, who, he hears, is this day to officiate yet once more before the altar in honour of his dead father. But the others have not yet finished their ministrations, and he gazes in mild wonder at Kundry, who pours some of the contents of a golden vial over his feet and wipes them with her unbound hair. Taking the vial from her he bids Gurnemanz anoint his head, thus consecrating him King of the Grail and its people. This is duly done, and the first use he makes of his authority is to baptize Kundry, who falls weeping on the ground.

It is here that the sweet, celestial strains of the Good Friday music begin to be heard, throwing a gentle radiance over the score. The words of Parsifal and Gurnemanz celebrating the joy of nature in man's gratitude for his redemption have given its title to this tender intermezzo. But it is of the fresh purity of the trees and flowers decked in their spring garment of green that the music sings to us in a pastoral symphony whose idyllic beauty is untroubled by any hint of grief or suffering.

Parsifal is invested with the mantle of a Knight of the Grail, and with Gurnemanz and Kundry in attendance sets out for the castle. A transformation scene, similar to that in Act I, takes place, while the orchestra commemorates the death of Titurel in a gloomy march. When we reach the Hall, which is only dimly lighted, we find the ceremony just starting. The knights advance in two processions, the one bearing Amfortas and the shrouded Grail, the others the coffin containing the body of Titurel. In a solemn antiphonal hymn they heap their grave reproaches on their recreant ruler, and in reply Amfortas, raising himself on his couch, invokes the soul of his father in an appeal for death in which the dignity of suffering and passionate despair are finely blended. But the impatient knight breaks in on his soliloquy,

bidding him perform his office. "Unveil the Grail!
Thou must! thou must!"

With a mighty "No!" Amfortas rises to his feet.
Maddened by pain and misery he rushes among them,
tearing open his garments and bidding them bury their
weapons in his sinful heart. His sudden movement and
the wild light of ecstasy burning in his eyes fill the knights
with consternation, and they shrink back in fear. We
have reached the supreme climax of the work. Parsifal,
who has entered unobserved, comes forward with quiet
confidence and touches with the Spear-point the wound
that Amfortas' gesture has revealed :

> Only one weapon serves :
> The Spear that smote must heal thee of thy wound.
> Be whole, absolved, and atoned !
> For I do hold thy office now.

Amfortas reels, his face transfigured with hope and holy
joy, while Gurnemanz supports him in his arms. Parsifal
moves toward the centre and displays on high the sacred
Spear. Then he ascends the altar steps and firmly bids
the esquires reveal the Grail. Amid murmurs of wonder
and thanksgiving he takes in his hands the holy Cup,
which shines softly in the growing darkness; the radiance descends from above, and in it a white dove is seen
hovering over Parsifal's head. Whilst all are kneeling,
wrapt in adoration, Kundry sinks lifeless to the ground,
a look of divine peace lighting up her face. The curse is
lifted, her expiation accomplished.

Whether Wagner has entirely succeeded in producing a
masterpiece out of this material may be doubted. To
many people the different elements in *Parsifal* appear
not only diverse but actually incongruous. It is true
that in mediæval times incidents from Holy Writ were

often presented in dramatic form, and there seems no logical objection to a composer taking a sacred theme for an operatic work. But since the time of the liturgical dramas the Church and the Theatre have become more and more sharply differentiated when regarded from an æsthetic standpoint. By the end of the 17th century opera and oratorio were already distinct, and the tendency since has been to emphasize the contrast. Wagner's methods, with his direct appeal to the emotions and his reliance on elaborate stage machinery, are utterly antagonistic to the restrained dignity that characterizes true ecclesiastical music.

The result is that *Parsifal* falls between two stools. In the Scenes in Acts I and III where the liturgical element is strong, the intensely theatrical management of the lighting (not to mention the appearance of the dove) strikes a jarring note that is unpleasant. The cathedral, we feel, and not the opera house, is the place for this music. And yet when we hear parts of it in a sacred building we are surprised to find how greatly it suffers from the absence of the setting designed for it by the composer.

We are thus faced at the outset by a serious dilemma regarding the presentation of the work. This would not greatly matter if the music were of the consistent excellence that we find in *The Mastersingers*. But, unfortunately, this is not so. There are moments in *Parsifal* (such as the Prelude and the Grail Scene in Act I, all the first half of Act II, and the Good Friday music and the *finale* in Act III) which will bear comparison with anything that Wagner wrote, but the rest shows a fitfulness of inspiration that is not without significance, perhaps, when we remember that this is the composer's last work. The arid wastes of Gurnemanz' discourses we may possibly pass over. There are things to match them elsewhere, notably in *The Ring*. But the lack of fertility in the invention of new *motifs* that is apparent in the last two Acts, and the scarcity of those great tunes that so amply compensate for the dull patches in the earlier works, are more difficult to account for on any supposition but that of waning genius. It is not that the master has lost his grip : his command of his material, his disposition of his orchestral forces, remain unimpaired, and the Scene in the Hall of the Grail and the Flower-maidens episode are examples of supreme craftsmanship such as he alone could give us. But though his foot does not falter, his step seems, at times, to have lost its spring.

And yet, when criticism has done its worst, we are left with something that the world cannot possibly afford to lose—and the world has a way of sticking to its treasures in spite of the critics. The method by which it will preserve the nobler parts of *Parsifal* it is impossible to predict. But the popularity of the concert hall excerpts may, perhaps, afford a hint.

HÄNSEL UND GRETEL

Music by HUMPERDINCK. *Words by* FRAU A. WETTE.
Weimar, 1893 ; *London,* 1895 ; *New York,* 1895.

*H*ÄNSEL UND GRETEL is a work that can safely be recommended to all opera-goers, young and old. The unsophisticated will enjoy the gentle, artless story and rich flow of easily grasped melodies, while the seasoned expert will find a rarer pleasure in seeing the Wagnerian method so happily adapted to such novel material. To a mind wearied by a sustained effort to grapple with the complications of Wagner's colossal masterpieces, nothing could be more refreshing than Humperdinck's little work. Anyone who goes once is sure to go again, and he will discover a new delight as he gradually realizes with what firm and cunning art the gossamer threads of the musical texture have been held and interwoven. But the atmosphere of freshness and innocent charm which struck him so pleasantly at the first hearing will still persist, as it is happily of a kind which does not soon grow stale.

It has been said that *Hänsel und Gretel* is the one successful opera based on a whole-hearted acceptance of Wagner's principles. The truth of this is too obvious to need discussion. Not only did Humperdinck openly avow his allegiance to Wagnerian methods and, in accordance with these, choose a story that is as much a part of Teutonic legend as the *Nibelungenlied*, but the music itself bears eloquent witness to his discipleship. The use he makes of the Prayer theme with which the Prelude opens, the way he builds up the whole of his first Scene

on the little melody to which Gretel sings her opening
song, are quite in the manner of Wagner. But the
differences between the two writers are hardly less interesting than the similarities. Wagner could never have set
Hänsel und Gretel; his methods were too heroic. Even
in *Die Meistersinger* his laughter is that of a giant, and
this fragile fairy-story of two children and a witch would
have crumpled and collapsed under the weight of his
prodigious genius; Humperdinck's gentler nature was
far better suited to deal with such materials. For evidence of this we need look no farther than the tunes he
uses. Nearly all of them are beautiful flowing melodies,
many of considerable length, and as different from the
short, pithy phrases that are characteristic of the Wagnerian *motifs* as can well be imagined. Occasionally, it is
true, Wagner uses a more lyrical type of utterance—the
Prize Song is a conspicuous example—but with him
this is exceptional. Humperdinck's themes are almost all
lyrical, as befits his subject, and two of them, Gretel's
songs at the beginning of Acts I and II, are genuine folk-
melodies.

The libretto is the work of Frau Adelheid Wette, the
composer's sister, and was originally written for performance at a private gathering. Humperdinck provided
music for it in this form, and was so charmed by the effect
that he induced his sister to remodel it for a public
production, himself rewriting the music, and the result
is the opera as we know it.

The Prelude prepares us for what is to come, being
constructed out of themes that play an important part
later on. The first of these is the simple and touching
Prayer theme to which I have already referred, and it
defines at once the childlike atmosphere in which the
opera is going to move. When the curtain goes up we

see Hänsel and Gretel in their parents' cottage. The
room is small and poorly furnished. By the door sits
Hänsel, making brooms. Gretel is knitting a stocking by
the fireplace, and as she knits she sings an old song. It
is about the geese ; why have the poor geese no shoes ?
The cobbler has plenty of leather, but, alack, he has no
last to fit a goose's foot. Hänsel takes up the same air,
but changes the words and says how hungry he is, and
this leads to a short dialogue on the subject of their
poverty, in which we should notice the appearance of the
Prayer theme to Gretel's words :

> When past bearing is our grief,
> God the Lord will send relief.[1]

She succeeds in chasing away her brother's fit of depression,
and then tells him a great secret : a neighbour has brought
them a jug of milk for their dinner ! Hänsel is tempted
to taste it, but is rebuked by his virtuous sister, who thinks
they ought to get on with their work. This isn't Hänsel's
idea at all—he would like to dance ; to this suggestion
Gretel succumbs, and there follows a charming duet and
dance, to music that is closely related to the song with
which the Act opened. At last in their excitement they
tumble over one another and fall on the floor, and it is
there that their mother finds them when she comes in a
moment later. She is tired after a hard day's work and
is naturally annoyed to find the children have been wasting
their time. Unfortunately, while she is lecturing them,
she knocks over the milk-jug. It falls with a crash,
spilling the milk down her dress, and is broken to bits
on the floor. Now what are they to have for supper ?
Despair is in her heart, but she pulls herself together

---

[1] These extracts from the English version are printed by kind permission of Messrs Schott and Co.

and sends Hänsel and Gretel out into the wood to gather a basket of strawberries. As soon as they have gone she bursts into tears, overcome with misery. At the same moment the voice of the father outside is heard; he comes in trolling a song, slightly tipsy, and in the highest spirits; he has had a most successful day, done a roaring trade selling his brooms, and brought home a whole load of delicacies for the family table. His wife is inclined to be sharp with him at first, but soon regains her temper when she hears his story and sees the contents of his basket. Then the conversation turns to the children, and the broom-maker indulges in a hearty laugh when he hears about the episode of the milk-jug. " But where are the children now ? " he asks. " At the Ilsenstein for aught I know," replies his wife. " The Ilsenstein ! " he repeats, horror-struck. What ? Doesn't she know ? That is where the witch lives, the ' Gobbling Ogress,' who catches little children, puts them into her oven, and bakes them into gingerbread! With a cry of dismay the mother, closely followed by the father, dashes out into the wood in search of Hänsel and Gretel.

Act II. The orchestra opens the Second Act with a very graphic picture of a witches' ride. This is quite an extended composition, but eventually the music becomes calmer and more pastoral in character until at last the curtain rises. We are in the heart of the forest; it is sunset; under a large tree sits Gretel, making a garland of wild roses, and singing another song from the treasure-house of German folk-lore. As soon as she has finished, Hänsel, who has been picking strawberries among the bushes, comes out, his basket nearly full. Playfully he crowns her Queen of the Wood, only admonishing her not to eat the fruit of his labours. The sound of a cuckoo is heard in the distance, and this gives them the idea of playing at being cuckoos who eat their neighbours' eggs. Unfortunately they pretend the strawberries are the eggs, and before they know where they are the basket is empty again. Their first idea is to gather some more, but suddenly they notice that it is already getting dark— there is nothing for it but to go home. They prepare to do so, but Hänsel is appalled to find that he has forgotten the way. For a moment he is horribly frightened, but he pulls himself together and puts on an affected boldness to reassure his terrified sister. He gives a shout, as much to keep up his own spirits as out of any hope of its being answered, but only the echoes reply, and Gretel's fears, which make her imagine that the shadows are peopled by all sorts of evil shapes, begin to communicate themselves to him. The climax is reached when there actually does appear a little grey man with a tiny sack on his back. However, he means them no ill. He is the Sandman, the Sleep-fairy, and as he draws near he soothes the children with friendly gestures and then, scattering some sand upon their eyes, sings them his lullaby of peace and security. By the time he has finished they are both half asleep, but before they lie down they fall on their knees and repeat their evening prayer, beginning :

> When at night I go to sleep
> Fourteen angels watch do keep.

It is the most charming moment in the opera.

Their little act of worship over, the children go to sleep in each other's arms, but the mists that have arisen at the back of the stage are pierced by a beam of light, and a stairway is revealed down which there come the fourteen angels of the prayer. They group themselves round the sleepers, while the light gets steadily brighter, and are joined by other angels, till at length the curtain descends upon a radiant scene of celestial glory.

Act III. It is in this final Act that most of the real drama takes place. The first strains of the orchestra give us the witch's theme, a concise phrase of seven notes, more closely resembling a Wagnerian *motif* than anything else in the opera. At the end of the Introduction we are shown the same scene as in the previous Act, only now it is early morning; the angels have vanished, and the background is wrapped in a mist, out of which there steps the Dew-fairy, singing a song not unlike the Sandman's, and shaking a dewdrop from a bluebell on to the children. Presently Gretel awakes, and rubbing her eyes looks round her sleepily. The Fairy has gone, and the girl is greeted by the song of the lark. Soon she rouses her brother; she has had a lovely dream of angels, she tells him, and is astonished when she hears that he has shared it. But at this moment Hänsel turns round and gives a cry of astonishment—the mist has cleared away, and in the background stands the witch's house, all made of tasty delicacies and surrounded by a fence of gingerbread children. On one side is a cage and on the other an immense oven. After a joyous duet they gain courage and trip forward to have a taste, while the trumpets in the orchestra give out a reference to the Prayer theme, as if to suggest that the children are still under invisible angelic protection. Soon the witch's voice is heard from the house, but they attribute the sound to their imagination and go on eating, so that she is able to steal up and throw a rope round Hänsel's neck before he realizes what has happened. To his horror he finds himself drawn close to her, Gretel following, and has to listen to her somewhat lengthy invitation to come and enjoy the delights that lie inside the house. But meanwhile he has managed to get clear of the rope, and he and Gretel suddenly start to run away, only to be stopped as the witch casts a spell upon them :

> Hocus pocus, witches' charm !
> Move not, as you fear my arm !

Hänsel is led into the cage, there to be fattened up, while Gretel remains to do the witch's bidding. All the boy can do is to take advantage of the hag's momentary absence to warn his sister to keep her wits about her with a view to saving them both. The witch comes out, and in order that Gretel may help her to get things ready she disenchants her :

> Hocus pocus, elder-bush !
> Rigid body loosen !

and sends her off to the kitchen. While she is away the old woman relieves her feelings by a really horrible broomstick dance. She then takes a look at Hänsel to see whether he is fat enough to be eaten. Gretel must go first, she decides ! At this moment the girl returns from the kitchen, and seizing her opportunity while the witch's back is turned, disenchants her brother with the counter-charm she has just heard used on herself. Presently the hag bids her have a look in the oven to see how the dough is getting on, but, warned by Hänsel, who perceives the danger, Gretel assumes a sham stupidity and thus persuades the witch to go and look for herself. The children come up behind, give her a push, and into the oven she goes while they hastily fasten the door upon her ! Then, leaving her to bake, they dance the delightful ' Witch Waltz.' Suddenly with a loud bang the oven bursts, and a moment later Hänsel and Gretel see with astonishment that they are surrounded by children, whose disguise of gingerbread has fallen from them with the witch's death.

The rest of the story is quickly told. Gretel awakes the children, Hänsel speedily disenchants them, and with a chorus of thanks they crowd round their rescuers. Soon the voice of the father is heard, and very shortly he and the mother appear on the scene. They are overwhelmed with joy to find their children, for whom they have been searching all night, safe and sound. From the ruins of the oven the witch is dragged, baked to a gingerbread; and finally, as the curtain descends, all unite in a hymn of thanks for their deliverance.

There are many operas more impressive and more ambitious than *Hänsel und Gretel*, but none that has caught so happily the simple charm of the fairy-story and the elusive freshness of childhood.

BORIS GODOUNOV

Music by MOUSSORGSKY. *Words from* PUSHKIN.
St Petersburg, 1874 ; *London,* 1913 ; *New York,* 1913.

THE widespread popularity of this opera is not easy to account for at first sight. It is hardly a play at all in the generally accepted sense of the word ; several of its many scenes are entirely taken up with elaborate *tableaux* that do nothing to forward the action of the drama, while others are occupied with picturesque incidents which, though interesting in themselves, bear little or no relation to the main outlines of the plot. Even the story itself, when we have succeeded in discovering it among the mass of irrelevant detail, appears extraordinarily austere. The love element which might have been used to lighten it is thrust remorselessly into the background, and the heroine (if such she can be called) is a lady with whom Moussorgsky has made it impossible for us to feel the slightest sympathy. We turn in dismay from the play to the music, only to encounter the same uncompromising sternness ; no overture, no orchestral interludes, grave, sparkling, or tender, as the occasion demands—nothing to break the monotony of the continuous recitative to which the dialogue is set but a few songs of the simplest possible kind, pleasant enough, no doubt, but entirely inadequate to leaven the huge mass in which they are embedded. Finally, we discover that the whole thing is marred by an angularity in the writing that often amounts to downright clumsiness. It must be a sovereign merit that can compensate for such an accumulation of defects. Where does it lie ?

To answer this question fully would require a more elaborate argument than there is space for in a book of this kind. But a few observations may not come amiss. In the first place let us remember that the main political events described in the opera actually took place much as Moussorgsky described them. Boris Godounov did in fact reign as Czar of Russia from 1598 to 1605. Modern research has, indeed, established that he was not implicated in the murder of Czarevitch Dimitri, for which the composer makes him responsible. But his guilt was widely believed at the time and for long afterward. We are thus witnessing a drama that is true in all but one of its main essentials.

This would signify little were it not for the peculiar cast of Moussorgsky's mind. The creator of *Boris Godounov* was, according to his lights, an ardent patriot, and a holder of democratic views, and a vehement believer in artistic realism. Beauty for beauty's sake meant little to him ; truth was his ideal, and in music and drama he identified truth with accurate representation. For a man of this sort the stock-in-trade of romantic opera possessed no attraction. The theme he sought must be true, or at least credible ; its material must be connected in some way with his beloved country ; and it should provide him with an opportunity for a display of that sympathy with an oppressed people that was one of the mainsprings of his character.

In the story of the Czar Boris as told by Pushkin he found what he wanted, and, undismayed by the vastness of his canvas or by the slenderness of his technical equipment, he set to work with all the eagerness of an enthusiast. But it would not do to treat it in the manner of conventional opera with overture, chorus, aria, and the rest: that would be artificial and unworthy of an honest

artist. The play must begin at once with the minimum
of orchestral prologue, and the instruments must confine
themselves throughout to supporting the tones of the
voice. The singers themselves must employ a recitative
approaching as near as may be to the modulations of
spoken speech. Set songs and choruses may be inter-
polated on occasion (as in a Shakespeare play), but only
when the dramatic situation permits. Nor must the
story itself be allowed to degenerate into a romantic
eulogy of a bloodthirsty tyrant; the real hero of the
piece must be the suffering, persecuted people, down-
trodden and harried, hopeless, without a leader, and yet
the one solid reality amid the welter of contending and
ephemeral faction. Crowded scenes will thus become an
important element in the work. As to the music, it will
maintain a distinctively Russian element throughout;
such songs as there are will generally be folk-songs or
composed in the folk style, while the choruses will consist
of well-known songs or hymns, except on such occasions
as it is desired to represent the wild shoutings of an
undisciplined crowd.

Except in the Third Act, which takes place in Poland,
and where, as we shall see, a more formal element crept
in, Moussorgsky was unswervingly faithful to his convictions. But his uncompromising honesty, while it accounts
for the character of the work, does not of itself explain
its greatness. To understand that we must realize first
that he was so saturated in the Russian folk music that
its idiom was to him, at least, as natural as the general
language of musical Europe. This in itself gives a
unique character to *Boris*. But there is something more:
Moussorgsky was a dramatic genius of the first order.
Not only does he share with other Russian composers
that gift for colour which enables him to deal effectively

with those scenes in which the crowd figures prominently; he is just as successful when there are only one or two characters on the stage. His recitative is so original, so powerful, that it never wearies us, even when labouring under the disadvantages inevitable to translation, and in the great moments, such as that of Boris' death, he rises to heights where he stands, in his own sphere, alone.

It has just been said that he was unswervingly faithful to his convictions. A single exception must be made. Moussorgsky seems to have been captivated to a certain extent by his tyrant, and Boris looms like a Titan over the whole drama. We may be grateful for this concession, since it provides a unifying element that is badly needed. But it has done more than this; it has provided an unparalleled opportunity to any singer who was great enough to act the part as well as sing it. How that opportunity was taken by Chaliapine many of us can remember. Certainly no one who saw his performance will ever forget it.

Prologue. The curtain rises on the courtyard of the monastery of Novodievich, near Moscow. Boris is supposed to be within the building. A bewildered crowd cries to him to have pity on his children, to accept the crown which is being offered to him and ascend the steps of the Russian throne. But there is no spirit in the singing at this ' officially arranged ' demonstration, and it is only the vigilant eyes of the police that keep things going. As to why they have been brought together or what it is they are praying for the poor folk have no idea. At last the clerk of the Duma comes out and announces that Boris has rejected the proffered honour. A band of pilgrims passes into the monastery. The curtain falls. When it rises again the people are once more assembled, this time in the courtyard of the Kremlin. Boris has now accepted the throne and his coronation is proceeding in the cathedral. The crowd are awaiting the conclusion of the ceremony and the return of the royal procession. Presently Boris appears, but the acclamations of his people are powerless to cheer the lonely, troubled heart of the new Czar. He offers up a short but impressive prayer for divine guidance, and passes on.

These two opening Scenes contain nothing in the nature of dramatic action and remind one more of episodes in a historical pageant than of the beginning of an opera. But they fulfil, nevertheless, the purpose that Moussorgsky had in view, and create a background that is never quite forgotten as the piece proceeds.

Act I. *Scene* 1. A cell in a monastery. Pimen, an old monk, is at work by lamplight, writing the last page of his chronicle, an account of the troubled times in which he has lived. A steadily moving, tortuous phrase in the orchestra represents his laborious penmanship. The silence of the night is unbroken but for some faint sounds from a choir that are heard for a moment in some distant wing of the building. In a corner of the room lies Gregory, a young monk, asleep. Suddenly he wakes, disturbed by an evil dream. Pimen calms him, and he questions the old man about his chronicle, about the past, and, above all, about the murdered Czarevitch, Dimitri. " He was about thy age—and would be reigning now," replies Pimen, " but God hath overruled it." The matin-bell begins to sound, and taking his staff the old man totters out. But his words have fired Gregory's imagination, and his last words before he follows his teacher are charged with import in view of what follows :

Boris ! Boris !   Princes may bow before thee,
And none so bold as to rebuke thee for
The death of that unhappy child.
Yet from the darkness of this lonely cell
A humble monk shall cry aloud thy secret !
Thou shalt not long escape from human justice,
And God from Heaven shall smite thee in his wrath ! [1]

Scene II. An inn on the Lithuanian frontier. The Hostess is sitting alone. To pass the time she sings a song :

I have caught a drake
With feathers of the blue !
Ah, what a joy to see
Is my little drake to me, etc.

She is interrupted by the entrance of two wandering friars, Missail and Varlaam. One must use the word friars, for there is no other that is appropriate ; but the reader must not be misled. The vagabond ruffians who roamed about Russia at this time calling themselves friars had little in common with the often saintly products of Western monasticism. Turbulent, unruly, and often actually criminal in their dispositions, they were one of the many scourges that flourished in a time when the government of the country was unsettled and the hand of authority weak. With them is Gregory. The young man has now definitely embarked upon his great adventure. He has left his monastery and is now on his way to Poland, where he intends to declare himself to be Dimitri the Czarevitch, escaped from the clutches of Boris and eager to unseat the usurper and regain the throne of his father.

The influence of the good wine which the Hostess sets before them makes Varlaam talkative. He was a soldier

[1] These extracts are from an English version by Paul England. All rights reserved.

once and served with the army of Ivan the Terrible at
the siege of Kazan. The song in which he describes
the capture of the city is a vigorous piece of work that
enjoys a well-deserved popularity. But the revels are
presently brought to a sudden conclusion. A knock is
heard heralding the arrival of the police, who have been
warned of Gregory's escape and have orders to apprehend
him. He is only saved by his quickness of wit. Taking
advantage of the fact that no one else can read, he takes
the warrant and so misrepresents its contents that suspicion
is momentarily diverted to Varlaam. Then, while all
are crowding round the friar, he makes a sudden dash for
the window and escapes into the night.

Act II. The interior of the Czar's apartments in the
Kremlin. Feodor and Xenia, Boris' son and daughter,
are shown in the charge of their old nurse. Xenia is
bewailing the loss of her affianced lover, and the nurse,
finding her attempts at consolation unavailing, tries to
distract her with a song. A charming interlude follows.
The nurse's song—a lot of absurd nonsense about a
midge, set to a lively tune—is capped by Feodor with a
' clapping song,' in which the nurse soon joins.

But now the little scene is brought abruptly to an end
by the entry of the Czar. Boris speaks a word of sympathy
to Xenia, and, bidding her seek solace among her young
companions, sends her to her chamber. Then he turns
to the Czarevitch. He is delighted to find that Feodor
has been studying a map ; the knowledge he is acquiring
will be useful to him some day—sooner, perhaps, than he
imagines. This train of thought leads to a magnificent
monologue beginning, " My power is absolute," in which
regret, remorse, terror, and an overwhelming sense of
guilt strive together in his tortured soul. He is interrupted by a sudden noise without and sends his son to

see what is the matter. The boy soon returns and relates the cause of the disturbance : it was only a parrot that flew at one of the nurses. But again the tender scene between father and son is broken into, this time by Prince Shouisky. He is the bringer of bad news : not only is there a revolt of Boyars, but a Pretender has arisen in Poland who calls himself Dimitri. At that name Boris sharply orders his son to withdraw. When they are alone he asks the Prince if he is quite sure the real Dimitri is dead. Shouisky reassures him on that point ; he actually saw the body of the murdered child and willingly describes the whole scene. But Boris, whose agitation is visibly increasing, cuts him short and dismisses him. The Czar is alone, and his overwrought nerves conjure up before him a hideous apparition of the boy he has so foully done to death. He starts back, clutches at his throat in an agony of terror, and then suddenly falls on his knees :

> God Almighty ! Thou that seekest not the death of a sinner,
> O spare thy servant. Have mercy on my guilty soul !

Act III transports us to Poland, and the curtain rises on the boudoir of Marina Mnishek, daughter of the Palatine of Sandomir. Her maidens attempt to amuse their Princess with a song, but she dismisses them abruptly when it is over and, left to herself, indulges in a long and rather tedious soliloquy. This is delivered to the rhythm of a mazurka, and in the course of it we learn that Gregory (who now calls himself Dimitri) is being sheltered by Marina's father and that the girl herself is inclined to look favourably upon him. This is in no way due to the promptings of her heart—Marina's hard nature is entirely incapable of any weakness of that kind. It is not on Dimitri himself that her desires are fixed, but on the throne of Moscow that he aspires to win.

And now comes a strange episode. Marina's agreeable reflections are put an end to by the sudden entrance of Rangoni, a Jesuit priest. He too has observed the fascination which Marina exerts upon Dimitri, and is determined to make use of it for his own purposes. Speaking with all the authority of his holy office he bids her use all her woman's wiles to captivate the Pretender, even to the sacrifice of her honour, and then, when she has brought him to the condition of being unable to refuse her anything, to extort from him a promise to bring heretic Russia into the Roman fold. This audacious scheme does not appeal to the pleasure-loving Marina and she refuses to have anything to do with it. But she is afraid of the Jesuit in spite of herself, and when he lets loose upon her all the thunders of the Church, threatening her with everlasting damnation, she is speedily cowed into submission.

Scene II. Dimitri is awaiting Marina in the moonlit garden of the castle. But there is no sign of the proud Princess, and it is Rangoni who presently steals out from the shadow of the wall. As soon as he hears that it is from his beloved that the priest has come, Dimitri plies him earnestly with requests to bring her to him. The Jesuit sees another chance of advancing his project : he will willingly assist the intrigue if the Czarevitch will grant him a boon in return. He wishes to become his intimate counsellor, watch over his comings and goings, and be the guardian of his inmost thoughts. Dimitri is well aware whither all this is tending, but his passion will brook no delay and reluctantly he agrees. At this moment a company of lords and ladies come out from the castle, Marina among them, to the strains of a polonaise, and for a while Dimitri withdraws. The guests, however, do not stay long, and as soon as they have gone he returns and is shortly joined by Marina. The girl has learnt her lesson well. While he speaks of love as the only object worth striving for she remains quite unmoved and taunts him with his baseness; but when, stung by her reproaches, he talks of Russia and the crown he will win, she yields at once, and the Act ends with a short love-duet.

This is undoubtedly the weakest portion of the opera. It is said that it did not form part of the composer's original plan and was only inserted by him when his friends complained of the lack of feminine interest in the piece. Be this as it may, Moussorgsky's genius certainly flags here; the soil of Poland is less congenial to it than that of his native Russia, and his mazurka and polonaise contrast very unfavourably with the Russian tunes he employs elsewhere. The historical Marina is a hard, unsympathetic character with whom he found it impossible to do much. The most successful scene is that between her and the Jesuit, and here for a moment the music lives. But, dramatically, the introduction of the Roman priest is unwarranted, for we hear no more of him and very little of his schemes after the end of the Act.

The final Act, however, makes full amends for the weakness of its predecessor. We have done with the Polish interlude, and back in his own country the composer finds his feet again at once. The first Scene is laid in a woodland clearing. A road runs across the stage. The frenzied whirling figures of the short introduction suggest the wild, tumultuous nature of the scene to come. The curtain goes up, and in there rushes a crowd of people dragging with them a captive Boyar of Boris' faction. Seating him on a log they proceed to mock and taunt him. After a while the Village Idiot shambles

up, pursued by a crowd of urchins who tease him and
filch from him his jealously guarded penny. The next
arrivals are the friars, Missail and Varlaam, who are now
loud in their praise of Dimitri and their curses of Boris.
They join the crowd, which welcomes them gladly. A
pair of Jesuits who appear a little later are not so fortunate. Neither the friars nor the people desire interfer-
ence from Rome, and the Jesuits are quickly bound and
led off to be hanged. A procession of troops goes by;
Dimitri himself crosses the stage, and on his departure
the crowd follows him. Snow has begun to fall. The
idiot boy, alone amid the fluttering snowflakes, searches
vainly for his lost penny, his clouded mind gazing hope-
lessly out into the future. He is the very symbol of
the oppressed, despairing people.

> Trickle, trickle, tears ! Bitter, bitter tears !
> Weep and mourn, ye true believers !
> For the foe will come with sword in hand,
> And a doom will fall on a darkened land !
> Then woe to the land, and woe to the folk,—
> Poor starving folk !

This last Scene was originally placed by Moussorgsky
at the very end of his score, and he could hardly have hit
upon a more finely artistic conclusion to his work. But
producers were nervous about a *finale* in which the
leading character did not appear at all, and so in the
Rimsky-Korsakoff edition, the one generally followed,
the death-scene of Boris, which we are about to describe,
was placed last.

We are in the Kremlin at a special meeting of
the Duma. The Boyars are assembled and engaged
in futile discussion. Presently Shouisky enters and
describes how Boris is haunted by visions of the murdered Dimitri. He is in the middle of his narrative

when Boris himself reels in, crying, "Avaunt! Avaunt!"
But he collects himself quickly and allows Shouisky
to summon an old monk who is waiting for an
audience. It is Pimen, who has come to relate to the
Czar the story of a miracle wrought at Dimitri's tomb.
Boris hears him to the end and then falls fainting into
the arms of the Boyars. Once more he recovers himself,
but now he feels that his end is near. Dismissing the
Duma he sends for his son and then, tenderly and with
words of wise advice, takes his farewell of him, bidding
him protect his sister and commending them both to
the care of the God who has deserted their father. The
funeral knell is heard and the Boyars re-enter in procession. Feodor makes an attempt to cheer his royal
parent, but Boris gently stops him : " Nay, nay, my son,
my hour has come." His agony is upon him, but he
has strength left for the one supreme effort. Summoning
all his ebbing forces the dying lion rises for the last time
to his full height, a king even in his mortal weakness,
and cries aloud, " While I have life I still am Czar!"
But Death is at his throat, and even as he speaks he sways,
stumbles, and sinks back into his chair gasping a broken,
incoherent prayer for mercy. A moment later all is
over. The horror-struck Boyars whisper, " He is dead!"
and the curtain falls.

LE COQ D'OR

Music by RIMSKY-KORSAKOFF. *Words by* BIELSKY,
from PUSHKIN.
Moscow, 1910; *London,* 1913; *New York,* 1918.

ALTHOUGH the number of operas composed by
Rimsky-Korsakoff in the course of his long life
runs well into double figures, it is only the first
and the last of them that are at all familiar to English
audiences. The first, *The Maid of Pskoff*, has become
remarkable from the performance of Chaliapine in the rôle
of Czar Ivan during the great 1913 season of Russian
opera in London, and this same season also saw the
production of *Le Coq d'Or*, the composer's last work,
which has since received a number of performances in
England at the hands of various companies. It is in
many ways a remarkable piece. With the single exception of Moussorgsky, Rimsky-Korsakoff is probably the
finest operatic composer that Russia has produced, while
as a master of orchestration he can stand comparison
with the greatest names in music. This is the work of
his old age, the matured vintage of a vast experience,
and his touch throughout is singularly sure. The story
by its very nature presents peculiar problems of musical and dramatic characterization, but he solves them
all with that ease and assurance that only come from a
complete mastery of his medium.

Realizing, however, that his work might easily be mis-
interpreted, he has published some " Remarks " at the
beginning of the score, from which it is worth quoting
an extract or two :

The composer does not sanction any 'cuts.'

The composer desires that the singers in all his works keep strictly to the music written for them.

An opera is first and foremost a musical work.

But even with hints like these *Le Coq d'Or* is difficult to produce in the right way. Not only is the music for the singers of a most exacting nature, demanding vocal and interpretive gifts of the highest order, but the artists who take the leading parts must also be actors of a kind rarely met with on the operatic stage, and skilful dancers to boot, otherwise the work will lose much of its point. So great have these difficulties appeared in the eyes of some people, that the experiment has actually been made of presenting *Le Coq d'Or* with a double cast, each character being represented by a singer standing in the orchestra or elsewhere and an actor or dancer upon the stage. This novel attempt to solve one of the stock problems of opera was never sanctioned by the composer, and is not likely to be widely followed, if only on account of the expense involved.

The story is adapted from a tale by Pushkin. It is described as a " fable," and such it certainly is ; but certain elements in the plot are left so obscure that one is almost compelled to accept the theory propounded in many quarters that it has a symbolical or satirical meaning. What that meaning may be it is hard to say, but it has been suggested that the clue is to be sought among the obscure pages of Russian political history. The preface by the author of the libretto does not really throw much light on the subject. He says (to quote from the translation) : " The principal charm of the story lies in so much being left to the imagination, but, in order to render the plot somewhat clearer, a few words as to the action on the stage may not come amiss.

" Many centuries ago, a wizard, still alive to-day, sought by his magic cunning to overcome the daughter of the Aerial Powers. Failing in his project, he tries to win her through the person of King Dodôn. He is again unsuccessful, and, to console himself, he presents to the audience in his magic lantern the story of heartless royal ingratitude."

A muted trumpet opens the proceedings with a phrase whose reference to the title of the work is unmistakable. It is soon joined by other instruments, and a curious, sinuous theme is heard whose wayward rhythm and strange intervals suggest the music of the East. This theme plays an important part in the opera and is associated with the Queen of Shémakâ ; presently it gives place to another, hardly less peculiar, which is first heard on the bells, and represents the Astrologer, who now appears in front of the curtain. In a few words he tells us that by his magic he will bring before our eyes an ancient fable, then suddenly he disappears and the curtain rises.

King Dodôn sits in state in his spacious audience-chamber. Beside him are his two sons, Afrôn and Guidôn. A crowd of counsellors and courtiers is present, among whom we recognize General Polkân, whose long beard and military bearing make him a conspicuous figure. At the doors stand sentries, fast asleep, while at the back we catch a glimpse of the strange city over which King Dodôn rules.

The King is troubled. In spite of the fact that he is not as young as he was, neighbouring nations will still insist on attacking him. He could weep with vexation. What is to be done ? Guidôn suggests that they lay in a store of provisions and vintage wines and entrench themselves in the capital. Afrôn inclines toward giving the whole army a month's leave, then suddenly assembling it and marching out to battle.

The King and his courtiers are full of admiration for both these plans, but the military soul of Polkân stirs him to angry speech, and he expresses his contempt in forcible language. This leads to a slight disturbance, while the courtiers catch Polkân and give him a good beating, but it is soon over and they return to their deliberations.

Suddenly there is seen approaching the old Astrologer of the Prologue. He kneels before King Dodôn and tells him that he comes with a solution of his difficulties. He has a Golden Cock which he will give the King; the moment anything happens that is likely to disturb the tranquillity of the kingdom this bird will cry out, "Cock-a-doodle-doo! Danger lies in wait for you!" Until it does that everyone can rest in security. So saying he produces the bird, which immediately crows, "Cock-a-doodle-doo! Peace and quietness for you!"

The King is delighted. Let the Cock be placed on a high point of vantage and start on his duties at once. He thanks the Astrologer, and at first offers him any reward he likes to name, but when the old man tries to extract from him a written promise to this effect, duly witnessed, he backs out hastily. The Astrologer bows and departs, the King dismisses the courtiers, stretches himself in the sun, and says he feels sleepy. His housekeeper, Amelfa, who has just come in, summons the servants, who appear bearing a huge bed. But first the King must take some refreshment. She offers him a dish of dainties. Before he eats he sends for his parrot to amuse him; but his drowsiness soon overcomes him, the parrot is removed, the King climbs into bed, and the orchestra lulls him to

sleep with a soothing *berceuse*, while Amelfa keeps the
flies off his face.

Presently we hear the theme of the Queen of Shémakâ,
indicating the nature of the royal dreams, but this is
rudely interrupted by the voice of the Golden Cock
calling his warning. A crowd assembles and Polkân,
rushing in, shakes his reluctant master into wakefulness.
The King gets up, addresses the people, and then turns
to his sons, who have come in fully armed. They are
each to take half the army and start at once. Unwillingly
they depart, and their father returns quietly to bed.
But what was it he was dreaming about ? Amelfa
eventually guesses and he goes happily to sleep.

Again the warning voice of the Cock is heard, and again
the people assemble. But the King sleeps on, and once
more it is Polkân who has to rouse him. This time
Dodôn will take the field himself. His armour is brought ;
it is very rusty and he has difficulty in donning it as he
has increased in girth since last he wore it. At length he
is ready, a horse sufficiently quiet for him to ride has been
provided, and with Polkân and the remaining troops he
passes from the stage followed by words of good advice
from the people.

Act II. It is night. By the faint light of the moon we
can discern a dark and gloomy gorge. On the hillside
lie the bodies of fallen warriors, and in the centre of the
stage those of King Dodôn's two sons. The background
is shrouded in mist, and the atmosphere of horror is
heightened by the sound of the orchestra, which discourses strange and sombre music. Presently we catch
the martial air to which the troops had marched off at
the end of the previous Act, but now it is heard in the
minor key, muffled and pregnant with foreboding. Two
at a time, the soldiers of Dodôn appear coming along the

gorge, only to halt in grief and terror at the sight before them. Their laments are cut short by the arrival of the King himself with Polkân. In the darkness he stumbles over the bodies of his sons, recognizes them, and breaks into a song of woe. They have quarrelled, he supposes, and this is the result. Polkân is beginning to rally the troops, who have all burst into tears, when the mist rolls away and in the increasing light of dawn there is seen in the background a gorgeously decorated tent. " This, then, is the treacherous enemy ! " cries the general. " Forward with the artillery ! " A large cannon is brought up and all is ready for its discharge, when the folds of the tent are seen to tremble, the soldiers run away, and there emerges, richly dressed and radiant with beauty, the Queen of Shémakâ, who from this moment onward dominates the action. She starts by singing her " Hymn to the Sun," a magnificent example of modern *coloratura* writing. The King and Polkân are astonished.

> DODÔN. 'Tis amazing for a woman !
> POLKÂN. Execution superhuman !
> She is fair and full of wit,
> Let us join her for a bit !

They do so. The Queen receives them graciously, though she makes no secret of her desire to ' subdue ' Dodôn. Polkân opens a conversation on conventional lines, but after a while she takes objection to his manners and he is sent away behind the tent, to stay there till the King says, " One ! " Then she moves her cushion nearer to Dodôn and begins her task of conquest in earnest. It is an easy matter. The poor old man is bewildered by her beauty, her strangeness, and the brilliance of her singing, for she pours forth song after song in an abundance that speaks much for the fertility of the composer and makes the highest demands on the

powers of the singer. But at last she grows tired. Will
not the King sing a song now ? Dodôn protests that he
has long given up singing, but she presses him, and at last
in despair he rises to his feet and bawls :

> Lady fair, through thick and thin,
> I will strive thy love to win,

to an air even more ridiculous than the words set to it.
She soon tires of this form of amusement, sings another
song herself, and then asks him to dance for her. Again
he protests, but she overcomes his opposition by threatening to call back Polkân. Then, removing his helmet and
breastplate, and thus leaving him in an absurd costume,
she ties a handkerchief round his head, puts a fan in his
hand, and bids her retinue come and see the fun. Desperately he dances, faster and faster grows the music, till at
last he falls to the ground panting for breath. Presently
he recovers a little and manages to summon up enough
courage to make his clumsy proposal. She hesitates, and
only yields on his promise that Polkân shall be condemned
to death ! The King's carriage is brought, he and the
Queen get into it, and the procession starts off for home,
but not before the Queen's retinue have had time to
make some caustic remarks about the unsuitability of the
match.

Act III. We are back in the capital. The street is
crowded with people asking for news, and sounds of
crowing in the orchestra show us that the Golden Cock
is still at his post. Amelfa appears, and in answer to
questions announces that the King and his army have
been victorious and are shortly returning with a Queen
whom they have rescued. Very soon the procession
arrives, and the Queen's retinue, which includes giants,
dwarfs, and other oddities, presents a spectacle much

appreciated by the people. Finally the King himself appears with the Queen, both still sitting in the carriage, and is loyally welcomed by his subjects. A sudden diversion, however, is produced by the appearance of the old Astrologer. He acknowledges the royal greeting, and announces that he has come to claim the fulfilment of the King's promise to reward him. He asks for—the Queen! Amid the general amazement Dodôn attempts to reason with him, offering him state appointments or anything else he likes. But he utterly fails to move him, and finally, losing his temper, strikes him dead with a blow of his sceptre. The Queen laughs, but the King already regrets his rash act, and turns to her for comfort. She rebukes him curtly, " Nay, the sorry jest is ended," and suddenly there rises the voice of the Cock. The bird flies off its perch, hovers over the crowd, and then, descending suddenly, pecks Dodôn violently on the head and kills him. A clap of thunder is heard, and in the sudden darkness that falls the Queen can be heard laughing. When it grows light again she has disappeared and the people have nothing else to do but weep over the death of their beloved ruler. But on the descent of the curtain the Astrologer appears for a moment in front of it, just as he did at the beginning of the opera. " Let no one be distressed at the tragic ending of the story," he says. " Of all the figures on the stage only two were real—the Queen and I." And so he bows and disappears, leaving us to make what we can of it. The whole-hearted admirers of *Le Coq d'Or* evidently agree with the composer's theory : " An opera is first and foremost a musical work." In other words : " Take care of the sounds and the sense will take care of itself."

DER ROSENKAVALIER

Music by RICHARD STRAUSS. *Words by* H. VON HOFMANNSTHAL.
Berlin, 1911 ; *London,* 1913 ; *New York,* 1913.

EACH of the three principal operas by Richard Strauss, *Salome, Elektra,* and *Der Rosenkavalier,* has in turn been condemned in certain quarters as being *contra bonos mores* ; on such a judgment in connexion with the first two works we shall offer no opinion, but all musicians must rejoice that the third and best of the three has already passed beyond the sphere of irrelevant censure into the world of accepted successes.

The description on the title-page—" A comedy for music by H. von Hofmannsthal. . . . Music by Richard Strauss "—is an indication that poet and composer must be considered as of equal rank—if, indeed, the former be not entitled, like his own Baron Ochs, to walk three paces in advance of the latter. In any case it is certain that no composer ever had so distinguished a collaborator.

As poet, dramatist, and prose essayist, Hugo von Hofmannsthal has long been a prominent figure in Continental literature ; he is less widely known in England than in the United States, where Mr Charles Wharton Stork's admirable translations of the lyrical poems have drawn attention to a very important aspect of his genius. Hofmannsthal is before all things a symbolist, and this fact must be kept in mind in estimating even the fantastical manner of *Der Rosenkavalier.*

(" The Rose-bearer " is the not very happy title of the English version. " The Silver Rose " would, perhaps, better convey the idea, since it is around such a Rose that the story is woven, and this Rose is the symbol of Love.)

This drama is many things in one ; it is a comedy of intrigue, after the Beaumarchais model, a comedy of manners, *à la* Congreve, it has grim touches of Hogarthian satire ; but all is permeated by the spirit of Hofmannsthal the poet, with his symbol of the Silver Rose—not to be denied his moments of tenderness and pathos, lifting a squalid situation into the realm of fantastic humour, intent often on showing us beauty even in the waste places. Through all these moods Strauss has followed the poet in complete sympathy, with the result that *Der Rosenkavalier* stands next to Humperdinck's *Hänsel und Gretel* in the direct line of the Wagnerian succession.

Act I. We must imagine ourselves in the great world of Vienna at the time when Maria Theresa was Empress —a world of elegant gallantry, into the atmosphere of which the dramatist plunges us at once, without preliminary or reserve. The scene is a large *salon* communicating with others in the private apartments of the Princess von Werdenberg, the most impressive and convincing figure of a *grande dame* to be found on the operatic stage.

The situation disclosed at the rising of the curtain is unusual, and what is generally described as ' piquant.' It is early morning, and the birds sing cheerily, yet the general impression is not so much that day is just beginning as that a happy night is hardly ended.

Stretched on a sofa, in elegant *déshabillé*, is the Princess von Werdenberg, while at her feet reclines Octavian, her boy-lover, still adoring the white arm she allows him to retain.

" *Bichette !* " says the boy.

" *Quinquin !* " says the Princess, as she strokes his hair. Octavian is in deadly earnest and too young to know better—this great and gracious lady is for him the immortal goddess, ever young and ever fair. But the Princess—'Marie Thérèse' she has been named, after a still greater lady—is a married woman of vast experience, and with a clear eye for the inevitable future. In the midst of the boy's too ardent worship, his little fits of jealousy, his protestations of a lifelong devotion, she realizes only too well that they are living in a fool's paradise ; his youth has just begun, her prime is nearly over ; the day will come—to-morrow, maybe—when he will leave her, to find his true affinity.

No need to speak of Octavian's indignant denial of such a possibility. One fact, however, cannot be gainsaid—the Princess has a husband, who may return at any moment from his hunting expedition. A commotion without suggests that her fears are realized, and Octavian takes refuge in a curtained alcove. Fortunately it turns out to be nothing worse than a certain country cousin of the Princess, a formidable bore, indeed, but not dangerous. Baron Ochs von Lerchenau—Squire Bull of Larksmead, we might render it in English—is the dominating personage in the opera, and a masterly creation. He has a certain likeness to the booby-squires of our eighteenth-century fiction, in some points he resembles the Falstaff of *The Merry Wives*—like Sir John he is a very mountain of lechery—while in the matter of pompous self-complacency he sets a standard of his own.

The Baron has come, it appears, on a matter of the highest family importance. He is about to be married. He has decided to bestow the overwhelming honour of his hand, with all the solemn dignity attaching to

his lengthy pedigree, upon the daughter of a certain
worthy citizen Faninal, who has only lately succeeded in
adding the indispensable ' von ' to his name, thanks to the
vast fortune he has made as an army-contractor.   The
Baron is full of apologies for such a *mésalliance*, but, as
he says, the fellow owns an immense property—and his
health, he hears, is none of the best.   As for the girl,
she is charming, and only just come from a convent-
school.   In any case, his mind is made up, and he has
come to ask his cousin's assistance in a very delicate
matter.   It is the custom, it seems, among families of
the highest rank, that the prospective bridegroom, before visiting his *fiancée*, should send her a silver rose as
the symbol of his love ; this must be presented in person
by a member of his family—can the Princess von Werdenberg suggest a suitable ambassador for the present occasion ?

As the Scene develops the Princess has need of all her
breeding to enable her to bear with the liberties in which
her too blue-blooded relation thinks fit to indulge.   The
foregoing voluble statement of the Baron's errand has
been constantly interrupted by his shameless flirtation
with the pretty serving-maid in attendance on the Princess—none other, in fact, than Octavian, who has taken
advantage of his concealment in the alcove to assume
this disguise, and now passes for ' Mariandel,' a country
girl, new to her Highness's service.   At the first sight of
the strapping wench the lustful Ochs is all on fire and, in
spite of the Princess's endeavours to get her out of the
room, persists in detaining her, and takes every opportunity of whispering proposals into her ear.   The
Princess can only resign herself to the situation, while
Octavian enjoys the fun and leads the Baron on to
commit himself still further.

At last the Princess hits upon a device by which to get

'Mariandel' out of the room ; she sends her to fetch
a miniature of a certain kinsman of the family who might
possibly act as the bearer of the Silver Rose. The portrait with which Octavian returns is actually one of
himself—the Princess has prepared a satisfactory explanation—and the Baron is well pleased that Count
Octavian Rofrano, younger brother of the Marquis, should
be his ambassador.

Now follows the most diverting scene of the opera—
the Princess's *levée*. The folding-doors are thrown open
and at once the stage is crowded by a clamorous mob of
candidates for her Highness's favour. A dressing-table is
brought prominently forward, at which the Princess sub-
mits herself to the operations of her *perruquier* and at
the same time endeavours to take some courteous notice
of each of her noisy petitioners. Among these we may
notice a French milliner (with a *chapeau Paméla*), an
Italian tenor with his flautist, a dealer in parrots and
monkeys, a scholar, a widow ' lady of quality' with her
three ' quality' orphans, to say nothing of what the
major-domo describes as " the usual pack of rubbish."
[We must keep an eye on two very suspicious-looking
Italians, man and woman, who would seem to be
always lurking, for some dark purpose of their own, in
places where they are least likely to be noticed ; their
names are Valzacchi and Annina, and their function is to
add a touch of grotesque fantasy to the action.]

While all these enact their little parts—the tenor has a
charming Italian song, and the four ladies a delicious
little quartet that irresistibly recalls Mozart—the Baron
Ochs is busy with an attorney over the marriage settle-
ment. Their business over, the Princess dismisses the
crowd, courteously retaining the scholar for a few
minutes' conversation. The mysterious Italians seize the

opportunity to commend themselves to the Baron's notice ; he is about to take a young and lovely bride ; their business is to supply secret information—who knows how soon he may require their services ? Ochs dismisses them, without the expected *douceur*, and turns to present the Silver Rose to the Princess, who now hurries him also out of the room—she must dress, or she will be late for Mass.

Whether her Highness ever gets so far as the confessional we do not know, but the rest of the Act is given up to a self-revelation on her part which would be invaluable to her spiritual director. She begins with an indignant denunciation of her unspeakable kinsman, Baron Ochs von Lerchenau ; she feels an intense loathing at the thought of the approaching alliance between such a brute with a young girl fresh from school. And yet, was not her own fate much the same ? What remains of the innocent child she herself can call to mind—how many years ago ! —where is she now ? Alas, she died so young !—but what of the years since then ? And soon they will be speaking of " the old Princess Theresia." . . .

It is in this mood that the boy Octavian finds her when he returns, dressed as himself once more. He cannot move her from her sadness—she is obsessed by the thought of

Time's wingèd chariot hovering near

—soon it will overtake them, and bear him away from her: "Now, or to-morrow—if not to-morrow, very soon." She soothes his passionate protests as best she may, and dismisses him—they will meet again that evening in the Prater.

Octavian leaves her—and, for the first time, without a kiss. Instantly she summons her footmen and orders them to call him back, but he has already galloped out of sight. Finally she rings for her little black boy, to whom she confides the Silver Rose, the symbol of love, to be delivered into the hands of the Count Octavian—he will understand.

The curtain falls on the Princess, with bowed head, gazing sadly into the darkening future.

From this mere summary of an extraordinarily complicated Scene much has necessarily been omitted; but attention must be drawn to Ochs' long and unctuous disquisition on the various kinds of women and the way to trap them: *Macht das einen lahmen Esel aus mir?* It might be called "The Profligate's Vade-mecum," so rich is it in the advice that can only come from a varied experience. Strauss, in his musical commentary, has not missed a single point of interest; so elaborate indeed is the orchestration, so rapid and emphatic the delivery of the vocal part, that it would seem to matter little whether it be sung or spoken. The words must be heard—the musical interest lies with the orchestra. Vocal compensation, however, is made in the delightful trio for Ochs, Octavian, and the Princess, *Nein, Er agirt mir gar zu gut*, which closes the episode.

It seems futile to compare Ochs' monologue, as some have done, with the famous *Madamina* of Leporello in *Don Giovanni*, since the two conceptions belong to entirely different worlds. Nor is much to be gained by suggesting that Octavian is a sort of grown-up Cherubino; the latter is a purely ideal figure, while "Mignon" is altogether too actual, and for this reason can never be a sympathetic figure on the operatic stage—he is better appreciated in the subtle pages of von Hofmannsthal's libretto.

That the composer had Mozart constantly in his mind is clear from many a passage, such as the little quartet already alluded to, and the breakfast-scene, in which Strauss, wisely eschewing comparison, gives us a charming waltz where Mozart might have written a minuet. But perhaps the loveliest thing in the whole Act is the Princess's soliloquy toward the end, *Kann mich auch an ein Mädel erinnern*, and that is Strauss' very own.

Act II. The present Act is comparatively simple after the crowded confusion of Act I ; it is really a passionate love-duet against a background of excellent comedy, with some splashes of rather biting satire. We are in the mansion of the newly ennobled Herr von Faninal, a very perfect snob indeed, but hardly so diverting a figure as the outrageous Ochs.

The family has been apprized of the coming visit of the young Count Octavian as the bearer of the Silver Rose to Sophie, the daughter of the house, and the bride-elect of Baron Ochs von Lerchenau. Faninal is just going out, for, as the major-domo reminds him, it is contrary to etiquette that he should be found on the premises when the ambassador arrives. Marianne, the duenna—a worshipper of rank—is at the window, in excited anticipation. Sophie's excitement takes another form. She, a young girl, with the influence of the convent still upon her, is about to be united in the holy state of wedlock with " the virtuous and noble Lord of Lerchenau," as Marianne describes him ; she is overwhelmed by the honour, she is dazzled by the splendour of the bridegroom she has never seen ; from a full heart she prays Heaven to keep her from the deadly sin of pride, and from loving too much the pomps and vanities of this world.

Outside we hear a noise of cheers and shouting that comes always nearer ; already they are calling, " Room for the Count Rofrano ! " beneath her windows. " And will they so call out all the grand titles of my husband-to-be when he comes to claim me ? " she wonders. That husband she has not yet seen, and even her imaginary portrait of him begins to fade from the moment that she sets eyes on the glittering apparition who now enters the room—not an angel from Heaven, as Marianne suggests, but the young Octavian, the bearer of the Silver Rose of love.

It is a beautiful and impressive scene as the young Count in silver and white advances with the Rose, like a pale silver flame, in his hand; his retinue are in green and white, and prominent among them are his Hungarian bodyguard, with their big' fur caps and crooked sabres; Faninal's household forms the background.

With an embarrassed reverence Octavian offers the flower to the girl, who stands entranced at the wonderful vision before her. The Rose would seem to exhale an influence as powerful as Isolde's love-potion; it requires a long passage of great lyrical beauty to express their first fantastic rapture. The fragrance, says Sophie, when first she bends over the silver filagree, is that of real roses; yet no! this is a gift from Heaven; only the roses of Paradise can smell so sweet. Octavian, too, feels that this is no earthly rose that can work such miracles in him; he has found himself at last : " I was a boy, until I saw her face ! " Toward the end of the duet, though each is singing ' aside ' they are allowed to use the same words : " There was once a time when I was blest like this—but where can it have been ? " Henceforth, at any rate, this blessed memory will never fade.

The first mysterious ecstasy is over ; the servants leave the room, and only Marianne remains while the two sit side by side, and Sophie discusses, with childish innocence, the subject of her approaching marriage, from which she promises herself such happiness. Does Octavian never long to marry ? But with him, of course, it is different ; a man is always a man—but a woman is nothing until she is married ; what does she not owe to her husband !

This dialogue, *Ich kenn' Ihn schon recht wohl*, is sung throughout to one of the many waltz-measures which, though a bone of contention among the critics, are an unquestionable factor in the popularity of this opera ; the present simple and elegant example of the form seems peculiarly appropriate to the situation.

The waltz changes to a march as the husband to whom Sophie is to owe so much is ushered into the room. A greater contrast between this procession and the one we have lately witnessed could hardly be imagined. The Baron, a gross and overbearing animal, is followed by some loutish retainers, apparently fresh from the plough and squeezed into ill-fitting liveries ; the obsequious Faninal, in attendance, seems the more respectable figure of the two.

Sophie's illusions are shattered at a glance, and every movement of the Baron but heightens her disgust. His first attempt at compliment is enough : carefully examining her hand as he kisses it, he remarks approvingly on the delicate wrist, " a thing," he adds, " rarely found in persons of your station." (" This might be some low horse-dealer ! " is Sophie's comment.) As he proceeds to put her through her paces, the poor girl grows hot with shame and anger, but her restiveness only excites the baser part of the Baron's nature. " That's just how I like 'em ! " he chuckles. " Egad ! I have the luck of all the Lerchenaus ! " Once they are married, he feels sure, she will make the most devoted of wives !

[It is here that we have the one really popular passage in the opera, the facile waltz-tune (*Mit mir, mit mir !*) to which Ochs expresses his maudlin sentiments ; it is exactly the sort of music that would make the fortune of any 'musical comedy,' and the composer of *Elektra* evidently wrote it to show how well able he was to carry on the old Strauss tradition and provide the Viennese public with its favourite fare.]

All this while Octavian has been boiling with indignation, and even the duenna (who is enchanted with the Baron's " easy ways ") begins to feel nervous at the turn things are taking, when Faninal fortunately enters with the notary, and the three men withdraw into the next room, Ochs leading the way and taking good care that his future father-in-law shall keep not less than three paces behind him.

An uproar among the Baron's drunken servants calls the duenna from the room, and the pair are left alone. Lovers at first sight, their recent experience has brought them closer together. All tumult dies away in the orchestra as we begin the long love-duet that works up to its climax in the passage *Mit Ihren Augen voll Tränen*. By this time the boy and girl are in each other's arms, and blind to all else, though for some time their actions have been watched by others. These are the Italian spies, Valzacchi and Annina, who have made a noiseless entry through secret panels on opposite corners of the room, and, choosing their moment, rush on their victims, hold them fast, and shout loudly for Baron Ochs von Lerchenau.

The Baron is rather amused than seriously annoyed when he grasps what he imagines to be the situation; but Octavian is in a very different mood—he has something that the Baron must hear without delay. " This young lady——" he begins, but Ochs will not listen—he affects to regard it all as a mere boyish freak—besides, Sophie is wanted in the next room. The girl flatly refuses to follow him, and Octavian stands in front of the door to bar the Baron's passage. "This lady," he says firmly, "has decided that under no circumstance will she marry you—and for my part I may tell you that I consider you a thief, a liar, a dowry-hunter, and a dirty clodhopper." [At this crisis we find ourselves once more away on the wings of the waltz-measures which pursue us throughout this Act.] The noble Ochs' reply is to whistle for his men, who appear at the folding-doors. But Octavian's blood is up; he forces the Baron to draw, and, closing with him, inflicts the slightest of wounds on his arm.

The Baron's cries of pain and alarm bring the whole household on the scene, and a very enjoyable *ensemble* follows (still in the liveliest waltz-time), while the booby is helped on to a couple of chairs, and fussed over by his attendants, the duenna, and Faninal. The latter now becomes the centre of interest; besides condoling with the Baron and expressing his pious horror at Octavian's audacity, he has Sophie also to deal with. Her quiet statement that she has no intention of proceeding with the match drives him to distraction—she *shall* marry the Baron, dead or alive! He will drive her to church himself—what! she will say "No!" at the altar! Then a convent, nay, a prison-cell, shall be her lot for the rest of her life.

Sophie makes her escape, Octavian has already left, Faninal hurries out to order the choicest of wines for the wounded man, who is now in the hands of a physician. Thanks to his attentions, the Baron soon begins to feel quite at his ease again; under the influence of some generous Tokay he hums his favourite waltz, *Mit mir*, and gives himself up to the agreeable imaginings which the words suggest.

The future glows with a still rosier light when the mysterious Annina enters and hands him a letter from —Mariandel! This non-existent personage writes to say that she will be free to-morrow evening, and entirely at his lordship's disposal. The Baron is in the highest of spirits : " Did I not say I have the luck of all the Lerchenaus ? " he chuckles, as he lumbers off to bed, filled with delicious anticipations of to-morrow's assignation with the Princess's servant-maid.

Only one thing Ochs has forgotten; when the go-between hands us a mysterious letter on the stage, we are expected to reply by pressing a purse of gold into her hand—this the Baron has, most unfortunately, omitted to do.

Act III. After a brilliant and elaborate introduction —a *fugato* in six parts—the curtain rises on a scene in dumb show which puzzles us sorely as to its purpose ; it is plain, however, that we must be prepared for any amount of trickery and illusion in the events which are to follow.

In semi-darkness and perfect silence mysterious figures move to and fro, apparently rehearsing for one of Messrs Maskelyne and Cooke's entertainments or a bogus spiritualist *séance*. Apparitions rise through trap-doors, faces peer out suddenly from panels which revolve noiselessly, while a 'blind' window is shown to be highly 'practicable.' The directors of these manœuvres are the two Italians, Valzacchi and Annina ; the latter is in widow's weeds, and is seen making-up her face and otherwise altering her appearance. Octavian, too, in his Mariandel disguise is here, but only for a short time ; the purse of gold he gives Valzacchi on leaving makes it plain in whose interest, and against whom, the two intriguers are " maturing their felonious little plans."

The silent conspirators having departed, servants come

and light the candles; we now see a large room in an old-fashioned hostelry, with a curtained recess and a table laid for two. We need hardly say that the expected guests are Ochs and Mariandel.

The Baron's first act on entering is to extinguish most of the candles; he declines the help of the officious waiters, and, left alone, proceeds to ply his companion with wine, in order to overcome the shyness which 'she' affects to feel. We soon begin to be thankful for the arrangements, of which we had glimpses at the beginning of the Act, whereby the room has been transformed into a sort of cabinet of mysteries; we see that this is one of many ingenious devices by which the threatened unpleasantness of the scene is constantly averted.

The first thing to awaken the Baron's uneasiness is the startling likeness between Mariandel's features and those of the young Count under whose punishment he is still smarting—he cannot banish Octavian from his thoughts. But more definite fears soon assail him. In the very act of embracing his Mariandel he is conscious of a face scowling at him from a corner of the room: the opposite wall seems alive with leering eyes: he turns just in time to see a man's form vanish through the floor. He is beside himself with fright when the situation takes on a more broadly comic aspect. The blind window opens, and a funereal figure with outstretched arms shrieks, " My husband! 'tis he! " and vanishes, only to reappear through the door, followed by four small children, deserted like herself, she explains, by the heartless Baron! The woman storms, the children bawl " Papa! " in chorus; the Baron demands that they should be thrown out of the room, but meets with little sympathy from the landlord, who talks darkly of bigamy, and complains bitterly of the scandal that threatens his respectable establishment. The tumult grows, until Ochs rushes to the window and shouts for the police.

This is the Baron's fatal mistake—he has overestimated his own importance. The Commissary of Police who comes in answer to his call knows nothing of Ochs von Lerchenau—a provincial nobody—he merely sees an irate and pompous personage in a compromising position. Who is he, pray ? And who is this young woman ? He must know that such things are not permissible in Vienna !

(At this juncture Octavian dispatches a secret messenger to Faninal, and the Baron's valet sends to implore the assistance of the Princess von Werdenberg.)

Driven into a corner, the Baron declares that the lady with him is his affianced bride, the daughter of that well-known citizen the noble Herr von Faninal. Unfortunately for the Baron, Faninal arrives at the moment to give an indignant denial to such a statement—his daughter Sophie is waiting down below. Before she can come up, the alleged widow with her abandoned brood renew their whining accusations, to which Faninal is quite ready to listen. Sophie arrives on the scene, only to express her joy at the turn events have taken—for her part she is glad to be definitely rid of the man she has no intention of marrying. These successive shocks, which mean the ruin of his dearest hopes, are too much for poor Faninal, who collapses and is taken to an adjoining room.

This prolonged series of fantastic events now culminate in a scene of the wildest farce. The Baron is about to leave, taking Mariandel with him ; that personage, how-ever, strongly objects, and claims the protection of the Commissary. A few whispered words are sufficient to fill that officer with amused surprise, as he hands the cheeky ' girl' to the curtained recess, into which she disappears.

The furious Baron has to be restrained while a complete set of female garments are flung out one by one into the room, to be made into a bundle by the smirking officer, while Octavian pushes a dubious head from time to time between the curtains.

The entrance of the Princess von Werdenberg clears the atmosphere and brings with it a welcome repose. A great lady by birth and tradition, a woman of the world by long experience, ' Marie Thérèse ' appears like the ' goddess from the car ' who is to unravel the tangled intrigue. The Commissary is well known to her, and after a short ' aside ' with him she is *au fait* with all that has happened. Anxious to avoid scandal, to hurt no one's feelings, she endeavours to make light of the whole affair : " It is just one of those trifling masquerades," she says, " of which we Viennese are so fond." Even with the Baron she is courteous, though firm. If he is wise, she hints, he will retreat without more ado. But the Ochs' hide is of a prodigious thickness ; even after Sophie has delivered a message from her father to the effect that never again will the Baron be allowed to darken his doors, he still fails to realize his true position. The Princess's patience is marvellous, but at last she tells him plainly that he must renounce all pretensions to the Faninal alliance, and had better not show his face in Vienna for some time to come.

The Baron's final discomfiture, played to the briskest of waltz-tunes, is a most joyous affair. As he turns toward the door the whole pack are on him—landlord, waiters, coachmen, boots, all crowd around with clamorous demands for money ; the brats, still wailing for " Papa ! " get between his legs, while Annina (her old self again) dances in front of him, maliciously repeating his favourite boast, " Egad ! I have the luck of all the Lerchenaus ! "

At last the Baron makes an ignominious bolt, with his pursuers at his heels.

Purged by so much hearty laughter of its grosser elements, the action proceeds leisurely to a tranquil close. On the stage are left Octavian, Sophie, and the Princess —grave, serene, and a great lady, she commands our sympathy. Face to face with the trial she had foreseen " now or to-morrow—if not to-morrow, very soon," she meets it bravely and with perfect dignity. But she is much more than a woman of the world ; she had vowed always to put Octavian's happiness before her own, and she will do so—it is her duty to smooth the way for the boy and girl she sees before her. She finds a way to soften Octavian's painful embarrassment—" Go, and do all that your heart commands ! " she bids him— she contrives to set even Sophie at her ease with words of commendation, and, as a crowning act of courtesy, undertakes to pacify her father by offering to drive him home in her own carriage. What the effort has cost her may be gathered from her share in the fine trio *Hab' mir's gelobt ihn lieb zu haben.*

She goes into the next room to speak with Faninal. With her departure all problems and complexities have vanished both from stage and orchestra, and the opera is vignetted off with a formal duet of Mozartian sweet-ness and simplicity, in which Octavian and Sophie enter upon that dream of a never-ending love which the Prin-cess dreamed so long ago, and which she still retains among her most sacred memories.

The two most significant operas that have appeared within the last thirty years are Debussy's *Pelléas et Méli-sande* and Strauss' *Rosenkavalier,* and in each case the words demand a more than usual amount of consideration. In the first-named work a drama of some literary pretensions has served as admirable material for a composer whose musical genius conceals the weakness of the text by making it an integral part of something far greater. With *Der Rosenkavalier* the case is very different. Hugo von Hofmannsthal belongs to the authentic race of poets, Richard Strauss ranks with the greatest of symphonic composers—the conjunction of the two results in a conflict of fairly equal forces in which the poet comes off the loser.

Von Hofmannsthal's work has in it so fine a literary quality that *Der Rosenkavalier*, if expanded for the stage, might well take its place among the classic comedies. His Baron Ochs is, as we have said, a great creation ; the Princess von Werdenberg, on a smaller scale, hardly less so ; on the stage Octavian might be made convincing, and Sophie would be seen in the right perspective. The whole conception of the play is a happy mingling of satirical comedy with delightful fantasy, not without passages of tender beauty, while the dialogue and the situations are contrived throughout with the most delicate subtlety.

All this, of course, the composer has absorbed and striven faithfully to express, but the matter is too complex for musical treatment, and Strauss' vigorous and exuberant methods seem particularly ill-suited to the task. Accustomed for so long to make thunder and lightning with his orchestra, he forgets that there are situations in which

> it is excellent
> To have a giant's strength, but tyrannous
> To use it like a giant.

Even in the quieter passages Strauss' orchestration too often resembles that favourite economy of our mid-

Victorian ancestors, the 'crossed' letter, which it required both time and patience to decipher ; in neither case can the meaning be apprehended at a cursory encounter, and in the traffic of the stage this must always prove a serious handicap. And far too often is the ocean of sound lashed to a fury which beats the life out of the poor singers struggling to make themselves heard. As we have already pointed out, this is generally the fate of Ochs—for him to trouble to learn his ' notes ' would almost seem to be labour thrown away ; he can only win through by means of the most strenuous declamation and an unremitting attention to by-play.

But one of the most striking instances of this overweening tyranny of the instruments is to be found at the end of the First Act. The Princess has just dismissed Octavian, who has gone quietly from the room, when we are lifted almost out of our seats by such a hullabaloo in the orchestra as suggests nothing less than an immediate catastrophe—say the outbreak of a revolution, or the fall of Dagon's Temple. And what does it actually signify ? Why, that " Mignon " has gone off without embracing his mistress ! Although the poor lady is trying to express that fact, and her consequent emotions, through the ordinary dramatic channels, not only are we unable to hear what she says, but our attention is distracted from the figure on the stage by the unaccountable uproar in the orchestra.

Confronted with such a lack of proportion, and recalling by what simple means and with what beautiful effect Gluck or Mozart, or Verdi in his maturity, would have expressed an equivalent situation, we are inclined to question whether Opera in these latter days has not gone somewhat astray. Surely it would be better to leave the emotional revelation to the singer's art, supported, not crushed, by the orchestra; while in the case of a 'character' part like Ochs it seems as if a welcome return might be made to the old *recitativo secco*, or even the device of speaking the words to music.

Indeed, Strauss himself appears to have realized that, after all, the orchestra was not the only means of expression at his command; in no other opera has he paid such attention to the voice, or given us so much genuine melody. For this we owe him a great debt of gratitude, and for much else besides—for not having hesitated to shock the 'serious' with the frivolity of his waltzes —for offering incense so freely at the shrine of Mozart, least 'serious' of musical divinities—and, more particularly, for the quiet and lovely close of the final scene. In writing *Der Rosenkavalier* Strauss seems to have paused for a while on the path he had so long pursued, resolved to look back and ponder over the past before proceeding farther. If our young composers will consent to profit by the ripe experience of so great a genius and imitate his example, the welcome day cannot be far distant when the tyranny of the orchestra in the domain of opera will at last be ended.

A SHORT HISTORICAL SUMMARY

ITALIAN Opera was the child of the Renaissance, conceived at the very end of the 16th century. The earliest opera that has come down to us is called *Euridice*, and was produced at Florence in 1600; Rinuccini was the author of the words, for which Peri and Caccini wrote the music.

They did not call their work opera, but 'drama for music'; their object was to write a play on a classical subject which could be sung throughout in what they called 'speaking music,' or recitative, this being, as they believed, the manner in which the ancient Greek Tragedy had been performed. It is interesting to note that though this experiment, like the whole of the Renaissance, was a protest against ecclesiastical tradition, the only existing model for their guidance was the plain-song of the Church liturgy.

Although their attempt to find the perfect fusion between sense and sound did not succeed, this idea has never ceased to be the inspiration of the noblest achievements in opera, as well as the guiding principle of its great reformers. " Take care of the sense and the sounds will take care of themselves " is a homely maxim, but one very necessary for opera-makers to bear in mind; its general neglect has invariably resulted in a period of decay.

The singers in *Euridice* were accompanied by four instruments; when, only seven years later (1607), Monteverde produced an opera on the same subject, entitled *Orfeo*, he increased the number to forty, thus early raising the still vexed problem of the relative importance of the singers and the orchestra. With Monteverde, too, the rather austere lines of the recitative began to put forth little blossoms of melody which were not long in attaining an almost too luxurious growth.

It must be remembered that for the first forty years opera was an affair solely of Courts and palaces; the first public opera house was opened in 1637 at Venice, which now became the centre for these exhibitions, and a place of pilgrimage for the whole of fashionable Europe.

Among the visitors to this primitive Bayreuth in 1645 was the famous diarist John Evelyn, who writes as follows:

" This night we went to the opera, where comedies and other plays were represented in recitative music by the most excellent musicians, vocal and instrumental, with variety of scenes painted and contrived with no less art of perfection, and with machines for flying in the aire, and other wonderful motions; taken altogether it is one of the most magnificent and expensive diversions the wit of man can invent."

After extolling the splendour of the production Evelyn goes on to speak of the performers: " Anna Rencia, a Roman, and reputed the best treble of women; but there was an eunuch who in my opinion surpassed her; also a Genovese that sang an incomparable base. They held us by the eyes and ears till two in the morning."

He refers again to " the famous Anna Rencia, whom we invited to a fish dinner after four daies in Lent, when they had given over at the theatre. Accompanied with an eunuch whom she brought with her, she entertained us with rare music, both of them singing to an harpsichord." We feel sure that Pepys would have added, "and all merry."

In this lively peep into the fashionable life of Venice in 1645 we see already established certain main features of the operatic world which have not changed with the centuries. Opera has generally been "a magnificent and expensive diversion," and although the 'eunuch,' or male soprano, has disappeared,[1] it has always had its Anna Rencia, with her taste for little supper-parties on off-nights. But at that time the harmful necessary prima donna, at once the glory and the bane of Italian Opera, was still in the bud—the next century was to witness her dazzling efflorescence.

It is interesting to note that, at this period, while the music was often left in manuscript, the 'book,' on the contrary, was invariably printed; this was evidently in response to popular demand, the extent of which may be inferred from the following facts. As the performances were given at night, in a dimly lighted theatre, the keen opera-goer would bring his own candle with him in order to follow the words, and librettos still exist in which the singed leaves and dropped wax clinging to the pages bear witness to the interest they once inspired, and raise more than a suspicion that even in those days the singers were not always articulate.

With the rapid growth of public support for opera the demand for spectacle, sensation, and frivolity gradually gained the upper hand; considerations of dramatic propriety were thrust aside, and by the end of the century the decay of the libretto was fairly complete. The music, too, had suffered changes; popular melodies of all kinds were introduced without justification; the chorus, which had grown to some degree of importance, now disappeared, and an opera consisted practically of one long chain of vocal solos. It was along these lines that Italian

[1] The last to be heard in England was Velluti, in 1825.

Opera was to move unchallenged till far into the 18th century.

While noting the general decadence that now set in, we must not forget that this very period witnessed the first, and possibly the fairest, flowering of that entrancing melody which was to become the peculiar glory of the Italian school. The works of such masters as Scarlatti, Cesti, Caldara, have long been shelved because of their lack of dramatic vitality, yet they abound in airs of a serene and noble beauty which have never since been surpassed.

With the 18th century the corruption went on apace. It was the age of the great singers; it witnessed the development of a vocal perfection almost unthinkable in our own day, and the consequent tyranny of the prima donna and the *castrato*. Operas were written simply as a medium for vocal display, and the patrons were apparently content to have it so. When Handel established Italian Opera in London in 1711 the wits as well as the public were not slow to make fun of its obvious absurdities; the amusing articles of Addison and Steele in the *Spectator* and *Tatler* on the zoological element, so popular in Italy, the (human) bears and lions, the " pretty warbling choir " of real birds let loose in the theatre, make excellent reading. But the chief cause of objection was, doubtless, the employment of a foreign language on the stage, and the strongest protest against this new exotic form of entertainment was the production in 1728 of the mock-heroic *Beggar's Opera*, the words by John Gay, the music consisting largely of popular songs and dance tunes, arranged by Dr Pepusch. This ran for sixty-two nights, and was the begetter of any number of so-called ballad-operas of a similar type.

However, the rising tide of Italian Opera was not to be

checked; although Handel, after a thirty years' fight
with opposition and intrigue, left the operatic field in
1740, the works of his rivals, Porpora and Buononcini,
of Hasse, Sacchini, Galuppi, and other half-forgotten
composers, continued to find favour with the fashionable
world. All the great singers flocked to London, where
they enjoyed the same idolatry and stirred up the same
strife as elsewhere; in fact, the history of opera for the
better part of a century is largely a chronicle of the doings
of these Madames and Signors, whose vocal feats as reported would seem incredible had we not the music to
convince us, with passage after passage of difficulties which
would prove insurmountable to any singer of the present
day.

The operas of that time are, like the singers, gone beyond recall; they served their turn by demonstrating the
perfection to which the human voice, as a musical instrument, may aspire; dramatically they can scarcely be said
to have existed. We must make an exception perhaps in
the case of Handel, whose virile genius and true dramatic
instinct could infuse life even into the flabby material in
which he had to work. There is a definite movement just
now, both in this country and in Germany, in favour of a
revival of Handelian opera; should it succeed it would
mean a welcome swing of the pendulum toward a higher
standard of vocal perfection.

Meanwhile France and Germany had dealt with the
problem of opera, each in her own way. Into both
countries the new entertainment from Italy had been
introduced before 1650, with very different results. In
the north of Germany several attempts had been made to
establish a native opera, or at least to have opera sung to
German words, yet in spite of the enormous reputation
of Reinhard Keiser, who was working with Handel at

Hamburg about 1700, and is credited with over a hundred German operas, the national movement collapsed, and by 1730 the whole of musical Germany was Italianized, and Vienna was on the way to become the chief seat of Italian Opera in all Europe.

In France things had gone very differently. When G. B. Lulli—generally known as Lully—was brought as a boy from Florence to the Court of Louis XIV, he found a sort of native opera already established, in spite of several early attempts to introduce the Italian style. The French variety had been developed from the earlier ballet with its song and dance, and it was by devoting himself to this brand of music that Lully won the favour of the Grand Monarch, who was passionately fond of dancing and would himself condescend to appear in the Court spectacles. Later, with the poet Quinault for his librettist, he produced a series of grand operas (1672–87) exactly suited to the pseudo-classical taste of the age. Far severer in style than the already decadent Italian School, with greater regard for just expression, these works would weary us by the formal dullness of their librettos; but they mark a great advance in the handling of the orchestra, and the form of overture devised by Lully served as a model for nearly every composer until the arrival of Gluck.

J. P. Rameau (1683–1764), Lully's successor, best known to us by his harpsichord pieces, was a genius who, with a finer sense for drama and a profounder knowledge of harmony, made a more solid contribution toward the formation of a national type of opera. Yet both Lully and Rameau are little more than names to-day; their works lie buried under the faded verbiage of the librettos, where everything is as 'calm and critical' as Mrs Jarley's waxworks. But the "low punches" to which that lady objected have in them a vitality which has outlived all waxwork shows, and it is interesting to note that a certain little comic opera introduced to Paris in 1752 by a troupe of Italians, with far-reaching results, is still alive in Italy to-day, and was only recently heard with delight in England. We refer to Pergolesi's dainty intermezzo, *La Serva Padrona*, which, written as long ago as 1733, may claim to be the oldest operatic work that still survives. Its interest in connexion with the French Opera lies in the fact that, like *The Beggar's Opera* in England, its immense popularity in Paris signified a revolt against the ' classical ' opera of the time. J. J. Rousseau followed it up with *Le Devin du Village*, a work of similar calibre, which remained high in popular favour for nearly eighty years. Moreover, the growing taste for this lighter form of entertainment led to the establishment in 1762 of a definite house for *Opéra Comique*, a term which has come to include many a masterpiece that is far from ' comic ' in character.

This same year, 1762, is still more memorable for the triumph of the first great reformer, Gluck (1715–87). A Bohemian by birth, he had studied in Italy, and produced his first Italian opera in 1741. Four years later he was in London, where he met Handel, by whom he seems to have been deeply impressed. That he was considered somewhat of a revolutionary so early as 1756 is plain from the remarks of Metastasio, his librettist, on the production of a new opera at Vienna. " The drama," says the poet, " is my *Re Pastore*, set by Gluck, a Bohemian composer, whose spirit, noise, and extravagance have supplied the place of music in many theatres of Europe." These remarks from the man who dominated Italian Opera for the greater part of the 18th century take us at once to the root of the matter.

Gluck, disgusted at the stagnant state of the Opera, saw

clearly that any reform had to start with the libretto, which must be a ' drama for music,' and not merely, as it had come to be, a patchwork of elegant verses made to suit the requirements of the singer rather than the composer. There is no doubt that the ' poets ' and singers had long since entered into a conspiracy which had reduced Italian Opera to little more than a concert of vocal music combined with spectacle ; dramatic truth and sincerity of expression were set aside—the essential task of the librettist was to provide a series of neat quatrains, mere commonplaces of sentiment or morality, which would serve the composer for the number of airs, of varied character, allocated by rigid convention to each of the singers. The ability to supply this unworthy material had been developed to such a diabolical pitch of perfection by one man that he seems to have got the business entirely into his own hands ; this was the Metastasio above referred to, who reigned for over fifty years (1730–82) as Court poet at Vienna.   His reputation and authority were so unquestioned that a ' book ' by this great man was considered essential to the success of any opera ; most of his works were set by several different composers, some as many as thirty times over.   Gluck in his earlier career had been obliged, like the rest, to put up with the Metastasian libretto, but as his plans for reform expanded, he realized that the old man of the sea must be got rid of before anything could be done.   Happily he found in the poet R. Calzabigi a reformer as enthusiastic as himself ; the result of their collaboration was the opera *Orfeo*, which is generally regarded as the oldest work in the repertory. In it we see recovered some of the principles, though not the methods, of the founders of Opera in 1600, while its serene loveliness is a nearer approach to the true classic spirit than is to be found in any product of the actual

Renaissance period. *Orfeo* makes many an opera of the following century look faded by comparison, and itself, one thinks, can never grow old. It has for its subject one of the great immortal truths, that love can triumph over death ; musically it excludes the elements of decay by insisting on two vital principles : that nothing is to be admitted which does not spring directly from the dramatic situation, and that the quality of sensuous beauty must always be given its lawful prominence.

Orfeo was produced in Vienna in 1762, and was followed by two other works, *Alceste* and *Paride ed Elena*, in both of which Calzabigi collaborated. Gluck then moved to Paris, where his new doctrines found a readier acceptance than in Southern Europe. It was there that the celebrated rivalry between him and Piccinni ran its course, resulting in the conversion of the latter, who continued to compose classical operas on the Gluck model after that composer's death.

But the day for such themes was almost over—the stale fumes of the Renaissance were rolling away ; a brisker, gayer atmosphere had been brought to Paris by the ' Bouffons ' with their dainty little *Serva Padrona*, and the new house for *Opéra Comique* had given fresh incentive to men like Monsigny, D'Alayrac, and Grétry, who exercised their genius or talent on subjects of light romance or fantastic comedy.

In Italy, too, the comedy element shone brightly in the operas of Cimarosa (1749–1801), whose *Matrimonio Segreto* still keeps the stage, and Paisiello (1741–1816), whose reputation was to be dimmed only by the brilliance of Rossini. But this is to run on too fast ; we must return to Vienna to assist at the rising of the splendid star that was to preside over the birth of real German Opera— the incomparable Mozart (1756–91), whose masterpieces, with the exception of *Don Giovanni*, were all produced in that city.

Not that Mozart can be classed as distinctively German; while he excelled Gluck in the ability to express emotion or sum up a dramatic situation by the simplest possible means, he could be as florid as Porpora when he chose, and he had all the southern gaiety of Cimarosa. Three of his greatest works, *Figaro*, *Don Giovanni*, and *Così fan tutte*, are classed with *opera buffa*, while his serious opera *La Clemenza di Tito* was written for one of Metastasio's frozen librettos, and suffered in consequence. So much for the Italian side; on the other hand his delightful little *Singspiel* (song-play), *Die Entführung aus dem Serail*, was written to German words, and *Die Zauberflöte* may be considered the first real German opera.

But, German or Italian, gay or serious, Mozart's dramatic music differs from any other in a certain constant quality of pure loveliness; it matters not what subject is presented to him, he will clothe it in its appropriate mantle of music, and the result is invariably a thing of beauty, glowing with " the light that never was on land or sea." Within the last decade three of his operas, *The Magic Flute* (*Die Zauberflöte*), *Figaro*, and *The Seraglio* (*Die Entführung*), have become for the first time widely known in this country; as a result we have an ever-growing number of opera-goers who are prepared to swear that over all composers Mozart is king—and who can blame them for so excellent a choice?

With the production in 1814 of Beethoven's *Fidelio*, the first work of which it may be said that the interest lies mainly in the orchestra, Vienna ceases to be the central seat of opera—we must look to Italy and to Paris for some time to come.

Rossini (1792–1868) and Meyerbeer (1791–1864) are

the two figures that dominate the operatic world from 1820 to 1870, roughly speaking. Their earlier successes were made in Italy, but both migrated later to Paris, and brought about that fusion of the French and Italian schools which lasted until the influence of Wagner began to make itself felt.

Rossini's masterpiece *Il Barbiere di Siviglia* was produced at Rome in 1816. Although an interval of thirty years separates this work from Mozart's *Figaro* (1786) the transition does not seem so very abrupt ; both are comic masterpieces in their varying degrees, and in each case the libretto is taken from one of Beaumarchais' great twin comedies. Yet in their musical effect the two operas are poles apart ; while Mozart delights and satisfies with a great variety of well-graduated *nuances*, Rossini excites and dazzles by an unceasing flood of brilliance.

The Barber is the gayest of operas ; it is also the most florid. Gluck's reforms had made but little impression in Italy, and Rossini was all on the side of the singers ; no composer has ever understood them better, none has written so sympathetically for every class of voice. The grace and sparkle of his music proved irresistible, and he and his successors, Bellini and Donizetti, dominated the world of opera completely for more than half a century. The result was the emergence of a number of exceptional singers whose enormous influence constituted a real danger to operatic progress. Pasta, Malibran, Grisi, Piccolomini, Alboni, Lind, Patti, and, of men, Mario, Rubini, Tamburini, Lablache, are names worthy of all honour in their own sphere ; but there can be no doubt that the public idolatry with which they were surrounded was largely responsible for the artistic decline of what we now call ' old-fashioned Italian Opera,' and delayed the progress of the coming great reform.

Il Barbiere has never lost its hold; the part of Rosina remains to this day the chosen battle-horse of any singer who wishes to assert her claim to be a *prima donna assoluta*. We may be thankful that it is so—this work, when rightly sung, can never fail to charm; one cannot help wishing that Rossini had given us another *Barber*, instead of being betrayed by the rivalry of Meyerbeer into writing *Guillaume Tell* in order to meet the grandiose demands of the Paris opera house.

Giacomo Meyerbeer (actually Jakob Beer) is one of those temporarily important figures in musical history whom it is impossible to ignore, and not easy to praise. A fellow-student with Weber under the Abbé Vogler, he began by writing Italian Opera in the manner of Rossini, whose rival he eventually became. In 1826 he settled in Paris, where all his best-known works were produced—*Robert le Diable* (1831), *Les Huguenots* (1836), *Le Prophète* (1849), *Dinorah* (1859), *L'Africaine* (1865). The prodigious success of *Robert* installed Meyerbeer as the autocrat of the Paris Grand Opera practically for the rest of his life. The reason for that success is well suggested by the writer of the article "Meyerbeer" in Grove's Dictionary: "With this strange picturesque medley all were pleased, for in it each found something to suit his taste." This is perhaps as far as commendation can go in Meyerbeer's case; brilliantly gifted, of astonishing industry, with every advantage of education and experience, he seems to have been utterly devoid of a musical conscience. Weber had tried in vain to influence him for good; Wagner's high ideals and absolute sincerity made no appeal to him. To quote again from Grove: "Meyerbeer's music now belongs to the past, and there is little chance of it ever coming into fashion again. . . . He strove to please his public, and he had his reward."

In spite of the fact that his style is an inorganic composition of various schools, Meyerbeer is sometimes referred to as the Father of Modern French Opera; it would be interesting to learn which of his many brilliant successors has ever acknowledged his parentage. Apologists are not lacking among his critics, but Wagner's well-known contemptuous estimate will probably stand in future histories. Not all Meyerbeer's prodigious cleverness and *flair* for effect could make up for his obvious lack of sincerity—and what must Wagner, the poet, have thought of a man who could stoop to such subjects as *Robert le Diable* and *Dinorah* ?

It is difficult to realize that MM. Barbier and Carré, who were responsible for the latter piece of imbecility, could also supply, and in the same year (1859), the 'book' for Gounod's *Faust*, surely one of the best that ever composer had to work on. Thanks to its excellence, Gounod was able to produce that fine and original work which entitles him, and not Meyerbeer, to be regarded as the originator of the modern French school developed by A. Thomas, Saint-Saëns, Delibes, and Massenet.

But Paris was not destined to occupy much longer that paramount position which the influence of Gluck, Rossini, and Meyerbeer had gained for her ; toward the middle of the century a power had arisen in Germany which was to challenge the attention of the musical world by upsetting all previous operatic standards.

Any notice of Wagner as the Great Reformer must be preceded by a reverential tribute to his precursor, Carl Maria von Weber (1786–1826), whose *Der Freischütz*, produced at Berlin in 1821, remains, with the exception of *Die Meistersinger*, the most intensely national opera that Germany possesses. It is now generally acknowledged that in this work of high genius Weber has anticipated, by intuition, many of the ideas which Wagner afterward developed with such marvellous results. But Weber worked from sheer inspiration rather than from any conscious theory, and in his other two operas, *Euryanthe* and *Oberon*, squandered his lovely music on such worthless librettos that both works are practically lost to the theatre. However, *Der Freischütz* remains, still fresh and fair, and, though only a *Singspiel*, the most perfect operatic embodiment of the old German spirit of Romance.

This same spirit was no small part of the inspiration of Richard Wagner (1813–83) whose daring originality had made its mark within a quarter of a century after Weber's death.

Der fliegende Holländer was produced at Dresden in 1843, *Tannhäuser* in 1845, and *Lohengrin* at Weimar in 1850. Although these works only partially embody those theories which later on were to transform ' opera ' into ' music-drama,' the new seed was sprouting in them, plain for all to see. The insistence on dramatic continuity, the rejection of the old cramping melodic formulas, of show-pieces or ornament of any kind merely for its own sake, the important part assigned to the orchestra in the unfolding of the story, the guiding-themes as a clue to the underlying emotions—all these things clearly portend a revolt against established traditions. Moreover, the glowing genius of Wagner, more precious than all his theories, was already present in its youthful vigour ; nothing had ever been heard remotely approaching, in descriptive power, the overtures to *The Flying Dutchman* and *Tannhäuser*, while the visionary beauties of *Lohengrin* served to bring all heaven before the eyes of many who had never previously looked to the opera house for such an experience.

The librettos alone were a revelation. Hitherto the

opera-'books' had been, for the majority, a negligible quantity, or for the more thoughtful a thing to be regarded with contemptuous tolerance ; there was in them no respect for dramatic probability, no standard of literary decency ; with hardly an exception they were intellectually disreputable. But here were skilfully constructed dramas of great interest, written in a literary style that did no discredit to the high romantic nature of the subject ; it seemed almost a misnomer to apply the word 'libretto' to works like these. Wagner, like Gluck, had realized that no reform was possible that did not begin with the words ; in his ideal 'drama for music' words and music were co-important, inseparable, and, if possible, should spring both from the same imagination ; fortunately he possessed a poetic faculty sufficient for the needs of his musical genius, and we see the result in such homogeneous creations as *Tannhäuser*, *Die Meistersinger*, and *Parsifal*.

This revolution in the 'book' of the opera created a new class of opera-goers ; the *intelligentsia* could now enter the temple of the lyric drama and still preserve their self-respect. As time went on and the cult of Wagner became almost a religion it cannot be said that the attitude of these highly intelligent worshippers was altogether a healthy one. Fascinated and led astray by the composer's insistence on the philosophical importance of his music-dramas, the Perfect Wagnerite came to regard a visit to the opera rather as an intellectual exercise than an artistic enjoyment ; *The Ring* in particular was looked upon as a sort of guide to the Higher Wisdom, and books have been written about it that can only be classed with the literature of the Great Pyramid and the Bacon-Shakespeare controversy.

But all this is merely amusing in retrospect ; Wagner's

nebulous philosophy has long ceased to be of interest, even some of his art theories have been given decent burial, but the splendour of his music remains undimmed, and the reforms which he carried through are perhaps the most far-reaching and at the same time the most valuable that were ever effected in any field of art. It is open to question whether in some cases Wagner did not allow his theories to obscure the brightness of his genius. *The Ring*, for instance, once so blindly worshipped, is now seen, as a music-drama, to be founded on too complex a basis; people are no longer interested in the elaborate mythological pantomime which does duty for drama, nor in the truths which it is supposed to symbolize. But the gorgeous music still entrances, and many are of opinion that this will survive among the treasures of the symphony concert when the work is no longer to be seen in the theatre. Already the tendency is to give performances of single sections of *The Ring* rather than of the complete cycle in its colossal entirety.

There remain the three unquestioned masterpieces in which plot, poetry, and music must remain for ever inseparable—*Tristan* (1865), *Parsifal* (1882), and, above all, *Die Meistersinger* (1868), which for mellow wisdom of conception combined with exquisite beauty of expression occupies a place in Wagner's works comparable to that of *The Tempest* among the plays of Shakespeare, and which, moreover, is full of just the sane and kindly humour which we find in Shakespearian comedy.

At the very time that Wagner was tearing up the past by the roots and changing the whole operatic outlook, another composer, still working in the long-established formulas, was infusing new life into the old Italian Opera. Giuseppe Verdi (1813–1901) is the only composer whose fame is commensurate with that of Wagner in the musical history of their time. Born in the same year as the German master, he had written several operas while Donizetti was still alive ; he survived Wagner by eighteen years, and in his last opera, *Falstaff*, written at the age of eighty, he showed that he had assimilated what was best in the Reformer's methods, while retaining all his old melodious charm, and revealing for the first time a rich vein of delicate humour.

But the peculiar genius of Verdi is seen at its best in the works which belong to the middle period of his long career. His first vital opera, *Rigoletto*, was produced in 1851 (a year after *Lohengrin*) ; this was succeeded by *Il Trovatore* and *La Traviata*, both in 1853 ; *La Forza del Destino* followed in 1862, and *Aïda*, the crowning achievement, in 1871.

Verdi brought into Italian grand opera the much needed elements of strength and sincerity. Rossini's natural genius had found its true expression in comedy ; Bellini's delicate flutings were sufficient for *La Sonnambula*, but hardly for such a subject as *Norma* ; Donizetti had written excellent comic opera, but his attempts at the grand style are merely weak and pretentious—we feel that, like Meyerbeer, who for our purpose may well be classed among the Italians, he is merely making up music according to a popular receipt.

But Verdi, in his maturer work, is always unquestionably sincere ; his principle seems to have been : " Look in thy heart and write ! " The libretto may be crude melo-drama, the situations absurd, but Verdi manages to seize and alchemize them, and the result is a spontaneous out-pouring of lovely and appropriate melody. His ' tunes,' as they are often called in derision, are sometimes blatant and banal, but seldom weak or sentimental—at their best they possess a certain glamour which belongs to the region of pure romance. Although in his latest operas Verdi shows himself in perfect sympathy with the modern principle which demands that the orchestra shall have its full share in the musical interpretation, it is as a master of dramatic vocal melody that Verdi occupies the high place assigned to him.

Among later Italian composers the best known are Ponchielli (1834–86), Mascagni (1863–1945), Leoncavallo (1858– 1919), and Puccini (1858–1924). The first three are all one-opera men; the rightful heir to Verdi's throne has not yet appeared.

Although Wagner's reforms may be said to have renewed the face of the operatic world, it has not been found possible to accept his principles in their entirety— composers in every country have adopted such features as appealed most to their individual genius. One of the earliest to profit by the new light was Bizet (1838–75), whose *Carmen*, produced in the year of the composer's death, was actually condemned at the time for being too Wagnerian; it has long since taken its place among the masterpieces of dramatic music—not strictly to be classed with ' music-drama,' it stands, with *Aïda*, on the bridge which separates the old world from the new.

The next French composer to make a striking success in the Wagnerian manner was Charpentier (1860–1956) with his opera *Louise* (1900), a work which conforms to Wagner's counsel of perfection that words and music should be the work of a single brain. The subject, it is true, is thoroughly un-Wagnerian, for *Louise*, described as a ' musical Romance,' is actually a realistic picture of modern Parisian life, farced with a certain amount of dubious ethical propaganda which has undoubtedly contributed largely to the popularity of the work.

In complete contrast to *Louise* is *Pelléas et Mélisande*

(1907), by Debussy (1862–1918). Maeterlinck's poem, in which we seem to catch the echoes from some dim region " out of space, out of time," offered the composer exactly the right material for the exercise of his extraordinary genius. In his handling of it Debussy seems to reach backward as well as forward ; while exactly preserving Wagner's principle of dramatic continuity he goes far beyond ' the Master ' in novel and audacious harmonic combinations ; at the same time, in the almost complete fusion of words and music, *Pelléas* comes nearer to the original intentions of the Florentine founders of 1600 than any opera that has yet been written.

In Germany the composer who has followed the Wagnerian model most closely and with the greatest success is Engelbert Humperdinck (1858–1921), who in *Hänsel und Gretel* has given us one of the loveliest of operas, worthy to stand beside *Der Freischütz* as an inspiration drawn from the traditional romance and mystery of the German forest.

Richard Strauss (1864–1949), the most significant composer who has appeared since the death of Wagner, and one of the greatest symphonists of all time, certainly laid himself open in his earlier works, *Salome* (1905) and *Elektra* (1909), to the charge of putting " the statue in the orchestra " and a most unsightly " pedestal on the stage." He seems, however, to have found his true measure in *Der Rosenkavalier* (1911), a brilliant piece of satirical humour which makes a deeper impression with every hearing. It is to be noted as of good omen for the future that this, the latest opera of first-class importance, recalls, in some of its most delightful moments, the sweetness and gaiety of Mozart.

The world of opera is ripe for a work worthy to take its place in the great line of musical comedies, with *Falstaff*,

The Mastersingers, *The Barber of Seville*, and *Figaro*. We have had enough of noisy sensation, of morbid psychology, of a too frank eroticism; nothing is more to be desired, for our present need, than a revival of comic opera in the grand style, and the rise of a school of composers prepared to maintain, with the Poet Laureate, that

> Howsoe'er man hug his care
> The best of his art is gay.

A CATALOGUE OF SELECTED DOVER BOOKS
IN ALL FIELDS OF INTEREST

A CATALOGUE OF SELECTED DOVER BOOKS
IN ALL FIELDS OF INTEREST

AMERICA'S OLD MASTERS, James T. Flexner. Four men emerged unexpectedly from provincial 18th century America to leadership in European art: Benjamin West, J. S. Copley, C. R. Peale, Gilbert Stuart. Brilliant coverage of lives and contributions. Revised, 1967 edition. 69 plates. 365pp. of text.
21806-6 Paperbound $3.00

FIRST FLOWERS OF OUR WILDERNESS: AMERICAN PAINTING, THE COLONIAL PERIOD, James T. Flexner. Painters, and regional painting traditions from earliest Colonial times up to the emergence of Copley, West and Peale Sr., Foster, Gustavus Hesselius, Feke, John Smibert and many anonymous painters in the primitive manner. Engaging presentation, with 162 illustrations. xxii + 368pp.
22180-6 Paperbound $3.50

THE LIGHT OF DISTANT SKIES: AMERICAN PAINTING, 1760-1835, James T. Flexner. The great generation of early American painters goes to Europe to learn and to teach: West, Copley, Gilbert Stuart and others. Allston, Trumbull, Morse; also contemporary American painters—primitives, derivatives, academics—who remained in America. 102 illustrations. xiii + 306pp.
22179-2 Paperbound $3.00

A HISTORY OF THE RISE AND PROGRESS OF THE ARTS OF DESIGN IN THE UNITED STATES, William Dunlap. Much the richest mine of information on early American painters, sculptors, architects, engravers, miniaturists, etc. The only source of information for scores of artists, the major primary source for many others. Unabridged reprint of rare original 1834 edition, with new introduction by James T. Flexner, and 394 new illustrations. Edited by Rita Weiss. 6⅝ x 9⅝.
21695-0, 21696-9, 21697-7 Three volumes, Paperbound $13.50

EPOCHS OF CHINESE AND JAPANESE ART, Ernest F. Fenollosa. From primitive Chinese art to the 20th century, thorough history, explanation of every important art period and form, including Japanese woodcuts; main stress on China and Japan, but Tibet, Korea also included. Still unexcelled for its detailed, rich coverage of cultural background, aesthetic elements, diffusion studies, particularly of the historical period. 2nd, 1913 edition. 242 illustrations. lii + 439pp. of text.
20364-6, 20365-4 Two volumes, Paperbound $6.00

THE GENTLE ART OF MAKING ENEMIES, James A. M. Whistler. Greatest wit of his day deflates Oscar Wilde, Ruskin, Swinburne; strikes back at inane critics, exhibitions, art journalism; aesthetics of impressionist revolution in most striking form. Highly readable classic by great painter. Reproduction of edition designed by Whistler. Introduction by Alfred Werner. xxxvi + 334pp.
21875-9 Paperbound $2.50

DESIGN BY ACCIDENT; A BOOK OF "ACCIDENTAL EFFECTS" FOR ARTISTS AND DESIGNERS, James F. O'Brien. Create your own unique, striking, imaginative effects by "controlled accident" interaction of materials: paints and lacquers, oil and water based paints, splatter, crackling materials, shatter, similar items. Everything you do will be different; first book on this limitless art, so useful to both fine artist and commercial artist. Full instructions. 192 plates showing "accidents," 8 in color. viii + 215pp. 8⅜ x 11¼. 21942-9 Paperbound $3.50

THE BOOK OF SIGNS, Rudolf Koch. Famed German type designer draws 493 beautiful symbols: religious, mystical, alchemical, imperial, property marks, runes, etc. Remarkable fusion of traditional and modern. Good for suggestions of timelessness, smartness, modernity. Text. vi + 104pp. 6⅛ x 9¼.
20162-7 Paperbound $1.25

HISTORY OF INDIAN AND INDONESIAN ART, Ananda K. Coomaraswamy. An unabridged republication of one of the finest books by a great scholar in Eastern art. Rich in descriptive material, history, social backgrounds; Sunga reliefs, Rajput paintings, Gupta temples, Burmese frescoes, textiles, jewelry, sculpture, etc. 400 photos. viii + 423pp. 6⅜ x 9¾. 21436-2 Paperbound $4.00

PRIMITIVE ART, Franz Boas. America's foremost anthropologist surveys textiles, ceramics, woodcarving, basketry, metalwork, etc.; patterns, technology, creation of symbols, style origins. All areas of world, but very full on Northwest Coast Indians. More than 350 illustrations of baskets, boxes, totem poles, weapons, etc. 378 pp.
20025-6 Paperbound $3.00

THE GENTLEMAN AND CABINET MAKER'S DIRECTOR, Thomas Chippendale. Full reprint (third edition, 1762) of most influential furniture book of all time, by master cabinetmaker. 200 plates, illustrating chairs, sofas, mirrors, tables, cabinets, plus 24 photographs of surviving pieces. Biographical introduction by N. Bienenstock. vi + 249pp. 9⅞ x 12¾. 21601-2 Paperbound $4.00

AMERICAN ANTIQUE FURNITURE, Edgar G. Miller, Jr. The basic coverage of all American furniture before 1840. Individual chapters cover type of furniture—clocks, tables, sideboards, etc.—chronologically, with inexhaustible wealth of data. More than 2100 photographs, all identified, commented on. Essential to all early American collectors. Introduction by H. E. Keyes. vi + 1106pp. 7⅞ x 10¾.
21599-7, 21600-4 Two volumes, Paperbound $11.00

PENNSYLVANIA DUTCH AMERICAN FOLK ART, Henry J. Kauffman. 279 photos, 28 drawings of tulipware, Fraktur script, painted tinware, toys, flowered furniture, quilts, samplers, hex signs, house interiors, etc. Full descriptive text. Excellent for tourist, rewarding for designer, collector. Map. 146pp. 7⅞ x 10¾.
21205-X Paperbound $2.50

EARLY NEW ENGLAND GRAVESTONE RUBBINGS, Edmund V. Gillon, Jr. 43 photographs, 226 carefully reproduced rubbings show heavily symbolic, sometimes macabre early gravestones, up to early 19th century. Remarkable early American primitive art, occasionally strikingly beautiful; always powerful. Text. xxvi + 207pp. 8⅜ x 11¼. 21380-3 Paperbound $3.50

ALPHABETS AND ORNAMENTS, Ernst Lehner. Well-known pictorial source for decorative alphabets, script examples, cartouches, frames, decorative title pages, calligraphic initials, borders, similar material. 14th to 19th century, mostly European. Useful in almost any graphic arts designing, varied styles. 750 illustrations. 256pp. 7 x 10.
21905-4 Paperbound $4.00

PAINTING: A CREATIVE APPROACH, Norman Colquhoun. For the beginner simple guide provides an instructive approach to painting: major stumbling blocks for beginner; overcoming them, technical points; paints and pigments; oil painting; watercolor and other media and color. New section on "plastic" paints. Glossary. Formerly *Paint Your Own Pictures*. 221pp.
22000-1 Paperbound $1.75

THE ENJOYMENT AND USE OF COLOR, Walter Sargent. Explanation of the relations between colors themselves and between colors in nature and art, including hundreds of little-known facts about color values, intensities, effects of high and low illumination, complementary colors. Many practical hints for painters, references to great masters. 7 color plates, 29 illustrations. x + 274pp.
20944-X Paperbound $2.75

THE NOTEBOOKS OF LEONARDO DA VINCI, compiled and edited by Jean Paul Richter. 1566 extracts from original manuscripts reveal the full range of Leonardo's versatile genius: all his writings on painting, sculpture, architecture, anatomy, astronomy, geography, topography, physiology, mining, music, etc., in both Italian and English, with 186 plates of manuscript pages and more than 500 additional drawings. Includes studies for the Last Supper, the lost Sforza monument, and other works. Total of xlvii + 866pp. 7⅞ x 10¾.
22572-0, 22573-9 Two volumes, Paperbound $10.00

MONTGOMERY WARD CATALOGUE OF 1895. Tea gowns, yards of flannel and pillow-case lace, stereoscopes, books of gospel hymns, the New Improved Singer Sewing Machine, side saddles, milk skimmers, straight-edged razors, high-button shoes, spittoons, and on and on . . . listing some 25,000 items, practically all illustrated. Essential to the shoppers of the 1890's, it is our truest record of the spirit of the period. Unaltered reprint of Issue No. 57, Spring and Summer 1895. Introduction by Boris Emmet. Innumerable illustrations. xiii + 624pp. 8½ x 11⅝.
22377-9 Paperbound $6.95

THE CRYSTAL PALACE EXHIBITION ILLUSTRATED CATALOGUE (LONDON, 1851). One of the wonders of the modern world—the Crystal Palace Exhibition in which all the nations of the civilized world exhibited their achievements in the arts and sciences—presented in an equally important illustrated catalogue. More than 1700 items pictured with accompanying text—ceramics, textiles, cast-iron work, carpets, pianos, sleds, razors, wall-papers, billiard tables, beehives, silverware and hundreds of other artifacts—represent the focal point of Victorian culture in the Western World. Probably the largest collection of Victorian decorative art ever assembled—indispensable for antiquarians and designers. Unabridged republication of the Art-Journal Catalogue of the Great Exhibition of 1851, with all terminal essays. New introduction by John Gloag, F.S.A. xxxiv + 426pp. 9 x 12.
22503-8 Paperbound $4.50

A HISTORY OF COSTUME, Carl Köhler. Definitive history, based on surviving pieces of clothing primarily, and paintings, statues, etc. secondarily. Highly readable text, supplemented by 594 illustrations of costumes of the ancient Mediterranean peoples, Greece and Rome, the Teutonic prehistoric period; costumes of the Middle Ages, Renaissance, Baroque, 18th and 19th centuries. Clear, measured patterns are provided for many clothing articles. Approach is practical throughout. Enlarged by Emma von Sichart. 464pp. 21030-8 Paperbound $3.50

ORIENTAL RUGS, ANTIQUE AND MODERN, Walter A. Hawley. A complete and authoritative treatise on the Oriental rug—where they are made, by whom and how, designs and symbols, characteristics in detail of the six major groups, how to distinguish them and how to buy them. Detailed technical data is provided on periods, weaves, warps, wefts, textures, sides, ends and knots, although no technical background is required for an understanding. 11 color plates, 80 halftones, 4 maps. vi + 320pp. 6⅛ x 9⅛. 22366-3 Paperbound $5.00

TEN BOOKS ON ARCHITECTURE, Vitruvius. By any standards the most important book on architecture ever written. Early Roman discussion of aesthetics of building, construction methods, orders, sites, and every other aspect of architecture has inspired, instructed architecture for about 2,000 years. Stands behind Palladio, Michelangelo, Bramante, Wren, countless others. Definitive Morris H. Morgan translation. 68 illustrations. xii + 331pp. 20645-9 Paperbound $3.50

THE FOUR BOOKS OF ARCHITECTURE, Andrea Palladio. Translated into every major Western European language in the two centuries following its publication in 1570, this has been one of the most influential books in the history of architecture. Complete reprint of the 1738 Isaac Ware edition. New introduction by Adolf Placzek, Columbia Univ. 216 plates. xxii + 110pp. of text. 9½ x 12¾. 21308-0 Clothbound $10.00

STICKS AND STONES: A STUDY OF AMERICAN ARCHITECTURE AND CIVILIZATION, Lewis Mumford. One of the great classics of American cultural history. American architecture from the medieval-inspired earliest forms to the early 20th century; evolution of structure and style, and reciprocal influences on environment. 21 photographic illustrations. 238pp. 20202-X Paperbound $2.00

THE AMERICAN BUILDER'S COMPANION, Asher Benjamin. The most widely used early 19th century architectural style and source book, for colonial up into Greek Revival periods. Extensive development of geometry of carpentering, construction of sashes, frames, doors, stairs; plans and elevations of domestic and other buildings. Hundreds of thousands of houses were built according to this book, now invaluable to historians, architects, restorers, etc. 1827 edition. 59 plates. 114pp. 7⅞ x 10¾. 22236-5 Paperbound $3.50

DUTCH HOUSES IN THE HUDSON VALLEY BEFORE 1776, Helen Wilkinson Reynolds. The standard survey of the Dutch colonial house and outbuildings, with constructional features, decoration, and local history associated with individual homesteads. Introduction by Franklin D. Roosevelt. Map. 150 illustrations. 469pp. 6⅝ x 9¼. 21469-9 Paperbound $4.00

THE ARCHITECTURE OF COUNTRY HOUSES, Andrew J. Downing. Together with Vaux's *Villas and Cottages* this is the basic book for Hudson River Gothic architecture of the middle Victorian period. Full, sound discussions of general aspects of housing, architecture, style, decoration, furnishing, together with scores of detailed house plans, illustrations of specific buildings, accompanied by full text. Perhaps the most influential single American architectural book. 1850 edition. Introduction by J. Stewart Johnson. 321 figures, 34 architectural designs. xvi + 560pp.

22003-6 Paperbound $4.00

LOST EXAMPLES OF COLONIAL ARCHITECTURE, John Mead Howells. Full-page photographs of buildings that have disappeared or been so altered as to be denatured, including many designed by major early American architects. 245 plates. xvii + 248pp. 7⅞ x 10¾.

21143-6 Paperbound $3.50

DOMESTIC ARCHITECTURE OF THE AMERICAN COLONIES AND OF THE EARLY REPUBLIC, Fiske Kimball. Foremost architect and restorer of Williamsburg and Monticello covers nearly 200 homes between 1620-1825. Architectural details, construction, style features, special fixtures, floor plans, etc. Generally considered finest work in its area. 219 illustrations of houses, doorways, windows, capital mantels. xx + 314pp. 7⅞ x 10¾.

21743-4 Paperbound $4.00

EARLY AMERICAN ROOMS: 1650-1858, edited by Russell Hawes Kettell. Tour of 12 rooms, each representative of a different era in American history and each furnished, decorated, designed and occupied in the style of the era. 72 plans and elevations, 8-page color section, etc., show fabrics, wall papers, arrangements, etc. Full descriptive text. xvii + 200pp. of text. 8⅜ x 11¼.

21633-0 Paperbound $5.00

THE FITZWILLIAM VIRGINAL BOOK, edited by J. Fuller Maitland and W. B. Squire. Full modern printing of famous early 17th-century ms. volume of 300 works by Morley, Byrd, Bull, Gibbons, etc. For piano or other modern keyboard instrument; easy to read format. xxxvi + 938pp. 8⅜ x 11.

21068-5, 21069-3 Two volumes, Paperbound $10.00

KEYBOARD MUSIC, Johann Sebastian Bach. Bach Gesellschaft edition. A rich selection of Bach's masterpieces for the harpsichord: the six English Suites, six French Suites, the six Partitas (Clavierübung part I), the Goldberg Variations (Clavierübung part IV), the fifteen Two-Part Inventions and the fifteen Three-Part Sinfonias. Clearly reproduced on large sheets with ample margins; eminently playable. vi + 312pp. 8⅛ x 11.

22360-4 Paperbound $5.00

THE MUSIC OF BACH: AN INTRODUCTION, Charles Sanford Terry. A fine, nontechnical introduction to Bach's music, both instrumental and vocal. Covers organ music, chamber music, passion music, other types. Analyzes themes, developments, innovations. x + 114pp.

21075-8 Paperbound $1.25

BEETHOVEN AND HIS NINE SYMPHONIES, Sir George Grove. Noted British musicologist provides best history, analysis, commentary on symphonies. Very thorough, rigorously accurate; necessary to both advanced student and amateur music lover. 436 musical passages. vii + 407 pp.

20334-4 Paperbound $2.75

JOHANN SEBASTIAN BACH, Philipp Spitta. One of the great classics of musicology, this definitive analysis of Bach's music (and life) has never been surpassed. Lucid, nontechnical analyses of hundreds of pieces (30 pages devoted to St. Matthew Passion, 26 to B Minor Mass). Also includes major analysis of 18th-century music. 450 musical examples. 40-page musical supplement. Total of xx + 1799pp.
(EUK) 22278-0, 22279-9 Two volumes, Clothbound $15.00

MOZART AND HIS PIANO CONCERTOS, Cuthbert Girdlestone. The only full-length study of an important area of Mozart's creativity. Provides detailed analyses of all 23 concertos, traces inspirational sources. 417 musical examples. Second edition. 509pp.
(USO) 21271-8 Paperbound $3.50

THE PERFECT WAGNERITE: A COMMENTARY ON THE NIBLUNG'S RING, George Bernard Shaw. Brilliant and still relevant criticism in remarkable essays on Wagner's Ring cycle, Shaw's ideas on political and social ideology behind the plots, role of Leitmotifs, vocal requisites, etc. Prefaces. xxi + 136pp.
21707-8 Paperbound $1.50

DON GIOVANNI, W. A. Mozart. Complete libretto, modern English translation; biographies of composer and librettist; accounts of early performances and critical reaction. Lavishly illustrated. All the material you need to understand and appreciate this great work. Dover Opera Guide and Libretto Series; translated and introduced by Ellen Bleiler. 92 illustrations. 209pp.
21134-7 Paperbound $1.50

HIGH FIDELITY SYSTEMS: A LAYMAN'S GUIDE, Roy F. Allison. All the basic information you need for setting up your own audio system: high fidelity and stereo record players, tape records, F.M. Connections, adjusting tone arm, cartridge, checking needle alignment, positioning speakers, phasing speakers, adjusting hums, trouble-shooting, maintenance, and similar topics. Enlarged 1965 edition. More than 50 charts, diagrams, photos. iv + 91pp.
21514-8 Paperbound $1.25

REPRODUCTION OF SOUND, Edgar Villchur. Thorough coverage for laymen of high fidelity systems, reproducing systems in general, needles, amplifiers, preamps, loudspeakers, feedback, explaining physical background. "A rare talent for making technicalities vividly comprehensible," R. Darrell, *High Fidelity*. 69 figures. iv + 92pp.
21515-6 Paperbound $1.00

HEAR ME TALKIN' TO YA: THE STORY OF JAZZ AS TOLD BY THE MEN WHO MADE IT, Nat Shapiro and Nat Hentoff. Louis Armstrong, Fats Waller, Jo Jones, Clarence Williams, Billy Holiday, Duke Ellington, Jelly Roll Morton and dozens of other jazz greats tell how it was in Chicago's South Side, New Orleans, depression Harlem and the modern West Coast as jazz was born and grew. xvi + 429pp.
21726-4 Paperbound $2.50

FABLES OF AESOP, translated by Sir Roger L'Estrange. A reproduction of the very rare 1931 Paris edition; a selection of the most interesting fables, together with 50 imaginative drawings by Alexander Calder. v + 128pp. 6½x9¼.
21780-9 Paperbound $1.25

AGAINST THE GRAIN (A REBOURS), Joris K. Huysmans. Filled with weird images, evidences of a bizarre imagination, exotic experiments with hallucinatory drugs, rich tastes and smells and the diversions of its sybarite hero Duc Jean des Esseintes, this classic novel pushed 19th-century literary decadence to its limits. Full unabridged edition. Do not confuse this with abridged editions generally sold. Introduction by Havelock Ellis. xlix + 206pp. 22190-3 Paperbound $2.00

VARIORUM SHAKESPEARE: HAMLET. Edited by Horace H. Furness; a landmark of American scholarship. Exhaustive footnotes and appendices treat all doubtful words and phrases, as well as suggested critical emendations throughout the play's history. First volume contains editor's own text, collated with all Quartos and Folios. Second volume contains full first Quarto, translations of Shakespeare's sources (Belleforest, and Saxo Grammaticus), Der Bestrafte Brudermord, and many essays on critical and historical points of interest by major authorities of past and present. Includes details of staging and costuming over the years. By far the best edition available for serious students of Shakespeare. Total of xx + 905pp. 21004-9, 21005-7, 2 volumes, Paperbound $7.00

A LIFE OF WILLIAM SHAKESPEARE, Sir Sidney Lee. This is the standard life of Shakespeare, summarizing everything known about Shakespeare and his plays. Incredibly rich in material, broad in coverage, clear and judicious, it has served thousands as the best introduction to Shakespeare. 1931 edition. 9 plates. xxix + 792pp. (USO) 21967-4 Paperbound $3.75

MASTERS OF THE DRAMA, John Gassner. Most comprehensive history of the drama in print, covering every tradition from Greeks to modern Europe and America, including India, Far East, etc. Covers more than 800 dramatists, 2000 plays, with biographical material, plot summaries, theatre history, criticism, etc. "Best of its kind in English," New Republic. 77 illustrations. xxii + 890pp. 20100-7 Clothbound $8.50

THE EVOLUTION OF THE ENGLISH LANGUAGE, George McKnight. The growth of English, from the 14th century to the present. Unusual, non-technical account presents basic information in very interesting form: sound shifts, change in grammar and syntax, vocabulary growth, similar topics. Abundantly illustrated with quotations. Formerly Modern English in the Making. xii + 590pp. 21932-1 Paperbound $3.50

AN ETYMOLOGICAL DICTIONARY OF MODERN ENGLISH, Ernest Weekley. Fullest, richest work of its sort, by foremost British lexicographer. Detailed word histories, including many colloquial and archaic words; extensive quotations. Do not confuse this with the Concise Etymological Dictionary, which is much abridged. Total of xxvii + 830pp. 6½ x 9¼. 21873-2, 21874-0 Two volumes, Paperbound $6.00

FLATLAND: A ROMANCE OF MANY DIMENSIONS, E. A. Abbott. Classic of science-fiction explores ramifications of life in a two-dimensional world, and what happens when a three-dimensional being intrudes. Amusing reading, but also useful as introduction to thought about hyperspace. Introduction by Banesh Hoffmann. 16 illustrations. xx + 103pp. 20001-9 Paperbound $1.00

POEMS OF ANNE BRADSTREET, edited with an introduction by Robert Hutchinson. A new selection of poems by America's first poet and perhaps the first significant woman poet in the English language. 48 poems display her development in works of considerable variety—love poems, domestic poems, religious meditations, formal elegies, "quaternions," etc. Notes, bibliography. viii + 222pp.

22160-1 Paperbound $2.00

THREE GOTHIC NOVELS: THE CASTLE OF OTRANTO BY HORACE WALPOLE; VATHEK BY WILLIAM BECKFORD; THE VAMPYRE BY JOHN POLIDORI, WITH FRAGMENT OF A NOVEL BY LORD BYRON, edited by E. F. Bleiler. The first Gothic novel, by Walpole; the finest Oriental tale in English, by Beckford; powerful Romantic supernatural story in versions by Polidori and Byron. All extremely important in history of literature; all still exciting, packed with supernatural thrills, ghosts, haunted castles, magic, etc. xl + 291pp.

21232-7 Paperbound $2.00

THE BEST TALES OF HOFFMANN, E. T. A. Hoffmann. 10 of Hoffmann's most important stories, in modern re-editings of standard translations: Nutcracker and the King of Mice, Signor Formica, Automata, The Sandman, Rath Krespel, The Golden Flowerpot, Master Martin the Cooper, The Mines of Falun, The King's Betrothed, A New Year's Eve Adventure. 7 illustrations by Hoffmann. Edited by E. F. Bleiler. xxxix + 419pp.

21793-0 Paperbound $2.50

GHOST AND HORROR STORIES OF AMBROSE BIERCE, Ambrose Bierce. 23 strikingly modern stories of the horrors latent in the human mind: The Eyes of the Panther, The Damned Thing, An Occurrence at Owl Creek Bridge, An Inhabitant of Carcosa, etc., plus the dream-essay, Visions of the Night. Edited by E. F. Bleiler. xxii + 199pp.

20767-6 Paperbound $1.50

BEST GHOST STORIES OF J. S. LEFANU, J. Sheridan LeFanu. Finest stories by Victorian master often considered greatest supernatural writer of all. Carmilla, Green Tea, The Haunted Baronet, The Familiar, and 12 others. Most never before available in the U. S. A. Edited by E. F. Bleiler. 8 illustrations from Victorian publications. xvii + 467pp.

20415-4 Paperbound $2.50

THE TIME STREAM, THE GREATEST ADVENTURE, AND THE PURPLE SAPPHIRE— THREE SCIENCE FICTION NOVELS, John Taine (Eric Temple Bell). Great American mathematician was also foremost science fiction novelist of the 1920's. *The Time Stream,* one of all-time classics, uses concepts of circular time; *The Greatest Adventure,* incredibly ancient biological experiments from Antarctica threaten to escape; The *Purple Sapphire,* superscience, lost races in Central Tibet, survivors of the Great Race. 4 illustrations by Frank R. Paul. v + 532pp.

21180-0 Paperbound $3.00

SEVEN SCIENCE FICTION NOVELS, H. G. Wells. The standard collection of the great novels. Complete, unabridged. *First Men in the Moon, Island of Dr. Moreau, War of the Worlds, Food of the Gods, Invisible Man, Time Machine, In the Days of the Comet.* Not only science fiction fans, but every educated person owes it to himself to read these novels. 1015pp.

20264-X Clothbound $5.00

THE RED FAIRY BOOK, Andrew Lang. Lang's color fairy books have long been children's favorites. This volume includes Rapunzel, Jack and the Bean-stalk and 35 other stories, familiar and unfamiliar. 4 plates, 93 illustrations x + 367pp.
21673-X Paperbound $2.50

THE BLUE FAIRY BOOK, Andrew Lang. Lang's tales come from all countries and all times. Here are 37 tales from Grimm, the Arabian Nights, Greek Mythology, and other fascinating sources. 8 plates, 130 illustrations. xi + 390pp.
21437-0 Paperbound $2.50

HOUSEHOLD STORIES BY THE BROTHERS GRIMM. Classic English-language edition of the well-known tales — Rumpelstiltskin, Snow White, Hansel and Gretel, The Twelve Brothers, Faithful John, Rapunzel, Tom Thumb (52 stories in all). Translated into simple, straightforward English by Lucy Crane. Ornamented with headpieces, vignettes, elaborate decorative initials and a dozen full-page illustrations by Walter Crane. x + 269pp.
21080-4 Paperbound $2.50

THE MERRY ADVENTURES OF ROBIN HOOD, Howard Pyle. The finest modern versions of the traditional ballads and tales about the great English outlaw. Howard Pyle's complete prose version, with every word, every illustration of the first edition. Do not confuse this facsimile of the original (1883) with modern editions that change text or illustrations. 23 plates plus many page decorations. xxii + 296pp.
22043-5 Paperbound $2.50

THE STORY OF KING ARTHUR AND HIS KNIGHTS, Howard Pyle. The finest children's version of the life of King Arthur; brilliantly retold by Pyle, with 48 of his most imaginative illustrations. xviii + 313pp. 6⅛ x 9¼.
21445-1 Paperbound $2.50

THE WONDERFUL WIZARD OF OZ, L. Frank Baum. America's finest children's book in facsimile of first edition with all Denslow illustrations in full color. The edition a child should have. Introduction by Martin Gardner. 23 color plates, scores of drawings. iv + 267pp.
20691-2 Paperbound $2.50

THE MARVELOUS LAND OF OZ, L. Frank Baum. The second Oz book, every bit as imaginative as the Wizard. The hero is a boy named Tip, but the Scarecrow and the Tin Woodman are back, as is the Oz magic. 16 color plates, 120 drawings by John R. Neill. 287pp.
20692-0 Paperbound $2.50

THE MAGICAL MONARCH OF MO, L. Frank Baum. Remarkable adventures in a land even stranger than Oz. The best of Baum's books not in the Oz series. 15 color plates and dozens of drawings by Frank Verbeck. xviii + 237pp.
21892-9 Paperbound $2.25

THE BAD CHILD'S BOOK OF BEASTS, MORE BEASTS FOR WORSE CHILDREN, A MORAL ALPHABET, Hilaire Belloc. Three complete humor classics in one volume. Be kind to the frog, and do not call him names . . . and 28 other whimsical animals. Familiar favorites and some not so well known. Illustrated by Basil Blackwell.
156pp. (USO) 20749-8 Paperbound $1.50

EAST O' THE SUN AND WEST O' THE MOON, George W. Dasent. Considered the best of all translations of these Norwegian folk tales, this collection has been enjoyed by generations of children (and folklorists too). Includes True and Untrue, Why the Sea is Salt, East O' the Sun and West O' the Moon, Why the Bear is Stumpy-Tailed, Boots and the Troll, The Cock and the Hen, Rich Peter the Pedlar, and 52 more. The only edition with all 59 tales. 77 illustrations by Erik Werenskiold and Theodor Kittelsen. xv + 418pp. 22521-6 Paperbound $3.50

GOOPS AND HOW TO BE THEM, Gelett Burgess. Classic of tongue-in-cheek humor, masquerading as etiquette book. 87 verses, twice as many cartoons, show mischievous Goops as they demonstrate to children virtues of table manners, neatness, courtesy, etc. Favorite for generations. viii + 88pp. $6\frac{1}{2}$ x $9\frac{1}{4}$.
22233-0 Paperbound $1.25

ALICE'S ADVENTURES UNDER GROUND, Lewis Carroll. The first version, quite different from the final *Alice in Wonderland,* printed out by Carroll himself with his own illustrations. Complete facsimile of the "million dollar" manuscript Carroll gave to Alice Liddell in 1864. Introduction by Martin Gardner. viii + 96pp. Title and dedication pages in color. 21482-6 Paperbound $1.25

THE BROWNIES, THEIR BOOK, Palmer Cox. Small as mice, cunning as foxes, exuberant and full of mischief, the Brownies go to the zoo, toy shop, seashore, circus, etc., in 24 verse adventures and 266 illustrations. Long a favorite, since their first appearance in St. Nicholas Magazine. xi + 144pp. $6\frac{5}{8}$ x $9\frac{1}{4}$.
21265-3 Paperbound $1.75

SONGS OF CHILDHOOD, Walter De La Mare. Published (under the pseudonym Walter Ramal) when De La Mare was only 29, this charming collection has long been a favorite children's book. A facsimile of the first edition in paper, the 47 poems capture the simplicity of the nursery rhyme and the ballad, including such lyrics as I Met Eve, Tartary, The Silver Penny. vii + 106pp. 21972-0 Paperbound $1.25

THE COMPLETE NONSENSE OF EDWARD LEAR, Edward Lear. The finest 19th-century humorist-cartoonist in full: all nonsense limericks, zany alphabets, Owl and Pussy-cat, songs, nonsense botany, and more than 500 illustrations by Lear himself. Edited by Holbrook Jackson. xxix + 287pp. (USO) 20167-8 Paperbound $2.00

BILLY WHISKERS: THE AUTOBIOGRAPHY OF A GOAT, Frances Trego Montgomery. A favorite of children since the early 20th century, here are the escapades of that rambunctious, irresistible and mischievous goat—Billy Whiskers. Much in the spirit of *Peck's Bad Boy,* this is a book that children never tire of reading or hearing. All the original familiar illustrations by W. H. Fry are included: 6 color plates, 18 black and white drawings. 159pp. 22345-0 Paperbound $2.00

MOTHER GOOSE MELODIES. Faithful republication of the fabulously rare Munroe and Francis "copyright 1833" Boston edition—the most important Mother Goose collection, usually referred to as the "original." Familiar rhymes plus many rare ones, with wonderful old woodcut illustrations. Edited by E. F. Bleiler. 128pp. $4\frac{1}{2}$ x $6\frac{3}{8}$. 22577-1 Paperbound $1.25

TWO LITTLE SAVAGES; BEING THE ADVENTURES OF TWO BOYS WHO LIVED AS INDIANS AND WHAT THEY LEARNED, Ernest Thompson Seton. Great classic of nature and boyhood provides a vast range of woodlore in most palatable form, a genuinely entertaining story. Two farm boys build a teepee in woods and live in it for a month, working out Indian solutions to living problems, star lore, birds and animals, plants, etc. 293 illustrations. vii + 286pp.

20985-7 Paperbound $2.50

PETER PIPER'S PRACTICAL PRINCIPLES OF PLAIN & PERFECT PRONUNCIATION. Alliterative jingles and tongue-twisters of surprising charm, that made their first appearance in America about 1830. Republished in full with the spirited woodcut illustrations from this earliest American edition. 32pp. 4½ x 6⅜.

22560-7 Paperbound $1.00

SCIENCE EXPERIMENTS AND AMUSEMENTS FOR CHILDREN, Charles Vivian. 73 easy experiments, requiring only materials found at home or easily available, such as candles, coins, steel wool, etc.; illustrate basic phenomena like vacuum, simple chemical reaction, etc. All safe. Modern, well-planned. Formerly *Science Games for Children*. 102 photos, numerous drawings. 96pp. 6⅛ x 9¼.

21856-2 Paperbound $1.25

AN INTRODUCTION TO CHESS MOVES AND TACTICS SIMPLY EXPLAINED, Leonard Barden. Informal intermediate introduction, quite strong in explaining reasons for moves. Covers basic material, tactics, important openings, traps, positional play in middle game, end game. Attempts to isolate patterns and recurrent configurations. Formerly *Chess*. 58 figures. 102pp. (USO) 21210-6 Paperbound $1.25

LASKER'S MANUAL OF CHESS, Dr. Emanuel Lasker. Lasker was not only one of the five great World Champions, he was also one of the ablest expositors, theorists, and analysts. In many ways, his Manual, permeated with his philosophy of battle, filled with keen insights, is one of the greatest works ever written on chess. Filled with analyzed games by the great players. A single-volume library that will profit almost any chess player, beginner or master. 308 diagrams. xli x 349pp.

20640-8 Paperbound $2.75

THE MASTER BOOK OF MATHEMATICAL RECREATIONS, Fred Schuh. In opinion of many the finest work ever prepared on mathematical puzzles, stunts, recreations; exhaustively thorough explanations of mathematics involved, analysis of effects, citation of puzzles and games. Mathematics involved is elementary. Translated by F. Göbel. 194 figures. xxiv + 430pp.

22134-2 Paperbound $3.00

MATHEMATICS, MAGIC AND MYSTERY, Martin Gardner. Puzzle editor for Scientific American explains mathematics behind various mystifying tricks: card tricks, stage "mind reading," coin and match tricks, counting out games, geometric dissections, etc. Probability sets, theory of numbers clearly explained. Also provides more than 400 tricks, guaranteed to work, that you can do. 135 illustrations. xii + 176pp.

20338-2 Paperbound $1.50

"ESSENTIAL GRAMMAR" SERIES

All you really need to know about modern, colloquial grammar. Many educational shortcuts help you learn faster, understand better. Detailed cognate lists teach you to recognize similarities between English and foreign words and roots—make learning vocabulary easy and interesting. Excellent for independent study or as a supplement to record courses.

ESSENTIAL FRENCH GRAMMAR, Seymour Resnick. 2500-item cognate list. 159pp.
(EBE) 20419-7 Paperbound $1.25

ESSENTIAL GERMAN GRAMMAR, Guy Stern and Everett F. Bleiler. Unusual shortcuts on noun declension, word order, compound verbs. 124pp.
(EBE) 20422-7 Paperbound $1.25

ESSENTIAL ITALIAN GRAMMAR, Olga Ragusa. 111pp.
(EBE) 20779-X Paperbound $1.25

ESSENTIAL JAPANESE GRAMMAR, Everett F. Bleiler. In Romaji transcription; no characters needed. Japanese grammar is regular and simple. 156pp.
21027-8 Paperbound $1.25

ESSENTIAL PORTUGUESE GRAMMAR, Alexander da R. Prista. vi + 114pp.
21650-0 Paperbound $1.35

ESSENTIAL SPANISH GRAMMAR, Seymour Resnick. 2500 word cognate list. 115pp.
(EBE) 20780-3 Paperbound $1.25

ESSENTIAL ENGLISH GRAMMAR, Philip Gucker. Combines best features of modern, functional and traditional approaches. For refresher, class use, home study. x + 177pp.
21649-7 Paperbound $1.35

A PHRASE AND SENTENCE DICTIONARY OF SPOKEN SPANISH. Prepared for U. S. War Department by U. S. linguists. As above, unit is idiom, phrase or sentence rather than word. English-Spanish and Spanish-English sections contain modern equivalents of over 18,000 sentences. Introduction and appendix as above. iv + 513pp.
20495-2 Paperbound $2.75

A PHRASE AND SENTENCE DICTIONARY OF SPOKEN RUSSIAN. Dictionary prepared for U. S. War Department by U. S. linguists. Basic unit is not the word, but the idiom, phrase or sentence. English-Russian and Russian-English sections contain modern equivalents for over 30,000 phrases. Grammatical introduction covers phonetics, writing, syntax. Appendix of word lists for food, numbers, geographical names, etc. vi + 573 pp. 6⅛ x 9¼. 20496-0 Paperbound $4.00

CONVERSATIONAL CHINESE FOR BEGINNERS, Morris Swadesh. Phonetic system, beginner's course in Pai Hua Mandarin Chinese covering most important, most useful speech patterns. Emphasis on modern colloquial usage. Formerly *Chinese in Your Pocket.* xvi + 158pp. 21123-1 Paperbound $1.75

How to Know the Wild Flowers, Mrs. William Starr Dana. This is the classical book of American wildflowers (of the Eastern and Central United States), used by hundreds of thousands. Covers over 500 species, arranged in extremely easy to use color and season groups. Full descriptions, much plant lore. This Dover edition is the fullest ever compiled, with tables of nomenclature changes. 174 full-page plates by M. Satterlee. xii + 418pp. 20332-8 Paperbound $2.75

Our Plant Friends and Foes, William Atherton DuPuy. History, economic importance, essential botanical information and peculiarities of 25 common forms of plant life are provided in this book in an entertaining and charming style. Covers food plants (potatoes, apples, beans, wheat, almonds, bananas, etc.), flowers (lily, tulip, etc.), trees (pine, oak, elm, etc.), weeds, poisonous mushrooms and vines, gourds, citrus fruits, cotton, the cactus family, and much more. 108 illustrations. xiv + 290pp. 22272-1 Paperbound $2.50

How to Know the Ferns, Frances T. Parsons. Classic survey of Eastern and Central ferns, arranged according to clear, simple identification key. Excellent introduction to greatly neglected nature area. 57 illustrations and 42 plates. xvi + 215pp. 20740-4 Paperbound $2.00

Manual of the Trees of North America, Charles S. Sargent. America's foremost dendrologist provides the definitive coverage of North American trees and tree-like shrubs. 717 species fully described and illustrated: exact distribution, down to township; full botanical description; economic importance; description of subspecies and races; habitat, growth data; similar material. Necessary to every serious student of tree-life. Nomenclature revised to present. Over 100 locating keys. 783 illustrations. lii + 934pp. 20277-1, 20278-X Two volumes, Paperbound $6.00

Our Northern Shrubs, Harriet L. Keeler. Fine non-technical reference work identifying more than 225 important shrubs of Eastern and Central United States and Canada. Full text covering botanical description, habitat, plant lore, is paralleled with 205 full-page photographs of flowering or fruiting plants. Nomenclature revised by Edward G. Voss. One of few works concerned with shrubs. 205 plates, 35 drawings. xxviii + 521pp. 21989-5 Paperbound $3.75

The Mushroom Handbook, Louis C. C. Krieger. Still the best popular handbook: full descriptions of 259 species, cross references to another 200. Extremely thorough text enables you to identify, know all about any mushroom you are likely to meet in eastern and central U. S. A.: habitat, luminescence, poisonous qualities, use, folklore, etc. 32 color plates show over 50 mushrooms, also 126 other illustrations. Finding keys. vii + 560pp. 21861-9 Paperbound $3.95

Handbook of Birds of Eastern North America, Frank M. Chapman. Still much the best single-volume guide to the birds of Eastern and Central United States. Very full coverage of 675 species, with descriptions, life habits, distribution, similar data. All descriptions keyed to two-page color chart. With this single volume the average birdwatcher needs no other books. 1931 revised edition. 195 illustrations. xxxvi + 581pp. 21489-3 Paperbound $4.50

AMERICAN FOOD AND GAME FISHES, David S. Jordan and Barton W. Evermann. Definitive source of information, detailed and accurate enough to enable the sportsman and nature lover to identify conclusively some 1,000 species and sub-species of North American fish, sought for food or sport. Coverage of range, physiology, habits, life history, food value. Best methods of capture, interest to the angler, advice on bait, fly-fishing, etc. 338 drawings and photographs. 1 + 574pp. 6⅝ x 9⅜.

22383-1 Paperbound $4.50

THE FROG BOOK, Mary C. Dickerson. Complete with extensive finding keys, over 300 photographs, and an introduction to the general biology of frogs and toads, this is the classic non-technical study of Northeastern and Central species. 58 species; 290 photographs and 16 color plates. xvii + 253pp.

21973-9 Paperbound $4.00

THE MOTH BOOK: A GUIDE TO THE MOTHS OF NORTH AMERICA, William J. Holland. Classical study, eagerly sought after and used for the past 60 years. Clear identification manual to more than 2,000 different moths, largest manual in existence. General information about moths, capturing, mounting, classifying, etc., followed by species by species descriptions. 263 illustrations plus 48 color plates show almost every species, full size. 1968 edition, preface, nomenclature changes by A. E. Brower. xxiv + 479pp. of text. 6½ x 9¼.

21948-8 Paperbound $5.00

THE SEA-BEACH AT EBB-TIDE, Augusta Foote Arnold. Interested amateur can identify hundreds of marine plants and animals on coasts of North America; marine algae; seaweeds; squids; hermit crabs; horse shoe crabs; shrimps; corals; sea anemones; etc. Species descriptions cover: structure; food; reproductive cycle; size; shape; color; habitat; etc. Over 600 drawings. 85 plates. xii + 490pp.

21949-6 Paperbound $3.50

COMMON BIRD SONGS, Donald J. Borror. 33⅓ 12-inch record presents songs of 60 important birds of the eastern United States. A thorough, serious record which provides several examples for each bird, showing different types of song, individual variations, etc. Inestimable identification aid for birdwatcher. 32-page booklet gives text about birds and songs, with illustration for each bird.

21829-5 Record, book, album. Monaural. $2.75

FADS AND FALLACIES IN THE NAME OF SCIENCE, Martin Gardner. Fair, witty appraisal of cranks and quacks of science: Atlantis, Lemuria, hollow earth, flat earth, Velikovsky, orgone energy, Dianetics, flying saucers, Bridey Murphy, food fads, medical fads, perpetual motion, etc. Formerly "In the Name of Science." x + 363pp.

20394-8 Paperbound $2.00

HOAXES, Curtis D. MacDougall. Exhaustive, unbelievably rich account of great hoaxes: Locke's moon hoax, Shakespearean forgeries, sea serpents, Loch Ness monster, Cardiff giant, John Wilkes Booth's mummy, Disumbrationist school of art, dozens more; also journalism, psychology of hoaxing. 54 illustrations. xi + 338pp.

20465-0 Paperbound $2.75

THE PRINCIPLES OF PSYCHOLOGY, William James. The famous long course, complete and unabridged. Stream of thought, time perception, memory, experimental methods—these are only some of the concerns of a work that was years ahead of its time and still valid, interesting, useful. 94 figures. Total of xviii + 1391pp.
20381-6, 20382-4 Two volumes, Paperbound $8.00

THE STRANGE STORY OF THE QUANTUM, Banesh Hoffmann. Non-mathematical but thorough explanation of work of Planck, Einstein, Bohr, Pauli, de Broglie, Schrödinger, Heisenberg, Dirac, Feynman, etc. No technical background needed. "Of books attempting such an account, this is the best," Henry Margenau, Yale. 40-page "Postscript 1959." xii + 285pp. 20518-5 Paperbound $2.00

THE RISE OF THE NEW PHYSICS, A. d'Abro. Most thorough explanation in print of central core of mathematical physics, both classical and modern; from Newton to Dirac and Heisenberg. Both history and exposition; philosophy of science, causality, explanations of higher mathematics, analytical mechanics, electromagnetism, thermodynamics, phase rule, special and general relativity, matrices. No higher mathematics needed to follow exposition, though treatment is elementary to intermediate in level. Recommended to serious student who wishes verbal understanding. 97 illustrations. xvii + 982pp. 20003-5, 20004-3 Two volumes, Paperbound $6.00

GREAT IDEAS OF OPERATIONS RESEARCH, Jagjit Singh. Easily followed non-technical explanation of mathematical tools, aims, results: statistics, linear programming, game theory, queueing theory, Monte Carlo simulation, etc. Uses only elementary mathematics. Many case studies, several analyzed in detail. Clarity, breadth make this excellent for specialist in another field who wishes background. 41 figures. x + 228pp. 21886-4 Paperbound $2.50

GREAT IDEAS OF MODERN MATHEMATICS: THEIR NATURE AND USE, Jagjit Singh. Internationally famous expositor, winner of Unesco's Kalinga Award for science popularization explains verbally such topics as differential equations, matrices, groups, sets, transformations, mathematical logic and other important modern mathematics, as well as use in physics, astrophysics, and similar fields. Superb exposition for layman, scientist in other areas. viii + 312pp.
20587-8 Paperbound $2.50

GREAT IDEAS IN INFORMATION THEORY, LANGUAGE AND CYBERNETICS, Jagjit Singh. The analog and digital computers, how they work, how they are like and unlike the human brain, the men who developed them, their future applications, computer terminology. An essential book for today, even for readers with little math. Some mathematical demonstrations included for more advanced readers. 118 figures. Tables. ix + 338pp. 21694-2 Paperbound $2.50

CHANCE, LUCK AND STATISTICS, Horace C. Levinson. Non-mathematical presentation of fundamentals of probability theory and science of statistics and their applications. Games of chance, betting odds, misuse of statistics, normal and skew distributions, birth rates, stock speculation, insurance. Enlarged edition. Formerly "The Science of Chance." xiii + 357pp. 21007-3 Paperbound $2.50

JIM WHITEWOLF: THE LIFE OF A KIOWA APACHE INDIAN, Charles S. Brant, editor. Spans transition between native life and acculturation period, 1880 on. Kiowa culture, personal life pattern, religion and the supernatural, the Ghost Dance, breakdown in the White Man's world, similar material. 1 map. xii + 144pp.
22015-X Paperbound $1.75

THE NATIVE TRIBES OF CENTRAL AUSTRALIA, Baldwin Spencer and F. J. Gillen. Basic book in anthropology, devoted to full coverage of the Arunta and Warramunga tribes; the source for knowledge about kinship systems, material and social culture, religion, etc. Still unsurpassed. 121 photographs, 89 drawings. xviii + 669pp.
21775-2 Paperbound $5.00

MALAY MAGIC, Walter W. Skeat. Classic (1900); still the definitive work on the folklore and popular religion of the Malay peninsula. Describes marriage rites, birth spirits and ceremonies, medicine, dances, games, war and weapons, etc. Extensive quotes from original sources, many magic charms translated into English. 35 illustrations. Preface by Charles Otto Blagden. xxiv + 685pp.
21760-4 Paperbound $4.00

HEAVENS ON EARTH: UTOPIAN COMMUNITIES IN AMERICA, 1680-1880, Mark Holloway. The finest nontechnical account of American utopias, from the early Woman in the Wilderness, Ephrata, Rappites to the enormous mid 19th-century efflorescence; Shakers, New Harmony, Equity Stores, Fourier's Phalanxes, Oneida, Amana, Fruitlands, etc. "Entertaining and very instructive." *Times Literary Supplement.* 15 illustrations. 246pp.
21593-8 Paperbound $2.00

LONDON LABOUR AND THE LONDON POOR, Henry Mayhew. Earliest (c. 1850) sociological study in English, describing myriad subcultures of London poor. Particularly remarkable for the thousands of pages of direct testimony taken from the lips of London prostitutes, thieves, beggars, street sellers, chimney-sweepers, street-musicians, "mudlarks," "pure-finders," rag-gatherers, "running-patterers," dock laborers, cab-men, and hundreds of others, quoted directly in this massive work. An extraordinarily vital picture of London emerges. 110 illustrations. Total of lxxvi + 1951pp. 6⅝ x 10.
21934-8, 21935-6, 21936-4, 21937-2 Four volumes, Paperbound $14.00

HISTORY OF THE LATER ROMAN EMPIRE, J. B. Bury. Eloquent, detailed reconstruction of Western and Byzantine Roman Empire by a major historian, from the death of Theodosius I (395 A.D.) to the death of Justinian (565). Extensive quotations from contemporary sources; full coverage of important Roman and foreign figures of the time. xxxiv + 965pp. 21829-5 Record, book, album. Monaural. $3.50

AN INTELLECTUAL AND CULTURAL HISTORY OF THE WESTERN WORLD, Harry Elmer Barnes. Monumental study, tracing the development of the accomplishments that make up human culture. Every aspect of man's achievement surveyed from its origins in the Paleolithic to the present day (1964); social structures, ideas, economic systems, art, literature, technology, mathematics, the sciences, medicine, religion, jurisprudence, etc. Evaluations of the contributions of scores of great men. 1964 edition, revised and edited by scholars in the many fields represented. Total of xxix + 1381pp. 21275-0, 21276-9, 21277-7 Three volumes, Paperbound $7.75

ADVENTURES OF AN AFRICAN SLAVER, Theodore Canot. Edited by Brantz Mayer. A detailed portrayal of slavery and the slave trade, 1820-1840. Canot, an established trader along the African coast, describes the slave economy of the African kingdoms, the treatment of captured negroes, the extensive journeys in the interior to gather slaves, slave revolts and their suppression, harems, bribes, and much more. Full and unabridged republication of 1854 edition. Introduction by Malcom Cowley. 16 illustrations. xvii + 448pp. 22456-2 Paperbound $3.50

MY BONDAGE AND MY FREEDOM, Frederick Douglass. Born and brought up in slavery, Douglass witnessed its horrors and experienced its cruelties, but went on to become one of the most outspoken forces in the American anti-slavery movement. Considered the best of his autobiographies, this book graphically describes the inhuman treatment of slaves, its effects on slave owners and slave families, and how Douglass's determination led him to a new life. Unaltered reprint of 1st (1855) edition. xxxii + 464pp. 22457-0 Paperbound $2.50

THE INDIANS' BOOK, recorded and edited by Natalie Curtis. Lore, music, narratives, dozens of drawings by Indians themselves from an authoritative and important survey of native culture among Plains, Southwestern, Lake and Pueblo Indians. Standard work in popular ethnomusicology. 149 songs in full notation. 23 drawings, 23 photos. xxxi + 584pp. 6⅝ x 9⅜. 21939-9 Paperbound $4.50

DICTIONARY OF AMERICAN PORTRAITS, edited by Hayward and Blanche Cirker. 4024 portraits of 4000 most important Americans, colonial days to 1905 (with a few important categories, like Presidents, to present). Pioneers, explorers, colonial figures, U. S. officials, politicians, writers, military and naval men, scientists, inventors, manufacturers, jurists, actors, historians, educators, notorious figures, Indian chiefs, etc. All authentic contemporary likenesses. The only work of its kind in existence; supplements all biographical sources for libraries. Indispensable to anyone working with American history. 8,000-item classified index, finding lists, other aids. xiv + 756pp. 9¼ x 12¾. 21823-6 Clothbound $30.00

TRITTON'S GUIDE TO BETTER WINE AND BEER MAKING FOR BEGINNERS, S. M. Tritton. All you need to know to make family-sized quantities of over 100 types of grape, fruit, herb and vegetable wines; as well as beers, mead, cider, etc. Complete recipes, advice as to equipment, procedures such as fermenting, bottling, and storing wines. Recipes given in British, U. S., and metric measures. Accompanying booklet lists sources in U. S. A. where ingredients may be bought, and additional information. 11 illustrations. 157pp. 5⅝ x 8⅛.
(USO) 22090-7 Clothbound $3.50

GARDENING WITH HERBS FOR FLAVOR AND FRAGRANCE, Helen M. Fox. How to grow herbs in your own garden, how to use them in your cooking (over 55 recipes included), legends and myths associated with each species, uses in medicine, perfumes, etc.—these are elements of one of the few books written especially for American herb fanciers. Guides you step-by-step from soil preparation to harvesting and storage for each type of herb. 12 drawings by Louise Mansfield. xiv + 334pp. 22540-2 Paperbound $2.50

CATALOGUE OF DOVER BOOKS

MATHEMATICAL PUZZLES FOR BEGINNERS AND ENTHUSIASTS, Geoffrey Mott-Smith. 189 puzzles from easy to difficult—involving arithmetic, logic, algebra, properties of digits, probability, etc.—for enjoyment and mental stimulus. Explanation of mathematical principles behind the puzzles. 135 illustrations. viii + 248pp.
20198-8 Paperbound $1.75

PAPER FOLDING FOR BEGINNERS, William D. Murray and Francis J. Rigney. Easiest book on the market, clearest instructions on making interesting, beautiful origami. Sail boats, cups, roosters, frogs that move legs, bonbon boxes, standing birds, etc. 40 projects; more than 275 diagrams and photographs. 94pp.
20713-7 Paperbound $1.00

TRICKS AND GAMES ON THE POOL TABLE, Fred Herrmann. 79 tricks and games— some solitaires, some for two or more players, some competitive games—to entertain you between formal games. Mystifying shots and throws, unusual caroms, tricks involving such props as cork, coins, a hat, etc. Formerly *Fun on the Pool Table*. 77 figures. 95pp.
21814-7 Paperbound $1.00

HAND SHADOWS TO BE THROWN UPON THE WALL: A SERIES OF NOVEL AND AMUSING FIGURES FORMED BY THE HAND, Henry Bursill. Delightful picturebook from great-grandfather's day shows how to make 18 different hand shadows: a bird that flies, duck that quacks, dog that wags his tail, camel, goose, deer, boy, turtle, etc. Only book of its sort. vi + 33pp. 6½ x 9¼. 21779-5 Paperbound $1.00

WHITTLING AND WOODCARVING, E. J. Tangerman. 18th printing of best book on market. "If you can cut a potato you can carve" toys and puzzles, chains, chessmen, caricatures, masks, frames, woodcut blocks, surface patterns, much more. Information on tools, woods, techniques. Also goes into serious wood sculpture from Middle Ages to present, East and West. 464 photos, figures. x + 293pp.
20965-2 Paperbound $2.00

HISTORY OF PHILOSOPHY, Julián Marias. Possibly the clearest, most easily followed, best planned, most useful one-volume history of philosophy on the market; neither skimpy nor overfull. Full details on system of every major philosopher and dozens of less important thinkers from pre-Socratics up to Existentialism and later. Strong on many European figures usually omitted. Has gone through dozens of editions in Europe. 1966 edition, translated by Stanley Appelbaum and Clarence Strowbridge. xviii + 505pp. 21739-6 Paperbound $3.00

YOGA: A SCIENTIFIC EVALUATION, Kovoor T. Behanan. Scientific but non-technical study of physiological results of yoga exercises; done under auspices of Yale U. Relations to Indian thought, to psychoanalysis, etc. 16 photos. xxiii + 270pp.
20505-3 Paperbound $2.50

Prices subject to change without notice.
Available at your book dealer or write for free catalogue to Dept. GI, Dover Publications, Inc., 180 Varick St., N. Y., N. Y. 10014. Dover publishes more than 150 books each year on science, elementary and advanced mathematics, biology, music, art, literary history, social sciences and other areas.